D0222011

GOETHE, KANT, AND HEGEL

Discovering the Mind

Walter Kaufmann

with new introductory essays by Ivan Soll

Volume I *Goethe, Kant, and Hegel*
Volume II *Nietsche, Heidegger, and Buber*
Volume III *Freud* vs. *Adler and Jung*

GOETHE, KANT, AND HEGEL

Discovering the Mind

Volume 1

Walter Kaufmann

with a new introduction by
Ivan Soll

Transaction Publishers
New Brunswick (U.S.A.) and London (U.K.)

New material this edition copyright © 1991 by Transaction
Publishers, New Brunswick, New Jersey 08903. Originally published
in 1980 by McGraw-Hill Book Company. Copyright © 1980 by
Walter Kaufmann.

All rights reserved under International and Pan-American Copyright
Conventions. No part of this book may be reproduced or transmit-
ted in any form or by any means, electronic or mechanical, including photocopy, recording, or any information storage and retrieval
system, without prior permission in writing from the publisher. All
inquiries should be addressed to Transaction Publishers, Rutgers-
The State University, New Brunswick, New Jersey 08903.

Library of Congress Catalog Number: 90-11108
ISBN: 0-88738-370-X
Printed in the United States of America

Library of Congress Cataloging-in-Publication Data

Kaufmann, Walter Arnold.
    Goethe, Kant, and Hegel/by Walter Kaufmann; with a new
introduction by Ivan Soll.
        p.   cm.
    Reprint. Originally published: New York: McGraw-Hill, 1980.
    Includes bibliographical references and index.
    ISBN 0-88738-370-X (pbk)
    1. Philosophy of mind—History. 2. Self-knowledge, Theory
of History. 3. Philosophy, German. I. Title.
[BD418.3.K38 1990]
193—dc20
    [B]   90-11108
                                                       CIP

Contents ▶▶▶

II. Influences: Herder, Lessing, Schiller, Fichte, Schopenhauer

III. Kant: The Structure of the Mind

ILLUSTRATIONS

Introduction
to the
Transaction Edition

Ivan Soll

Toward the end of an unflaggingly vital and productive life that was to be tragically truncated in an abrupt and unanticipated way, Walter Kaufmann wrote *Discovering the Mind*. Erudite but animated, monumental but not at all ponderous, it is, among other things, Kaufmann's final reconsideration of an intellectual tradition that had been the abiding source and focus of his own prolific writing.

The subject of the work is explicitly defined, not in terms of a historical tradition, however, but of an enterprise, "discovering the mind," which Kaufmann conceives broadly, using "mind" as "an inclusive term for feeling and intelligence, reason and emotion, perception and will."[1] And Kaufmann's avowed "central aim throughout" is "to contribute to the discovery of the mind."[2] But he also claims that, "It should be one of the compensations of this study that it leads to a new and better understanding of a good deal of the intellectual history of the past two hundred years."[3]

What he in fact deals with historically is an intellectual tradition developed principally by thinkers who wrote in German. Since Kaufmann defines his subject matter in terms of its intellectual aim rather than its historical period, we are confronted by his implicit suggestion that in the last two hundred years most of the interesting developments in the discovery of the mind have, in fact, taken place among those who have written in German. Given the list of thinkers who are included in his discussion, this provocative suggestion is not without some plausibility.

The work is divided into three volumes. Each deals with three major figures: the first with Goethe, Kant, and Hegel; the second with Nietzsche, Heidegger, and Buber; the third with Freud, Adler, and Jung. There are also a number of other figures, such as Lessing, Schiller, Kierkegaard, and Schopenhauer, who are treated far more briefly, often by way of illuminating the writers receiving fuller analysis.

Each volume has a hero. A case is made that Goethe, Nietzsche, and Freud were in significant ways admirable human beings who made important contributions to the discovery of the mind. The other six do not come off nearly as well. Hegel and Buber receive mixed reviews. The rest are severely criticized as being both of unadmirable character and as having contributed little to the discovery of the mind, indeed, as having seriously impeded it. We are presented with an intellectual landscape in which what is not a help is usually a hindrance, in which an author's character is usually relevant to his contribution, and in which intellectual interventions are rarely ever impersonal.

Kaufmann makes no attempt to depict this landscape in muted tones, as he allows both his enthusiasms and distastes full expression. Whether one always agrees with him is beside the point. His judgments are generally supported with cogent argumentation, and the passion with which he embraces and rejects thinkers and their thought seems appropriate to the importance of the issues at stake. Kaufmann's extremely frank and personal expression of his passions and preferences is unusual in academic writing. This should not be taken as a ground for criticism, but rather as an essential part of his unique contribution to the discussion of these matters.

Kaufmann closely links the process of discovering the

mind with the attainment of self-knowledge. He insists on this linkage not only in the unexceptionable but special case of our coming to know our own minds as individuals but also where it less obviously obtains, in the process of discovering the nature of the human mind in general. In closely connecting all knowledge of the mind with self-knowledge, Kaufmann is doing more than recalling Socrates's injunction, "Know thyself!," and allying this enterprise with it. He is calling attention to often overlooked or suppressed links between knowing one's own mind in particular and the human mind in general, between self-deception and the misunderstanding of others, between self-knowledge and the knowledge of selves. Kaufmann argues with reference to a number of thinkers, that flaws in one's understanding of oneself are usually obstacles to one's understanding of others, that the failure of a theory about the human mind often mirrors a failure of the theorist to come to terms with himself.

This consideration of theories about the human mind in conjunction with an examination of the mentality or character of the theorist constitutes another salient feature of Kaufmann's method, and one which again puts him at odds with standard academic practice. Kaufmann unabashedly breaches the prevalent prohibition against any *ad hominem* approach to philosophers, explicitly calling this taboo into question. Starting with the reasonable but rather general assumption that "the ideas of these men are not totally unrelated to their mentalities," he repeatedly offers evidence and hypotheses specifically linking their particular theories to their personalities. He thinks it imperative and enlightening to discover the minds of those who discovered the mind.

In entering upon this terrain, Kaufmann is careful and quick to distance himself from "reductionism," which he defines with admirable and delightful concision as "the claim that something is 'nothing but' something else."[4] In the context of exploring the relation between the personalities and theories of those who wrote about the mind, reductionism consists in the claim that conceptions of the human mind are *nothing but* reflections of the personalities of their authors.

Although Kaufmann does not spell out the reasons for rejecting reductionism, they are not difficult to locate. The kind of reductionism here at issue is objectionable in that it tends to have disastrous methodological consequences. If this type of reductionism were accepted, tracing the way in which any conception of the human mind is anchored in the personality of its author would become the central or even the sole question to be investigated. And it would tend to be pursued to the neglect or even exclusion of other issues, particularly those concerning the intrinsic plausibility and merit of the conceptions under investigation. I think that the widespread and tenaciously rooted resistance to any analysis of conceptions and theories as reflections of the character of their authors stems from a fear that the legitimation of such investigations would undermine the traditional assessment of the intrinsic value of the ideas.

Kaufmann does not, however, intend his analyses of the relation between a writer's ideas and his personality as a replacement for traditional investigations of the intrinsic merit of the ideas, but as a supplement to them. Having explicitly rejected reductionism, he is not committed to replacing the assessment of the ideas themselves by accounts of their genesis out of the personalities of their authors. His program entails only enriching the accounts and assessments of the works themselves with considerations of the authors' personalities. And indeed, such considerations do sometimes help to explain cases of otherwise puzzling adherences to implausible ideas and unpromising intellectual practices, to account for opinions rigidly held and curiously impervious to the claims of competing views, and to illuminate strong intellectual commitments made in the absence of decisive evidence.

Discovering the Mind as a whole constitutes a plea as well as a paradigm for the introduction of such considerations into the standard repertoire of historians and interpreters of philosophical and psychological theories. This program is certainly not without precedents, but they are not usually to be found among professional philosophers, and even more rarely among those of repute, like Kaufmann.

The most notable exception and the principal inspiration of this and several other of the book's remarkable qualities is Friedrich Nietzsche. It was Nietzsche who argued that a philosophical theory was to be best understood as being primarily the expression of the philosopher's basic personality, rather than as the result of his impersonal consideration of data and arguments. Though Nietzsche was not as careful as Kaufmann to avoid the reefs of reductionism, his analyses of the relation between the character of various thinkers and their thought clearly constitute the model for Kaufmann's own excursions into this area. Kaufmann, in venturing hypotheses about various ideas and theories as *reflections of* as well as *reflections by* the minds that produced them, is reviving a promising type of Nietzschean analysis, generally neglected and taboo.

Nietzsche's influence can also be discerned in Kaufmann's masterfully rapid but penetrating approach, his refusal to get bogged down in the morass of his material, his deliberate decision not to attempt to offer an overly full account of the material in which his major theses and insights would lose a great deal of their force in a sea of related but not directly relevant detail. This is a quality that Nietzsche had himself displayed and singled out for discussion as the all-important "tempo" of a work. Though *Discovering the Mind*, like all of Kaufmann's work, is remarkably well informed and informative, it aspires neither to be complete nor compendious. In fact, it is one of Kaufmann's theses that the ideal of offering complete accounts of intellectual developments owes much of its influence to Hegel and has been in some ways an unfortunate development, an unrealizable goal and requirement that creates pressure to mask the inevitable incompleteness of the narratives of intellectual history by recourse to obscurity.

The Nietzschean influence is also clear in Kaufmann's deliberate rejection of a dispassionate tone. Nietzsche was not only the subject of Kaufmann's first book, *Nietzsche: Philosopher, Psychologist, Antichrist* (1950), the philosopher much of whose work Kaufmann translated into English, and one of the three acknowledged heroes of *Discovering the Mind*. He was also the major influence on Walter Kaufmann's philosophic work, and his imprint on the conception and style of Kaufmann's last book is unmistakable.

The tradition that Kaufmann reconsiders, that of "discovering the mind" in German letters of the last two hundred years, clearly crosses or ignores the boundaries among the disciplines as they have come to be defined and established in the academy. Some of the figures he discusses, such as Kant, Hegel, and Heidegger, have been clearly defined, by themselves as well as the tradition, as philosophers. Others, such as Goethe and Schiller, despite their historically influential and intrinsically valuable theoretical writings, have been usually categorized as being essentially writers of "literature," that is, of "imaginative literature," whose works are studied primarily in departments of literature and written about by people who consider themselves literary critics and historians. Others, such as Freud, Adler, and Jung, find their niche in our established order of the disciplines among the "psychologists," even though not all of their neighbors in this edifice are particularly happy about the proximity.

Still others, like Nietzsche and Buber, have been harder to place. Nietzsche, who preferred to identify himself as a "good European" rather than as a German, led a life in which he had no fixed abode in any one country (or academic discipline)—a life in which he continually moved across borders, both geographical and intellectual. His work has suffered and enjoyed a similar fate. Because of its highly literary, metaphorical, and aphoristic style, its lack or avoidance of fully spelled-out argumentation for its positions, its vehement and personal tone, its unorthodox set of concerns; it was long rejected by a majority of the philosophical establishment in the English-speaking world—not as being bad philosophy, but as not being philosophy at all. And not even Nietzsche's recent prominence has dissolved the problem of his marginality. In the English-speaking world, his new popularity finds its center of gravity somehow still on the periphery of the discipline of philosophy or in other disciplines, in those, for example, that concern themselves with the theory of literature and art.

Buber's position in the world of academic philosophy is surely even more marginal and obscure than Nietzsche's. As in the case of Kierkegaard (who is also discussed, albeit briefly), there remains uncertainty as to whether he belongs to philosophy or theology.

Walter Kaufmann's *Discovering the Mind* speaks in an important way to these issues of disciplinary identity. As is usually the case in Kaufmann's work, the discussion has both a historical and a philosophical dimension. The historical dimension concerns the two-hundred-year tradition of German letters taken up for consideration in this book. The interdependence of philosophy, literature, and psychology in this tradition is so obvious and well documented, that one is tempted to say that it cannot be ignored, except that it has been ignored, particularly, though not exclusively, in the English-speaking world.

In this German tradition, those who produced literary works and those who produced philosophical works regularly read each other and drew inspiration for their own work from this cross-disciplinary reading. (Kant is perhaps the one notable exception: Though he was widely read by literary figures in the tradition, he did not read them.) Some of the central figures in the tradition, notably Goethe, Schiller, and Nietzsche, produced both significant theoretical and literary work. The literary work of Goethe and Schiller, as well as their theoretical work, importantly influenced the development of German philosophy. Most importantly, there was a strongly sensed community of purpose that transcended the barriers of genre and discipline. "Discovering the mind," Kaufmann argues, was an important aspect of what was viewed as a common enterprise, to which literature, philosophy, and psychology all contributed. We should not forget that psychology only gradually emerged as a separate discipline in the course of this period.

Though there has been some awareness and acknowledgment of the organic cohesiveness and interdependence of literature, philosophy, and psychology in this tradition, the awareness remains for the most part superficial, undetailed, and without consequence in our approach to the period. Professional philosophers still tend to study the philosophical texts in abstraction from those literary works, which often inspired them or to which they are a response. Although some literary critics do acknowledge the influence of philosophical works upon literary ones, they rarely analyze the philosophic texts in sufficient detail and almost never incorporate careful *philosophic* assessment of these texts into their accounts. Among psychologists, who are typically concerned with the legitimation of their discipline as a "science" on the basis of its similarities with the paradigmatic physical sciences, psychology's common origin with philosophy and literature and its long intermingling with them tend to be deemphasized, depreciated, and suppressed. Their enduring and intimate association tends to be viewed as a primitive and unproductive confusion, which we have fortunately now overcome by finally separating out what are essentially distinct enterprises.

This tendency toward fragmentation is the reflection of a general trend toward deeper and more numerous institutional divisions among the disciplines. Without taking a stand on the purported advantages and inevitability of this intellectual Balkanization, one cannot help but see how our present state of academic and disciplinary division tends to warp our understanding of a tradition in which what is now dispersed among different disciplines existed as an intermingled whole.

Kaufmann's *Discovering the Mind* has the merit of refocussing our attention upon the remarkable integration of philosophical, literary, and psychological work in the tradition of German letters from the Enlightenment to the Second World War. In our recent treatment of this period, we have tended to overlook or ignore its remarkably high degree of organic unity, in part because this sort of integration has been lost in our own literary culture. *Discovering the Mind* should make it harder for us to continue approaching with good conscience this literary-philosophical-psychological tradition from the exclusive perspective of a particular discipline. It impedes the facility and narrowness of approach that is the consequence of our own cultural fragmentation. Kaufmann has achieved with respect to our study of this period in German intellectual history what Kierkegaard wanted to achieve with respect to our embracing religious faith: He has made things more difficult for us—but also more rewarding. And we are in his debt for this difficulty.

The philosophical dimension of Kaufmann's emphasis on the integration of philosophy, literature, and psychology transcends the question of the interpretation of a particular period of intellectual history, or that of the appropriate methodology for intellectual history in general. It also consists in the implicit thesis, that this former integration of what is currently separated furnishes the most fruitful context for discovering the mind. It suggests that it is in the interplay of literature, philosophy and psychology that the best insights concerning mind have been, and will likely be, obtained. His historical interpretation, in as much as the period interpreted is presented as exemplary, also furnishes the basis of an intellectual program.

Discovering the mind is too important and central a human concern, Kaufmann implies, to be left exclusively to the "psychologists," that is, to those who have come to carry this institutionally and narrowly defined title of relatively recent origin, the professional psychologists. The major insights into the nature of the mind have often come, he argues, from thinkers who were not psychologists so defined, and the greatest of the professional psychologists have drawn heavily on the insights of those who were not in the profession.

The refusal to abandon the discovery of the mind to the guild of professional psychologists is not just an insistence on the rights of writers and philosophers to address themselves to this task, justified by their traditional presence on this turf and their considerable contributions. It is also a reminder to philosophers and writers that involvement in this enterprise has been and should remain a central aspect of their vocation—a duty as well as a right. The lamentable tendency to relinquish psychology to the psychologists is not just the result of their presumptuous and aggressive appropriation of what is by nature an intellectual and existential concern common to all human beings. There has been complicity on the part of philosophers and writers who wanted to rid themselves of the burden of having to work at discovering the mind. In addition to the effective pursuit of prerogatives by a guild, there has been an all too willing retreat from this former common ground by those who found it easier not to maintain a presence there. We should chastise and lament the retreat as well as the aggression.

In this first of three volumes, Kaufmann provides a bold historical hypothesis about the last two centuries of intellectual life in the German speaking world: the development of theories and conceptions of the mind and of philosophy in general is presented as having taken place in an intellectual space defined overwhelmingly by those two giants of German letters, Johann Wolfgang von Goethe (1749–1832) and Immanuel Kant (1724–1804). Other figures of the period are discussed and, in some cases, even allowed to have had considerable influence and intellectual virtue—Lessing, Schiller, and Hegel, for example. But Kaufmann is unwavering in his insistence that no other figure of the period even remotely compares in influence to Kant or Goethe. Some who have been put forward as major influences, like Herder, are argued to have had less influence than has been supposed. Still others, like Schiller and Hegel, are presented as themselves recipients and transmitters of the two major influences.

It is to be predicted that such a stark structuring of a complex subject will generate the protest that these matters cannot not be so simply viewed. No doubt the proponents of various figures in this tradition (particularly those scholars who have written about other figures) will feel that the importance of these figures has not been fully appreciated. Confronted with these misgivings, one should not forget that Kaufmann's picture of Goethe and Kant as by far the two most important influences on subsequent intellectual life in Germany is not created by presenting the other leading contenders as pygmies. We should also keep in mind that the thesis concerns subsequent influence, not intrinsic merit. Lessing, Schiller, and Hegel are all treated with enormous respect. And Kant, despite and because of his great influence, is severely criticized and viewed as the source of much that went wrong in German philosophy and intellectual life.

We should also not forget that the thesis is clearly offered as a hypothesis, as an interesting proposal of considerable plausibility, to be pushed as far as it will go. It is a hypothesis of considerable synthetic power, supplying a well-defined perspective from which a bewildering amount of historical material can be systematically viewed. Whatever one decides about its ultimate adequacy, it furnishes a valuable focus for the further study and debate of this rich chapter of intellectual history. The thesis is certainly both arguable and debatable. That it has been so forcefully argued by Kaufmann and will be heatedly debated by others is all to the good.

To put Kaufmann's historical interpretations in this book in perspective, we should consider some of his previous contributions to the subject matter. For example, in *Hegel: Reinterpretation, Texts and Commentary* (1965), he argued for Hegel's philosophical merit and historical importance to an audience that needed some convincing. With this in mind, his insistence that Kant and Goethe were still more influential than Hegel is less likely to be seen as an advocacy that springs from a failure to consider the alternatives seriously. In general, it would be well to remember that this eagle's-eye view of an extensive period in intellectual history was preceded by two substantial studies of major figures in the period (Hegel and Nietzsche) and a number of essays on related topics, particularly some of those in *From Shakespeare to Existentialism* (1959). Only one acquainted with these earlier contributions will fully appreciate the effort and power of synthesis, the admirable abbreviation, the simplicity and austerity of presentation arising from what had to be complex considerations and hard choices. Kaufmann's last, long-ranging look at his cultural heritage is a masterful distillation of an extensive erudition, effectively brought to bear upon specific and important issues, but never flaunted.

Kaufmann's conception of the place of Kant and Goethe in German culture is remarkable and provocative, not only because of the extraordinary influence he attributes to them, but also because of his evaluation of their respective influences. That Goethe is praised, not only as an enormous, but also as an enormously positive influence, is not at all unusual. But that a substantial part of Goethe's importance and merit is located in his having developed an alternative model for science in his *Theory of Colors*, written as a critique of Newton, is a significant hypothesis.

Unlike the Newtonian conception of science, in which quantification and measurement occupy a central position, Goethe offers us an alternative model for "science" in which these are not essential, and which Kaufmann finds to be preferable in some contexts of inquiry, like that of discovering the mind. Kaufmann is using the term "science" in the broad German sense of "*Wissenschaft,*" which includes humanistic disciplines as well as the natural and social sciences, and which applies to anything that is a *rational inquiry.* The crucial issue raised by Kaufmann's championing of a Goethean model of science is not, however, whether one should or should not extend the word "science" to these other disciplines and inquiries. It is rather whether or not the discovery of the mind (and by extension—the discovery of other human truths) is best pursued by adhering to quantitative methods.

Kaufmann's dismissal of the results of quantitative methodology in psychology as insignificant is simply stated, not argued. This dismissal and the accompanying lack of argument are sure to raise the hackles and voices of the proponents of quantitative methods in psychology. Of course, the bold claim that quantitative studies have not substantially contributed to the discovery of the mind calls for a lot of further consideration and argument. Kaufmann does not make any pretense of argument; he advances this as a radical hypothesis, worthy of further consideration and argument, and worthy of enunciating because it calls into question prevalent and largely unquestioned beliefs. He devotes his energies rather to arguing for the correlative thesis, that some of the greatest contributions to the discovery of the mind have come from thinkers, like Goethe, Nietzsche and Freud, who did not use quantitative methods.

The convincingly argued claim, that Goethe's importance and influence flowed as much from his person as from his works, is put forward as being generally instructive. Kaufmann, citing other examples in the history of philosophy, such as Socrates, J. L. Austin, and Ludwig Wittgenstein, plausibly makes the case that it is not uncommon in the history of philosophy that one's influence often depends upon personal charisma or in conveying the impression that one is in some way an exemplary human being. Using the model of the exemplary Goethe, Kaufmann wants to move us away from the prevalent idea that the history of ideas is only the history of ideas. It is also the history of individuals, whose manner of living or being, at least as it is publicly perceived, is to a great extent responsible for their influence.

This insistence upon the importance of the stature and personal force of the writer, as perceived through and apart from his writings, for determining his influence upon the history of thought contributes to a larger and more important issue. It opens the way to a discussion of what constitutes not just the influence of a thinker but his actual merit, contribution, and greatness. It opens the way, moreover, to a discussion liberated from the narrowing constraints of the prevalent notion that philosophical excellence is primarily, or even exclusively, a matter of the excellence of the argumentation, of impeccable logic, and the marshalling of all the relevant evidence.

By pointing out that Socrates and Wittgenstein do not offer complete and rigorous demonstrations for their views, Kaufmann is not suggesting that their reputation for greatness is undeserved, but rather that excellence and greatness in philosophy (and in discovering the mind) does not depend exclusively upon the definitiveness of the demonstrations for one's views. But neither is he suggesting that rigor and adequacy of argumentation are irrelevant considerations. In calling attention to what he argues to be an astounding lack of rigor in both Kant and Hegel, he not only tries to correct common misconceptions about them, but also to suggest that they were great philosophers *despite* this lack of rigor, which he clearly considers a serious flaw, though one not incompatible with philosophic greatness. Kaufmann does not attempt to develop a positive and systematic account of what constitutes excellence or greatness in philosophy, but by rejecting an overly narrow conception of the matter that enjoys some currency, he implicitly encourages his readers to explore the question from a richer and more varied perspective than they might have otherwise adopted.

Kaufmann's treatment of Kant is far more startling than his treatment of Goethe. Kant, who has enjoyed respect and praise almost universally, and from the most diverse philosophical directions, is here astonishingly and unqualifiedly branded as a disastrous influence upon the subsequent development of German thought. Though it has been common enough to call attention to some of the obvious failings of Kant's writing style and even, to some extent, the content of his philosophy, this has generally occurred as a series of marginal comments in the context of an overwhelming reverence for his achievement, in an atmosphere of overall admiration that remains in no way challenged by the critical marginalia. Kaufmann makes no bones about his opinion of Kant as having been on the whole a catastrophe for German philosophy. His critique of Kant is radical and unorthodox, yet another philosophical heresy from the author of *The Faith of a Heretic* (1961), a book in which he locates the central virtue of our philosophical tradition in its ever renewed criticism of whatever has become generally accepted as true, authoritative, and canonical.

His case against Kant involves not so much new revelations of hidden flaws, but a clear-eyed assessment of fairly obvious failings and unfortunate influences, relatively unburdened and unblurred by the conventional pieties concerning Kant's unquestionable overall greatness and positive contribution to philosophy. Once again the value of Kaufmann's thesis lies primarily in the raising of an important issue that that has rarely, if ever, been raised, in the consideration of a plausible hypothesis that has rarely, if ever, been seriously considered.

Kant is blamed for a being *the major source* of at least two disastrous traditions in German philosophy. First, he is seen as the source of a continuing tradition of obscurity and obscurantism. He is also faulted as the fountainhead of an inappropriate insistence on certainty and necessity in our investigations and theories and, correspondingly, of unfounded claims to have achieved such rigor. One of Kaufmann's most intriguing ideas is that the two tendencies are actually connected. Having accepted the unrealizable requirement of certainty and necessity, one naturally resorts to obscurity to conceal from oneself and others that one has failed to fulfill it.

Kant is blamed for yet another misguided requirement: that philosophy should endeavor to attain completeness. The requirement of completeness, like the demand for certainty and necessity, it is suggested, being gratuitous and unattainable, naturally produces a tradition characterized by the pretentious counterfeit of the misguided ideal and the attempt to conceal the failure and fakery by willful, though not necessarily conscious, obscurantism.

Some will no doubt want to question whether Kant is really the primary source of all these subsequent ills of German intellectual life. The quest for certainty can be easily traced back to Descartes and to Newton, and, despite some foreshadowings in Kant, the ideal of completeness seems to have emerged in full force only with Hegel's *Phenomenology of Spirit*. But such disputes about the exact origins of these false ideals for philosophy are much less important than the crucial thesis that they have indeed proven to be counterproductive requirements, that they have become pernicious and enduring afflictions of our intellectual life.

With respect to these flaws, so fateful for the subsequent course of German philosophy, Goethe is presented as Kant's antipode. If Kant began the process of teaching the German language to speak philosophically (his notable German predecessors had used Latin and French), he taught it to speak badly—that is, obscurely. Goethe, on the contrary, used, and indeed himself developed, a German in which one could express one's ideas clearly. While Kant carried on the unfortunate tradition of Descartes, misguidedly seeking an absolutely certain foundation for our knowledge, Goethe emphasized that the true mark of a fruitful scientific procedure was the formulation and testing of hypotheses that always remain open to further questioning.

The subsequent development of German philosophy can be viewed, argues Kaufmann, as largely determined by these polar opposites and the tension between them. Hegel can be understood as having acquired his notoriously obscure style and his false claims to having achieved necessity and completeness in his "dialectical demonstrations" in imitation of Kant. Hegel's developmental approach, which so influenced the intellectual methodology of the nineteenth century, is argued to have derived from Goethe. Heidegger's obscurity and apodictic tone are also seen as part of the unfortunate legacy of Kant. The admirable writing styles of Schopenhauer and Nietzsche, as well as the latter's experimental spirit and constant questioning of everything, is attributed to Goethe's influence. Even if one finds this somewhat Manichean conception of the development German thought problematic or simplistic, it is an original and not implausible hypothesis, which, like a number of Kaufmann's central claims in this work, is fruitful in the crucial sense, that critically considering it, independently of whether we ultimately accept, reject, or modify it, will deepen our understanding of the subject matter to which it pertains.

Although Kaufmann presents Kant as the primary source of major ills in German thought, he constantly maintains that, despite Kant's bad qualities and his disasterous influence on subsequent philosophy, he was a great philosopher. Kaufmann does not himself make the case for Kant's greatness or for the significance of his positive contributions. No doubt he thought it unnecessary to convince our philosophical culture of what it already believes—almost without question. But after his devastating criticism and his rejection, not only of some of Kant's ideas but of the whole manner in which Kant philosophized, some of us will be curious as to what Kaufmann took to be Kant's redeeming virtues.

He does make some scattered remarks, admiring Kant's crushing criticisms of the proofs for God's existence and the unsurpassed philosophic drama of Kant's "antinomies," a presentation on facing pages of what he claimed were perfectly valid arguments for each of two opposing positions ("theses" and "antitheses") on four classical problems in philosophy. But these few and fragmentary admirations do not constitute a counterpoise to the sweeping criticisms. How can Kant have had those particularly general vices, with which he is here convincingly charged, and still have been a great philosopher? Is he really the dark angel of German philosophy or simply its devil?

Usually it is easier for us to explain and defend our negative judgments than our enthusiasms. But this does not seem to be Kaufmann's problem. With respect to those figures he thinks made major contributions to the discovery of the mind— Goethe, Hegel, Nietzsche, and Freud (and obviously not Kant)—he sticks his neck out, listing with admirable concision, clarity, and intellectual courage, point by point, what he takes to be those contributions. These unusually unambiguous *prises de position*, like much else in this work, will form ideal foci for further discussion and debate.

Considerable space is devoted to a recounting of the story of the composition and publication of Kant's *Critique of Pure Reason* and Hegel's *Phenomenology of Spirit*. Here, as elsewhere in Kaufmann's work, the erudition and information is not an end in itself. Although his account of these matters appears at first to be overly detailed and even gratuitous (even considering the fact that we are dealing with what is arguably each philosopher's most important work), it actually turns out to serve an important purpose. He presents ample evidence that Kant's *Critique* and Hegel's *Phenomenology* were both, though the products of long reflection, written in extreme haste and published pretty much without revision. Kaufmann thinks it important to emphasize that these works were hurriedly produced and never carefully vetted or reworked, for he wants to overcome the awe in which these texts have traditionally been treated. He wants to prepare us to accept his appraisal of them as severely flawed masterpieces, rich in ideas but very badly written and organized, and remarkably lacking in rigor.

This is meant to be a liberating corrective to the prevalent practice of approaching these (and other philosophical masterpieces) as if the failure to find an interpretation that reveals the rigor of the argumentation, the deep aptness of the organization, and truth in the conclusions, or at least an impressive plausibility in these matters, must be a failure of the reader and not of the text. It is an attempt to free us from the oppressive tradition of having to treat what are admitted to be great philosophical works as *authoritative texts*, that is, as texts which, despite appearances to the contrary, are always able to yield, given the appropriate interpretation, coherence, significance, and truth.

It is meant to relieve us of the obligation to undertake prodigious hermeneutic exertions, even when they promise to be futile. These obligatory and often interminable efforts at interpretation are aimed at revealing supposedly hidden virtues of texts, virtues whose veiled presence is often assumed in an act of unfounded and implausible faith. In denying these two books some of their generally presumed virtues Kaufmann is clearly not denying them all virtue or greatness. Nor is he suggesting that they are not worth studying. He is rather calling attention to the complexity and variation of what makes philosophical works great and addressing the related existential question of how we should approach those texts that merit our attention and respect.

The question of style, particularly of the clarity of style, is a central aspect of Kaufmann's program. Goethe is praised for his clarity; Kant is criticized for his obscurity. Implicit in the discussion of the writing styles of the various figures considered is the rejection of the idea that clarity or obscurity of style is something with which one is blessed or cursed: something that is a given. Kaufmann approaches the style of a writer as Freud approached dreams, parapraxes, and neurotic symptoms, with the fundamental suspicion that it is something willed, that obscure writing is usually also intentionally, if unconsciously, obscurantist.

He suspects obscure philosophical writers, such as Kant, Hegel, and Heidegger, of wanting to hide something from themselves as well as from others, in some cases, the unsoundness of their positions; in others, their triviality. Obscure writing, he suspects, is a tool of deception, the deception of others and ourselves. And those who deceive themselves, not knowing their own minds, are usually in a bad position to know and write about the human mind in general. For Kaufmann, there is an intrinsic connection between the failure of style and the failure to know the mind. It is no mere coincidence that Kaufmann finds that those who write badly usually do not have much of value to say. With the exception of Hegel, he finds those who have written unclearly (Kant, Heidegger, Adler, and Jung) not to have made significant contributions to the discovery of the mind. Correspondingly, those who, in his opinion, have made major contributions (Goethe, Nietzsche, and Freud), were all masterful writers.

This attack of obscure writing is particularly significant with respect to a tradition, like that of German philosophy, in which there is not only a great deal of obscure writing, some of it extremely obscure, but also a remarkable toleration of obscurity and even a perverse tendency to find some virtue in it. How often complaints about the grotesque syntax and seemingly insurmountable opacity of these authors is met with lame excuses and hackneyed justifications: "The text may indeed be ferociously difficult, but the effort will be repaid by the excellence of the ideas it contains." "Keep reading! If you are tenacious and intelligent, you shall be rewarded. If you are not rewarded by hard-won but important revelations, you were obviously not tenacious and intelligent enough." "Given the complexity of the ideas, there is no simpler way to express them." "Given the *depth* of the ideas, there is no way to express them more clearly." "Considering the recondite content of the text, this is, despite appearances to the contrary, the best of all possible prose."

Kaufmann is not buying any of this. What seems to be bad writing, he suggests, *is* usually bad writing—and should not be tolerated or justified. Convolutedness and obscurity in writing are hardly ever the ineluctable reflections of corresponding complexities of content and of depths beyond the reach of direct illumination. They are more often subterfuges. Often the prolonged study of devilishly difficult texts does not repay the effort. It is high time someone confronted, as Kaufmann does, the existential issues raised by this body of almost impenetrable classics.

This concentration on writing style is a significant part of an attempt to capture the overall style of the thinkers discussed, a unifying style that includes the way they wrote, thought, and lived. To this admirable end, the analysis of specific texts almost always serves to reveal more general textures. The microscope is almost always a prelude to the telescope. The aim is always the large view, in which the trees do not obscure the forest. In this way, Walter Kaufmann made his last and grandest attempt to appropriate—and contribute

to—his cultural heritage. *Discovering the Mind* was for Kaufmann, though in a much more modern and modest manner,
what *The Phenomenology of the Spirit* had been for Hegel.
Following the advice of Goethe's *Faust*, he too "took what he
had inherited from his fathers and made it his own."

Ivan Soll
Bad Homburg

Notes

1. *Discovering the Mind* (New York: McGraw-Hill, 1980) p. 4.
2. Ibid. p. 7.
3. Ibid. pp. 6–7.
4. Ibid. p. 8.

Prologue ▶▶▶

1 ▶▶▶ Few people know their own minds. Many, though by no means all, would like to. Many more would like to know the minds of others. And philosophers and psychologists have long dreamed of understanding how the human mind works generally.

The imperative "Know thyself!" goes back to the ancient Greeks, and several Greek philosophers alluded to it. But the surviving evidence does not suggest that they reached any great heights of self-knowledge. The most profound exploration of this subject in antiquity was written not by a philosopher but by Sophocles, whose tragedy *Oedipus Tyrannus* suggests forcibly that self-knowledge might be a scarcely endurable torment. Oedipus is determined to find out who he is and how he is really related to those closest to him, and when he does he despairs.

What I am concerned with is self-knowledge, meaning knowledge both of our own minds and of the human mind in general. And when I speak of the mind I am not contrasting it with the heart or soul, as do those who associate the mind with the intellect and the heart or soul with emotion. I use "mind" as an inclusive term for feeling and intelligence, reason and emotion, perception and will, thought and the unconscious.

My usage, which is in accord with the best dictionaries and encyclopedias, does not commit me to the belief that minds exist, any more than Freud's use of "soul" committed him to a belief in souls. Pascal's "the heart has its reasons" did not entail any belief that these reasons were really situated in the heart. "Heart," "soul," and "mind" are ways of speaking of aspects of ourselves that seem to be mysterious and elusive.

2 ▶▶▶ Why is it that we have made so little progress in the discovery of the mind when we have done so much better in gaining knowledge of the outside world? We have discovered laws to which distant stars and galaxies seem to conform, but we do not understand the human mind nearly as well although it is so much closer to home and we seem to have privileged access to it.

The most obvious answer is that until recently the mind has been the province of philosophers and other humanists, and that the humanities are in a bad way compared to the natural sciences, and quite especially to astronomy and physics. Attending the Einstein Centennial Symposium in Princeton, in March 1979, soon after this book was finished, and going on from there to hear a humanities seminar at which a historian presented a paper, I could not help sharing this widespread feeling. The difference in standards was frightening.

This sense of an appalling disparity between the humanities and the natural sciences is nothing new. Immanuel Kant shared it when in 1787, in the preface to the second edition of his *Critique of Pure Reason*, he spoke more than a dozen times of "the secure stride of a science," contrasting it with the groping and fumbling that seemed to him to characterize much of the work in his own discipline. Exactly twenty years later, Hegel insisted in the preface to his first book that everything depended on elevating philosophy to the rank of a science.

Both Kant and Hegel were concerned specifically with the discovery of the mind, but they fell pitifully short of their avowed intentions. Why? I hope to show that this was due in large measure to the fact that they operated with a mistaken conception of science. As a result, they provided models that were almost as harmful as those which Kant cleared out of the way. We owe Kant an immense debt for making a clean sweep of so many fruitless speculations, and we can apply to him a remark the young Nietzsche once jotted down without ever publishing it himself: "The errors of great men are venerable because they are more fruitful than the truths of little men."[1] For all that, they do not cease to be errors, and one shows little respect for a thinker if one does not take his ideas seriously enough to ask whether they stand up under criticism.

In many ways, Kant was, despite his virtues, a disaster. The lack of progress we have made in the discovery of the mind was due in several ways to his fateful influence. That he was a great and brilliant man is no sufficient reason for dealing at length with his shortcomings. Is not this kind of antiquarianism one of the curses that keep the humanities from getting anywhere? Entirely too much energy is devoted to clearing up what happened long ago. Would it not be far better to start right off with a more positive approach?

I shall do precisely that and begin my story not with Kant, who is widely considered Germany's most renowned philosopher, if not the greatest philosopher since Plato and Aristotle, but with Goethe who is, by

[1] *Werke*, I, p. 393. All translations from the German are mine.

common consent, Germany's greatest poet. And I aim to show that Goethe did more than any man before him to advance the discovery of the mind. I shall be specific and spell out what I consider his major contributions. But then I shall turn to Kant and present him not merely as a dead philosopher who lived a long time ago but rather as the best possible representative and embodiment of ways of thinking that are still very much alive today.

I shall not tarry over faults peculiar to him and of no special relevance now. The major shortcomings on which we shall concentrate still impede the discovery of the mind today. And it is helpful to see how they existed together in a single mind, and how this mind was in ever so many ways the diametrical opposite of Goethe's. Here we have two ideal types, and if they had not actually existed, I doubt that anyone could have invented a more striking pair of opposite mentalities.

Goethe and Kant were contemporaries and wrote in the same language. To be more precise, they both wrote German but hardly the same language. Kant was twenty-five years older, but Goethe became world famous several years before Kant did, and their contemporaries were troubled by these two divergent models. Even before the end of the eighteenth century, Friedrich Schiller, the great poet who was Goethe's close friend as well as a devoted admirer of Kant's philosophy, tried to reconcile the irreconcilable. A great many others, from Hegel to Sartre, have tried to do this too in different ways. Thus Kant's disastrous influence was not by any means confined to his out-and-out followers but also marred the work of many important thinkers who tried somehow to mediate between him and Goethe.

Once this is recognized clearly, ever so many obscurities in the works of later thinkers are illuminated. It should be one of the fringe benefits of this study that it leads to a new and better understanding of a good deal of the intellectual history of the past two hundred years. But my central aim throughout is to contribute to the discovery of the mind.

3 ▶▶▶ Insofar as many highly intelligent people are still caught in fruitless approaches and follow paths that get lost in the woods without ever leading anywhere, it should be helpful to show what specifically is wrong with these approaches. The mere fact that they have not worked very well on quite a number of occasions leaves open the possibility that perseverance may pay after all. Hence it is essential to demonstrate what is wrong in principle. To put it more plainly and concretely, it needs to be shown how Kant's ways are really quite opposed to the ways that have led to the triumphs of modern science. It may sound almost too neat to say that for Kant science was Newtonian science while Goethe exerted himself to develop a non-Newtonian science, but we shall see that this contrast is indeed relevant though it does not explain everything by any means.

One can also advance the discovery of the mind by seeing as part of a single picture the major contributions made by Goethe and Hegel, and then later on by Nietzsche and Freud. Scholars have become such specialists that those who are experts on one of these men rarely know the others very well. It should prove helpful to show how their insights supplement each other.

Finally, the ideas of these men are not totally unrelated to their mentalities. The nature of this relationship is a touchy issue. For a long time, philosophers not only shied away from any study of it but actually branded even the least concern with it as a fallacy. In this way they set bounds to the inquiring mind. Some of the first attempts to breach this taboo have been rather crude and unilluminating, but the problem is of immense interest.

Why should students of the mind concern themselves only either with neurotics and sick people or with the run-of-the-mill perceptions of ordinary people, and not at all with the minds of great philosophers, psychologists, and poets? We should inquire into the relationship of Kant and C. G. Jung or Martin Heidegger and Martin Buber to their theories.

In attempting to do just that, I shall stay clear of reductionism, by which I mean the claim that something is "nothing but" something else. In the last volume of this trilogy we shall have occasion to consider a letter in which Jung said on February 28, 1943: "In the critical philosophy of the future there will be a chapter on 'The Psychopathology of Philosophy.'" What he went on to call for was a reductionist science that would show how various philosophies were, in his own words, "nothing but" neurotic symptoms. Even when turning the tables on him and showing that a psychopathology of *psychology*—and of *his* psychology in particular—could be every bit as interesting, I hope to avoid reductionism. A poem that expresses the highly individual sensibility and experience of a poet is not for that reason worthless, and a mask can be a work of art while the face behind it may be commonplace.

In short, we are embarking on a voyage of discovery. And it may not be inappropriate to anticipate one major point: Kant's insistence that in the philosophy of mind we cannot tolerate anything less than absolute certainty, necessity, and completeness was disastrous. To make discoveries one must not be too anxious about errors. One must be willing to state a theory clearly and crisply and say as the physicists do: I have worked on this for a long time, and this is what I have come up with; now tell me what, if anything, is wrong with it. And before one ever gets that far, one has usually found many of one's own attempts faulty and discarded them. What is most needful is by no means certainty but rather, to quote

Nietzsche's happy phrase, "the courage for an attack on one's convictions."[2] There are few areas, if any, where such courage is needed more than in the discovery of the mind.

[2] *Werke*, XVI, p. 318.

PART ▶ **I**

Goethe and the
Discovery of the Mind ▶▶▶

4 ▶▶▶ We possess an account of Goethe at twenty-one, before he became famous. It is found in a draft for a letter written in May 1772 by Johann Christian Kestner, who eleven months later married Charlotte Buff, with whom Goethe was also in love. Deeply upset by this marriage, Goethe wrote *The Sufferings of the Young Werther,* which ends with Werther's suicide. Once that novel appeared, if not a year earlier, in 1773, when *Götz* was published, people who met the author had preconceptions based on his writings. Kestner's description is invaluable because it is based solely on his impression of the young Goethe himself.

> In the spring a certain Goethe came here from Frankfurt, by profession a doctor of laws, aged 23 [actually 21], the only son of a very wealthy father, to look around here for some practice—that was his father's purpose, but his own was rather to study Homer, Pindar, etc., whatever his genius, his way of thinking, and his heart might inspire him to do. . . .
>
> . . . I got to know Goethe only late and by chance. . . .

You know that I do not form judgments hastily. I did find that he had some genius and a vivid imagination, but I did not consider that enough to esteem him highly.

Before I continue I must attempt some description of him, as I later got to know him very well.

He has a great many talents, is a true genius and a man of character. Possesses an extraordinarily vivid imagination and expresses himself for the most part in images and metaphors. . . .

He is violent in all of his emotions but often has a great deal of self-control. His way of thinking is noble; free of prejudices, he acts as he feels without caring whether others like it, whether it is the fashion, whether the way one lives permits it. All compulsion is hateful to him.

He loves children and can occupy himself with them extremely well. He is bizarre, and some features of his behavior and appearance could make him disagreeable; but children, women, and many others think very well of him.

The female sex he holds in very high esteem.

In principles he is not yet firm and is still striving for a system of sorts.

To say something about that, he has a high opinion of Rousseau but is not a blind admirer of him.

He is not what one calls orthodox. But not from pride or caprice or to make an impression. About certain very important issues he speaks to few and does not like to disturb others in their calm ideas.

. . . He does not go to church, not even for the sacraments, also prays rarely. For he says, for that I am not enough of a liar. . . .

I wanted to describe him, but it would become too lengthy, for there is much that could be said about him. *He is, in one word, a very remarkable human being.*[1]

What does all this have to do with the discovery of the mind? One of Goethe's friends, F. H. Jacobi, whose

[1] *Amelung,* # 24.

book *On the Doctrine of Spinoza* (1785) provoked a major controversy and altered the course of German philosophy, answered that question in one line, in a letter to a friend, August 10, 1774. He said of Goethe: "This man is autonomous [*selbstständig*] from tip to toe."[2]

5 ▶▶▶ Goethe's first major contribution to the discovery of the mind is that he provided a new model of autonomy or freedom. "Freedom" sounds less technical but is less clear and invites needless controversies; for example, about free will or politics. "Autonomy" suggests, strictly speaking, that one gives or has given laws to oneself; that one is self-governing; that in essentials one obeys one's own imperatives. Kant made "autonomy" the centerpiece of his philosophy and discussed the term at length in his first major work on ethics, in 1785. Even his enthusiastic admirers, however, did not accept his conception of autonomy. Goethe had refuted it not by argument but by his example; or, to be more precise, without as much as mentioning Kant, Goethe had exhibited the absurdity of Kant's notion of autonomy. At the heart of Nietzsche's philosophy and Freud's psychology we still find Goethe's version of autonomy, not Kant's.

Kant's fundamental intention was to show how human autonomy was possible in a deterministic, Newtonian universe. His commitment to human freedom as well as science had a great deal to do with the enormous impact of his philosophy. Nevertheless, his conception of autonomy was stillborn and largely ignored because his readers felt that, knowing Goethe, they knew what it really meant to be autonomous.

Philosophy students are taught the importance of proofs and refutations, and these are indeed invaluable

[2] *Amelung,* # 68.

for the training of undisciplined minds. But crucial philosophical claims have rarely been proved, nor do they generally die by refutation. Kant's celebrated refutations of the three traditional proofs of God's existence may seem to be notable exceptions, but what he refuted were supposedly rigorous proofs; he neither refuted nor claimed to refute the belief that God exists.

Kant's notion of autonomy will be considered in Chapter IV; Goethe's, here and now. Consider a remark Goethe made in a conversation with Eckermann, May 2, 1831. It was not published by Eckermann until 1836, but the point was implicit, if not explicit, throughout Goethe's life, and not lost on his more intelligent admirers: "Thus one also finds in life a mass of people who do not have enough character to stand alone; they throw themselves at a party, and that makes them feel stronger and allows them to be somebody."

This idea became central in Nietzsche's work and has become familiar to many readers through Jean-Paul Sartre's "Portrait of the Anti-Semite" and Eric Hoffer's *The True Believer.* The other side of the coin is equally well known. At the end of Ibsen's *An Enemy of the People* the hero makes what he calls "a great discovery," namely "that the strongest man in the world is he that stands most alone." In the same play we encounter "the compact majority." Near the beginning of a brief autobiography Sigmund Freud said: "Early in life I became familiar with the lot of standing alone among the opposition and being placed under a ban by the 'compact majority.' This laid the foundation for a certain independence of judgment."

Ibsen knew that Kierkegaard in "That Individual" (1859) had sounded the refrain "The crowd is untruth," and the demand to stand alone is one of the central motifs of the work of both. When Kierkegaard spoke of "becoming the individual" he in effect sided with Goethe against Kant. He probably did not know that

Goethe had said (*Sprüche in Prosa*, # 945):

> Nothing is more revolting than the majority; for it consists of few vigorous predecessors, of knaves who accommodate themselves, of weak people who assimilate themselves, and the mass that toddles after them without knowing in the least what it wants.

It was Schiller, Goethe's close friend, who first popularized the crucial idea in his most popular play, *Wilhelm Tell*. Despite his admiration for Kant, he proclaimed in the third scene of the first act: *"Der Starke ist am mächtigsten allein."* (The strong individual is most powerful when standing alone.)

Kant himself was a loner and did not derive his sense of identity from membership in any group; yet he associated morality with universality, and autonomy with universal laws that are binding for all rational beings, not with individuality. Goethe taught by example that autonomy involves going it alone.

6 ▶▶▶ The extent of Goethe's alienation from the compact majority has been obscured both by historical distance and by the myth that pictures him as a pillar of society, at least during his later years. That the young author of *Götz*, *Werther*, and the original version of *Faust* was a rebellious individualist is a point that does not need laboring. But he never ceased to be the passionate man who knows how to employ his passions creatively instead of making war on them; he always remained, as Nietzsche put it after calling Kant "the antipode of Goethe," a human being "who might dare to afford the whole range and wealth of being natural, being strong enough for such freedom."[3] His autonomy did not consist, as Kant's did, of being governed at every

[3] *Twilight of the Idols*, sec. 49.

turn by some maxim and of always doing what one *always* does, thus making a virtue of routine and repetition (See Section 31 below). On the contrary, Goethe kept astonishing people by doing again and again what neither he nor anyone else had done before. His works were not extrapolations from his first major success, like Kant's, nor did he keep imitating the style of his first masterpiece, like Kant, nor did he have a horror of change, like Kant. In all of these ways Goethe's autonomy was the opposite of Kant's.

Of course, he was a cabinet minister in a grand duchy and in many ways exceedingly respectable; and in his later years he had a·title and was made a member of the nobility: Herr Geheimrat von Goethe. But in what mattered to him—love and works—he was his own law. In 1788, the year Kant published his *Critique of Practical Reason*, his major work on ethics, Goethe wrote his *Roman Elegies*, celebrating carnal love, and began his affair with Christiane Vulpius, whom he married in 1806 when their son August was seventeen. Until then Goethe and Christiane had lived together without the benefit of the clergy. The day after the wedding the poet took the new Geheimrätin von Goethe to a reception, "not one given by a member of Weimar society, it is true, for those ladies continue their resistance for a long time yet, but by . . . Frau Schopenhauer, mother of the philosopher . . ."[4]

In 1789 Goethe turned forty. During the following year he published, among a great many other things, *Torquato Tasso* (one of his best plays, which consummates his "classicism," being composed in iambic pentameter and confined to five dramatis personae), *Faust: A Fragment* (which helped to launch German romanticism), *Attempt to Explain the Metamorphosis of Plants*, and two volumes of *Contributions to Optics*. Also in

[4] Friedenthal, *Goethe*, p. 263.

1790 he finished his *Roman Elegies* and composed his *Venetian Epigrams,* heaping scorn on Christianity and its founder, and he assumed the directorship of the Weimar court theater. That he had the courage to publish the epigrams he did publish is more surprising than that he should also have written the ones suppressed until the twentieth century. Here are two he published:

Every enthusiast nail to the cross in his thirtieth year!
  Once they see through the world, those taken in become knaves.

Much there is I can stand, and most things not easy to suffer
  I bear with quiet resolve, just as a god commands it.
Only a few I find as repugnant as snakes and poison—
  these four: tobacco smoke, bedbugs, garlic, and cross.

And here are two he did not publish:

What applies to the Christians is also true of the Stoics:
  Free human beings could not choose to be Christian or Stoic.

You are deceived by statesmen, priests, and the teachers of morals;
  and this cloverleaf, mob, how you like to adore it!
Even today there's, alas, little worth thinking and saying
  that does not grievously flout mores, the state, and the gods.[5]

None of this may strike many modern readers as especially bold. The best way of showing how all of it bears on Goethe's autonomy may well be to recall how the first translators of his *Faust* into English reacted to that play, which has come to be regarded as the quintessence of dignity. What is apt to shock readers today is not one or another Venetian epigram but the prudery of Goethe's contemporaries; and to understand his autonomy we must form some conception of the world in which he lived.

The first English version, *Faustus from the German,* appeared in London in 1821. The translator remained anonymous and informed the reader at the out-

[5] For these and many more examples see Kaufmann, *Twenty-five German Poets: A Bilingual Collection.*

set that "some parts are omitted which, it was felt, would be offensive to English readers." These parts, it turns out, include the "Prologue in Heaven" because it "is repugnant to notions of propriety such as are entertained in this country."

Two years later, Lord Francis Leveson Gower also omitted most of the Prologue from his version because he found that in the dialogue between Mephisto and the Lord "there is a tone of familiarity on both sides which is revolting in a sacred subject." Before I had read the prefaces to these translations, I assumed that Shelley translated the "Prologue in Heaven" merely because he found it exceptionally beautiful. But the fact that he also translated the Walpurgis Night leaves little doubt about his reasons. It is doubly noteworthy that both the Prologue and the Walpurgis Night were first published by Goethe in 1808, just before he turned sixty.

It is also a measure of Goethe's alienation from society as well as his autonomy that, having finished *Faust: The Second Part of the Tragedy* at the age of eighty-two, he tied it up in a parcel and refused to discuss the ending even with friends who inquired about it. It was to be published after his death. It was not that he was afraid of anyone, nor was there anything to be afraid of. He simply did not write to please others, least of all the public. He did not care to know how others might react to his work. He was not heteronomous but autonomous.

7 ▶▶▶ That a human being could have a significant impact on human thought by virtue of his character or personality may seem strange to many professors who assume that contributions must be made in terms of articles or books. Even those who do not sacrifice character to scholarship are apt to feel that personality is something private that has no place in their

writings. It is assumed that science is impersonal and that scholarly work ought to be scientific.

One might call this attitude positivistic, but it actually antedates the emergence of positivism, and Kant embodied it as well as anybody. In this respect, too, Goethe was Kant's antipode. Goethe was an exceptionally strong personality, and in his works he made no effort to hide his light under a bushel. Reversing the practice of many others, he came to hide himself more and more in social situations—behind the mask of the Herr Geheimrat von Goethe—while he revealed his character in his writings.

Of course, Goethe was not by any means the first human being to have influenced human thought through his character. Leaving aside religious figures, who pose special problems, and characters in the Bible and in Greek tragedy, such as Samson, Saul, and David, Aeschylus' Prometheus, and Sophocles' Oedipus, paradigmatic individuals who have changed our perception of what it means, or could mean, to be human include Socrates and Caesar, Napoleon and Lincoln, Rembrandt and Beethoven, Nietzsche and van Gogh.[6] Socrates may be the most obvious example, and the pertinent points can be summed up in a few words:

> The ethics of Plato and Aristotle, the Cynics and the Cyrenaics, the Stoics and the Epicureans was largely inspired by the personality, the life, and the death of Socrates. The image of the proud, ironic sage who found in wisdom and continual reflection that enduring happiness that riches cannot buy and whose character had somehow had such power that a despot, lacking self-control, seems like a slave compared with him—this wonderful embodiment of human dignity captivated all the later thinkers of antiquity, became their ethical ideal, and led to a new conception of man. Socrates' fearlessly questioning iconoclasm and his defiant decision to die rather than to

[6] See my *What Is Man?*, Chapter V: "Ecce Homo."

cease speaking freely had an equal impact on the modern mind. His character and bearing have influenced the history of philosophy as much as any system.[7]

Socrates also provided a decidedly un-Kantian paradigm of autonomy, but Goethe's version of autonomy differed from Socrates'. Socrates did not write, while Goethe was above all else a writer. What is more, Goethe was a poet who excelled at finding words for feelings, emotions, and passions, while Socrates inspired ever so many philosophers who believed as the Stoics did, partly under his influence, that happiness requires the subjugation of emotion and passion. To quote Nietzsche once more, Goethe could "dare to afford the whole range and wealth of being natural, being strong enough for such freedom" because he knew "how to use to his advantage even that from which the average nature would perish."[8] To enjoy and explore the passions without becoming their slave, to employ them creatively instead of either being dominated by them or trying to resist them, was of the essence of Goethe's autonomy.

8 ▶▶▶ The second point about Goethe's influence on the discovery of the mind can be made briefly. It can actually be summarized in a four-word epigram: *Man is his deeds.* This formulation is widely associated with existentialism and specifically with Sartre's influential lecture *L'Existentialism est un humanisme* (1946). In this lecture Sartre actually fell back on Kant in his attempt to defend existentialism against the charge of irresponsibility: "Nothing can be

[7] This is the penultimate paragraph of "Goethe and the History of Ideas," reprinted as Chapter IV in my *From Shakespeare to Existentialism.*

[8] *Twilight of the Idols,* section 49.

better for us unless it is better for all," he said, and "in choosing for himself he [man] chooses for all men." Moreover, Sartre gave his last major philosophical work a Kantian title: *Critique de la raison dialectique* (1960). One might therefore be inclined to see Sartre as a philosopher in the Kantian tradition. But his claim to fame rests as much on his plays, short stories, and novels as on his philosophical tomes, and the hero of what Sartre himself considered his best play,[9] *Le Diable et le Bon Dieu* (1951), is Götz, the hero of the play that made Goethe famous. Sartre is clearly one of the many thinkers who have tried—and failed—to reconcile Kant and Goethe.

The idea that man is his deeds is not an existentialist innovation but found in Goethe, who rejected the belief that man has an essence along with Kant's and Plato's doctrines of two worlds. Goethe repudiated Kant's notion of a noumenal self that lies beyond or behind the world of experience. Indeed, he went further and rejected any form of essentialism. In the fascinating preface to his *Doctrine of Colors* (1810) he put the point concisely:

> We really try in vain to express the essence of a thing. We become aware of effects [*Wirkungen*], and a complete history of these effects would seem to comprehend the essence of the thing. We exert ourselves in vain to describe the character of a human being; but assemble his actions, his deeds, and a picture of his character will confront us.

As a dramatist and novelist Goethe naturally knew that the way to depict or create a character is not to enumerate qualities but to depict or create actions. But Goethe does not claim in this passage that this is what distinguishes human beings. On the contrary, he speaks

[9] For Sartre's opinion of this play see "Sartre at Seventy," p. 14.

of things, and his very next sentence begins: "Colors are the deeds of light." In effect, Goethe denies that there are essences apart from appearances.

Kant considered the essence of a man unknowable because it transcended all possible experience. The same consideration applied to our ultimate motives, according to Kant. This did not keep Kant from offering an anatomy of the mind, based not on experience but on what *must* be the case to make possible human experience and knowledge, including what Kant took to be scientific and moral knowledge.

Goethe implicitly calls into question the existence of the mind. Neither the Buddhist doctrine that there is no mind nor William James' essay "Does Consciousness Exist?" (in *Essays in Radical Empiricism*) would have startled him. To know Faust's mind, we observe what he says and does; and to create Faust's mind, the poet invents speeches and deeds for him. But that means that we can dispense with the concept of mind as an entity. Mind becomes an inclusive term for feeling and intelligence, reason and emotion, perception and will, thought and unconscious. If we see things that way, does it make any sense to speak of discovering the mind? It does, as a kind of shorthand.

In this connection it is worth noting that the German language lacks an equivalent for "mind." Kant, who tried to give us an anatomy of the mind, lacked a term for that of which sensibility, understanding, reason, the inclinations, and the power of judgment were supposed to be parts. Sometimes he called it *Gemüt,* which sounds quaint today and brings to mind very dated poetry; rarely, *Seele* (soul). Some of the German philosophers who followed him employed a word that Goethe and Schiller used frequently: *Geist* (spirit). Freud, a century later, used *Seele (psyche* in Greek) and developed psychoanalysis. In an important sense, of course, Freud did not believe that we have souls, yet he needed a word for what he analyzed. Similarly, Goethe and Schiller did not believe in spirits, but used "spirit" (*Geist*) nevertheless, mindful that it was a poetic rather than a scientific term.

This multiplicity of terms has obscured the crucial fact that all of these men shared a fundamental concern that can be described as the discovery of the mind. But the use of this term does not entail any Cartesian dualism of mind and body. Most of these men opposed any such dualism.

It is far from entirely accidental that Kant featured reason and the power of judgment in the titles of his three "critiques," while Freud, though opposed to religion, preferred to speak of the soul. Kant was interested mainly in the rational part of the mind while Freud gave us, in effect, a critique of unreason, concentrating on the irrational and unconscious part of the mind. Unlike either of them, we shall be concerned with the whole mind.

9 ▶▶▶ Goethe's greatest contribution to the discovery of the mind was that, more than anyone else, he showed how the mind can be understood only in terms of development. In Kant's conception of the mind, as we shall see, development has no place. He claimed to describe the human mind as it always is, has been, and will be. There is no inkling that it might change in the course of history, not to speak of biological evolution or the course of a person's life.

Goethe did not prove the opposite view by argument, but he showed and made people see how the mind develops and needs to be understood in terms of development. He was not a philosopher and did not claim to be one. But the question whether showing something is inherently inferior to proving it or deducing it from pure concepts is part of Goethe's legacy.

Goethe, who was born in 1749, commanded the attention of his contemporaries from 1773, when his *Götz* appeared, until his death in 1832, over a period of almost sixty years. As soon as Schiller and Fichte, Hegel, Schelling, and Schopenhauer became aware of literature in their youth, they began to follow Goethe's development; and there was no blinking the fact that Goethe did develop. Nobody could see his more recent works as extrapolations from his earlier writings, as could be done in Kant's case. Goethe's style kept changing, but the changes were not gratuitous. He was no chameleon, no weathervane, and did not bow to fashion. His development gave every appearance of being organic, and his contemporaries witnessed it with their own eyes, with growing fascination. Every new work by Germany's greatest poet and writer was read as soon as it appeared and was totally unpredictable.

Having consummated first the so-called Storm and Stress and then German classicism, Goethe all but created German romanticism by publishing *Faust: A Fragment* and then following it with a novel, published in installments in the 1790s, *Wilhelm Meisters Lehrjahre.* This novel dealt, as the title declares, with the hero's years of learning or apprenticeship. Ever since, most of the major German novels down to the best-known works of Thomas Mann and Hermann Hesse have been so-called *Bildungsromane,* which relate the development of the hero or, to cite the subtitle of Nietzsche's *Ecce Homo:* "How One Becomes What One Is."

It is not enough to note that in the 1790s the budding German romantic movement developed a taste for fragments, though Goethe himself was not satisfied until he finally succeeded in completing his *Faust.* The play itself came to be understood more and more as a celebration of ceaseless striving, and what Goethe stimulated

Fauſt.

Eine Tragödie.

von

Goethe.

K. Tübingen.
in der J. G. Cotta'ſchen Buchhandlung.
1808.

was an overwhelming interest in becoming rather than being, in processes rather than results.

Carrying Goethe's suggestions a step further, we might say: There is no mind, and the way to discover the mind is to study feelings and emotions, thoughts and desires, dreams and acts. Or we could dispense with the paradox and say that mind is no substance or thing but a name for all of these phenomena, and that the way to comprehend them is to consider their sequence in time. The sequence or development is essential.

Apart from his *Wilhelm Meister,* Goethe impressed these ideas upon his contemporaries in three major ways: through his *Faust,* his life, and his autobiography. The impact of Goethe's *Faust* on German thought has no parallel in French, British, or American literature.

Had Goethe seen fit to publish the original version in 1775, its effect would have been overwhelming. Goethe's reasons for not doing this and publishing *Faust: A Fragment* in 1790 and *The First Part of the Tragedy* in 1808 were as honorable as could be and illustrate his autonomy. He did not publish what did not come up to his own standards. As he developed, he was no longer satisfied with the style of the original, which seemed too close to the period of Storm and Stress. But by initially publishing a fragment, it being known that there was more even then, and by letting people hope that eventually the sequel would appear, Goethe compelled his public to see a literary masterpiece not as a finished product, perfect and complete, but as something that was developing. Moreover, the hero, Faust, changed even in the fragment, and the reader was led to wonder how he would develop—not merely what might still happen to him, but what kind of a person he would become.

After eighteen years in which Faust had come to be acknowledged as the most fascinating and representative character in German literature, the whole First Part finally appeared with its overpowering conclusion, but it left this riddle unsolved. The work and the hero were still evolving, and that was how matters still stood when Hegel died in 1831.

At the beginning of the drama, Faust in his study seems stunted and incomplete, stuck in a static existence, a travesty of a man as long as he remains only a scholar. He has long ceased to develop, and his life is a mockery of life. Could Goethe have been thinking of Kant when he wrote the original version in the early 1770s? Kant was not yet widely known at that time, and yet Johann Gottfried Herder, who had been one of Kant's students in Königsberg, could have told Goethe about him in Strassburg in the early seventies. It is unlikely that Goethe's picture of Faust was inspired by Herder's reports because Herder's later account of Kant in the 1760s is quite different.[10] But if Goethe had known of Kant, how could he have done better? Faust's first monologue begins with a curse on Kant's kind of existence—a life without development, a life of routine, a death in life. Faust is a great scholar who lives in books and concepts without knowing anything of love and women.

"That is your world! A world indeed!" (line 409). What Faust craves is what Kant sought at all costs to avoid: change. The reader is made to feel that without development, without living dangerously in the world and risking love and the unforeseen, the great scholar is a human failure if not a caricature of a man. No attempt at a philosophical refutation of Kant could have approximated the impact of Faust.

The inexhaustible richness of the play has given rise to an immense secondary literature, and one could easily

[10] *Briefe zur Beförderung der Humanität, Werke,* ed. Suphan, XVIII, p. 324f. Quoted in Kantzenbach (1970), p. 18f., and Schultz (1965), p. 30.

go on and on about points that have left a mark on subsequent thought and contributed to the discovery of the mind. Above all, Goethe's Mephistopheles is a keen psychologist, a forerunner of Nietzsche, Freud, and Gide, who sees through Faust's constant self-deceptions and punctures them mercilessly with his deadly wit. That is a large part of his function in the play; he helped to sensitize generations of readers to self-deception. Hegel already spoke of Mephistopheles as generally a good authority and liked to quote him. Moreover, there is the conception of Mephistopheles that is spelled out by the Lord in the Prologue in Heaven:

> I never hated those who were like you:
> Of all the spirits that negate
> The knavish jester gives me least to do.
> For man's activity can easily abate,
> He soon prefers uninterrupted rest;
> To give him this companion hence seems best
> Who roils and must as Devil help create (lines 337ff.).

And in his first dialogue with Faust, Mephistopheles calls himself

> Part of that force which would
> Do evil evermore, and yet creates the good.
> . . .
> I am the spirit that negates (1335ff.).

In Goethe's profoundly anti-Manichaean conception, evil and the evil one are integrated in a vast cosmic design and contribute to development—and without that there would be uninterrupted rest, which is dismissed with contempt. What is wanted is development.

Goethe cannot be identified with Faust. Clearly, he is Mephistopheles as well as Faust, which is to say that he is unlike both. Neither Faust nor Mephistopheles could have written *Faust*. But the insistence on the need for development is very much Goethe's own and was impressed on his contemporaries and on later generations by his life as well as his work.

Internationally famous at twenty-five, Goethe never copied past successes, never got stuck in a rut, but always kept developing. We have noted some of the high points of his artistic development through the publication of *Faust: A Fragment* in 1790 and his great *Bildungsroman* of the nineties, *Wilhelm Meister*. It was also in 1790 that he began to introduce his conception of development into the natural sciences, in his *Attempt to Explain the Metamorphosis of Plants,* followed by his *Contributions to Optics* and eventually his *Doctrine of Colors*. But none of his works ever rivaled the impact of *Faust*, except his poems. He was far and away the greatest German poet, and many of his poems achieved enormous popularity. As a poet, too, he kept developing, and at the age of seventy he revolutionized German poetry once more with the publication of his *West-Eastern Divan*, a collection of his most recent poems in which he imitated Persian and other Near Eastern models, thus contributing to a lively concern with what he himself called, coining this term, "world literature."

In 1823, at seventy-four, he fell in love with the daughter of a woman whom he had loved in his youth, and he would have liked to marry her. But he parted from her and in desperation wrote his "Marienbad Elegy," expressing the hopeless love of an old man for a young woman. As an epigraph he used two lines from his *Tasso:*

> *And when man in his agony grows mute,*
> *A god gave me to utter what I suffer.*

Two years before his death, Goethe said in a conversation with Frédéric Jacob Soret, a scientist from Geneva who translated Goethe's *Metamorphosis of Plants* into French:

I have never affected anything in my poetry. What I did not live and what did not well up from inside me [*was mir nicht auf die Nägel brannte und zu schaffen machte*] I did not express in poetry. Love poems I wrote only when I loved. How then could I have written hate poems when I did not hate! And between us, I did not hate the French . . .

The relationship of some of Goethe's works to his life and loves was so striking that a hundred years after his death boys like myself were still taught the names of the women he had loved along with the works they had helped to inspire. Nor was Goethe himself innocent of this development. In 1811 he began to publish his autobiography, *Out of My Life: Poetry and Truth.* The German subtitle, *Dichtung und Wahrheit,* which is usually cited as if it were the main title, is ambiguous. *Dichtung* could mean fiction as well as poetry. The second volume appeared in 1812, the third in 1814—and eventually the sixth and last in 1822. The impact of this work was immense. It pointed the way for subsequent studies not only of Goethe but also of other poets and artists, and eventually of every human being.

10 ▶▶ In 1899 Otto Pniower assembled in a book materials bearing on the *Entstehungsgeschichte* (the history of the genesis) of Goethe's *Faust* and used as an epigraph, which he placed on the title page, a quotation from a letter Goethe had written to his friend Zelter, a composer, August 4, 1803: "Works of nature and art one does not get to know when they are finished; one must catch them in their genesis to comprehend them to some extent."

Goethe himself had intended his correspondence with Zelter for publication, and this striking quotation is merely a particularly pithy and, I think, exaggerated formulation of a point implicit not only in his autobiography but in ever so much of his work. Goethe's great example persuaded generations of German scholars to study not only Goethe and his works by paying attention to his development but to use the same approach in studying Plato and Aristotle, Michelangelo and Rembrandt, Mozart and Beethoven, Kant and Hegel, Shakespeare and Dostoevsky. It became a commonplace that great writers and artists could not be understood well until one had determined the sequence of their works and studied them as stages in a lifelong development.

Is it true that unless we "catch them in their genesis" we cannot understand works of art or nature even "to some extent"? To me it seems quite sufficient to insist that the genetic or developmental approach can enrich our understanding enormously. I *can* understand a poem or a painting, a novel, a sculpture, or a philosophical book "to some extent" without knowing its approximate date or its place in the artist's or writer's development, but when I see it in its temporal context I gain invaluable new perspectives. We shall return to this problem in the Hegel chapter.

In the English-speaking world, both the so-called new criticism and analytical philosophy represent twentieth-century revolts against this developmental approach. Neither of them can be comprehended when this is overlooked. In other words, both have to be understood in the context of a historical development, as protests against stupid excesses in which works were drowned in their background. These revolts in turn led to excesses that may seem to be specifically modern but were actually mocked already in the 1770s by Goethe's Mephistopheles in his conversation with a newly arrived student:

> The philosopher comes with analysis
> And proves it had to be like this:

> *The first was so, the second so,*
> *And hence the third and fourth was so,*
> *And were not the first and the second here,*
> *Then the third and the fourth could never appear.*
> *That is what all the students believe,*
> *But they have never learned to weave.*
> *Who would study and describe the living, starts*
> *By driving the spirit out of the parts:*
> *In the palm of his hand he holds all the sections,*
> *Lacks nothing except the spirit's connections.*

A few lines later, Mephistopheles adds, still giving advice to the student:

> *Yes, stick to words at any rate;*
> *There never was a surer gate*
> *Into the temple, Certainty.*

The student replies:

> *Yet some idea there must be.*

Mephisto retorts:

> *All right. But do not plague yourself too anxiously,*
> *For just where no ideas are*
> *The proper word is never far.*
> *With words a dispute can be won,*
> *With words a system can be spun,*
> *In words one can believe unshaken,*
> *And from a word no tittle can be taken.*

We shall have to see later to what extent these three Mephistopheles quotations apply to Kant. They are certainly far from dated. Many philosophers still stick to words and "creep" along "on the road of thought" as slowly as if philosophy were a game of chess, albeit without a queen. They come with analysis and try to prove things but miss out on the spirit that develops and defies certainty.

Microscopes are useful, but not for the discovery of the mind or spirit. While we cannot dispense with close attention to details, their meaning depends on the context. And the context cannot be understood solely in spatial terms; it is also temporal and developmental. That is a lesson Goethe impressed on all who immersed themselves in his work.

11 ▶▶▶ Goethe's opposition to Newton has not been appreciated sufficiently. Although Goethe himself considered his scientific work as important as anything he had done, his admirers are for the most part embarrassed by his polemics against Newton and either ignore them altogether or concede quickly that Newton was right about colors, and then change the subject. But even if we grant that Newton was right about colors—for our purposes it does not matter who was right—Goethe's refusal to equate science with Newtonian science represents his fourth major contribution to the discovery of the mind.

Kant equated science with Newtonian science, and many philosophers still feel that in the late eighteenth century this was reasonable. However that may be as long as "science" means physics, Kant and many of his successors wanted to make philosophy scientific and applied themselves specifically to the discovery of the mind; and that made the equation of science with Newtonian science disastrous. Goethe's notion of a non-Newtonian science was taken up in different ways by Hegel, Nietzsche, and Freud.

Hegel, like Schelling and Schopenhauer, admired Goethe's anti-Newtonian *Doctrine of Colors* and said, for example (in the Addition to Section 215 of his *Philosophy of Right*): "The physicists were peeved by Goethe's *Doctrine of Colors* because he did not belong to the guild and was on top of that a poet."

Goethe's conception of science is enormously interesting. It seems best to quote at length from Goethe's

Zur

Farbenlehre.

---

von Goethe.

Erster Band.

Nebst einem Hefte mit sechzehn Kupfertafeln.

Tübingen,

in der J. G. Cotta'schen Buchhandlung.

1810.

Preface to his *Doctrine of Colors,* cited once before about essences and deeds. The quotation that follows is long but also very beautiful, very important, and hardly known at all today. It merits attention, and Goethe put his points better than we could hope to put them if we had recourse to paraphrase.

> ... It is surely an exceedingly strange demand that is made sometimes but not fulfilled even by those who make it: that one should present experiences without any theoretical bond and leave it to the reader, the student, to form any conviction he pleases. For merely looking at something cannot get us anywhere. All seeing becomes contemplation; all contemplation, musing [*ein Sinnen*]; all musing, combination [*ein Verknüpfen*]; and so it can be said that every attentive look into the world involves theorizing. But to do this consciously, with self-knowledge, freedom, and, to use a daring word, irony— that skill is needed if the abstraction we are afraid of is to be harmless and the experienced result for which we hope is to be vital and useful.
>
> In the second part we occupy ourselves with the exposé of the Newtonian theory which has so far obstructed with force and prestige a free view of color phenomena; we fight against a hypothesis [!] that, although it is no longer found useful, still retains a traditional respect among men. ...
>
> But since the second part of our work might seem dry in content and perhaps too violent and passionate in execution, we may be permitted a cheerful parable to prepare for this more serious material and to excuse to some extent this vivid treatment.
>
> We compare the Newtonian color theory with an old castle that was initially planned by its builder with youthful haste, but by and by amplified by him and furnished in accordance with the needs of the time and circumstances and, in the course of skirmishes and hostilities, fortified and secured more and more.
>
> His heirs and successors proceeded likewise. It was considered necessary to enlarge the building, to build an

addition here, a wing there, an annex there, now because one's own needs increased, now because external adversaries exerted pressure, or owing to other accidents.

All these alien parts and additions then had to be related to each other by means of the strangest galleries, halls, and corridors. All damage, whether inflicted by enemies or by the force of time, was quickly repaired. As it became necessary, one dug deeper trenches, made the walls higher, and added towers, bay windows, and battlements. This care and these efforts produced and preserved a prejudice that the fortress was extremely valuable, although the art of building and fortifying castles had long developed much further, and people elsewhere had learned to construct far superior places for living and fighting. Above all, however, one venerated the old castle because it had never been conquered, because it had repulsed so many attacks, frustrated so many enemies, and retained its virginity. This claim, this reputation still endures. Nobody notices that the old building has become uninhabitable. . . .

This, then, is not a case of a long siege or a doubtful battle. Rather we encounter this eighth wonder of the world as an ancient relic that is already abandoned and threatens to collapse, and so we begin right away, without further ado, to reduce it, beginning with the roof, to let the sun shine at long last into the old rats' and owls' nest and reveal to the eyes of the surprised wanderer how labyrinthine and disconnected the building style was, how narrow and needy, accidental and artificial, deliberately contrived and wretchedly patched up. To show this, however, wall upon wall and vault upon vault must fall, and the rubble must be removed as quickly as possible.

To accomplish this and, if possible, to level the place while ordering the materials in such a way that they can be used again for a new building, that is the arduous task we have set ourselves in this second part. If we should succeed by the use of our utmost power and skill to reduce this bastille and to gain a free space, it is by no means our intention to cover it up and molest it again

dahin; flüchtige Abrisse zeigt man in allen Schu-
len herum und empfiehlt sie der empfänglichen Ju-
gend zur Verehrung, indessen das Gebäude bereits
leer steht, nur von einigen Invaliden bewacht,
die sich ganz ernsthaft für gerüstet halten.

Es ist also hier die Rede nicht von einer lang-
wierigen Belagerung oder einer zweifelhaften Fehde.
Wir finden vielmehr jenes achte Wunder der Welt
schon als ein verlassenes, Einsturz drohendes Al-
terthum, und beginnen sogleich von Giebel und
Dach herab es ohne weitere Umstände abzutragen,
damit die Sonne doch endlich einmal in das alte
Ratten- und Eulennest hineinscheine und dem Auge
des verwunderten Wanderers offenbare jene laby-
rinthisch unzusammenhängende Bauart, das enge
Nothdürftige, das zufällig Aufgedrungene, das
absichtlich Gekünstelte, das kümmerlich Geflickte.
Ein solcher Einblick ist aber alsdann nur möglich,
wenn eine Mauer nach der andern, ein Gewölbe

nach dem andern fällt und der Schutt, soviel sich thun läßt, auf der Stelle hinweggeräumt wird.

Dieses zu leisten und wo möglich den Platz zu ebnen, die gewonnenen Materialien aber so zu ordnen, daß sie bey einem neuen Gebäude wieder benutzt werden können, ist die beschwerliche Pflicht, die wir uns in diesem zweyten Theile auferlegt haben. Gelingt es uns nun, mit froher Anwendung möglichster Kraft und Geschickes, jene Bastille zu schleifen und einen freyen Raum zu gewinnen; so ist keinesweges die Absicht, ihn etwa sogleich wieder mit einem neuen Gebäude zu überbauen und zu belästigen; wir wollen uns vielmehr desselben bedienen, um eine schöne Reihe mannigfaltiger Gestalten vorzuführen.

Der dritte Theil bleibt daher historischen Untersuchungen und Vorarbeiten gewidmet. Aeußerten wir oben, daß die Geschichte des Menschen den Menschen darstelle, so läßt sich hier auch wohl

right away with a new building. We prefer to use it in order to present a series of beautiful forms.

The third part is therefore devoted to historical investigations and preliminaries. If we said above that the history of man shows us man, one could now claim that the history of science is science itself. One cannot gain pure recognition of what one possesses until one knows how to recognize what others have possessed before us. One will not truly and honestly enjoy the advantages of one's own time if one does not know how to appreciate the advantages of the past. But to write a history of the doctrine of color or even to do no more than to prepare the ground for one was impossible as long as the Newtonian doctrine held the field. For no aristocratic conceit has ever looked down with as much intolerable arrogance upon those who did not belong to the same guild as the Newtonian school has always condemned everything that was achieved before or beside it.

12 ▶▶▶ This text requires no close analysis. Goethe's style is not obscure. Unlike Kant, he says what he means so well that it would be the height of presumption to try to improve on it. There are mainly two reasons why he wrote so much more clearly.

First, he thought more clearly than Kant. What he wrote about he *saw* in concrete detail, and he was able to find words to communicate to others what he saw. One might call the approach he embodied visual and concrete, and Kant's conceptual and abstract. But my own approach is visual and concrete, and I am inviting you to see these two different approaches embodied in two human beings.

Secondly, Goethe had the courage to reread what he had written and to go over it again and again until it met the highest standards. As long as it did not, he was in no hurry to publish it. This was a crucial aspect of his autonomy: he did not write to please others or to enhance his status but to satisfy himself. The original version of the First Part of *Faust,* culminating in the dungeon scene whose power has never been equaled by any other German poet, was completed by 1775, but when Goethe finally published *Faust: A Fragment* in 1790 he held it back because he was not satisfied with it, and it did not appear in print until 1808, when he had succeeded in reworking it.

Many people suppose that poets and artists are impetuous and impatient while philosophers take their time to consider and reconsider every idea they have again and again. In fact, Kant was the fountainhead of a philosophical tradition that belies this popular assumption, and thinkers as diverse as Hegel and Buber followed his example rather than Goethe's.

Even Goethe's first great success, *Götz,* an exuberant work of a youthful rebel, represented a reworking of a complete draft, the so-called *Ur-Götz.* The same was true of *Iphigenie* and *Faust.* "Prometheus," the great poem first published by Jacobi in his book *On the Doctrine of Spinoza* in 1785, had been written in 1773 as part of a play that Goethe had been unable to finish. His creativity was as organic as Kant's was forced; he wrote easily but was far from accepting all that he had written as finished, even when it was far better than anything anybody else had ever done in German. In effect, he treated what he wrote as so many hypotheses that needed testing.

Having this perspective on his own work, he could see, as Kant could not, that Newton, too, though certainly a genius if there ever was one, had offered us hypotheses and by no means knowledge that was certain for all time. Goethe noted further that a hypothesis—and it should be noted that he used that word—can be "patched up" indefinitely like an old castle, but that this does not prove its truth. After a while it becomes "uninhabitable."

Much of what Goethe says in the long passage

quoted here has been widely discussed since Thomas Kuhn restated it, without citing Goethe but with many more examples, in *The Structure of Scientific Revolutions* (1962). Goethe clearly said—and said clearly—that science does not furnish certainty but only hypotheses; that it is not altogether continuous and cumulative but, after a hypothesis has been patched up to the point of becoming uninhabitable, requires a drastically new start; and that this development does not involve either conclusive proof or conclusive refutations.

As a "whole" human being, not divided against himself like Kant, he assimilated science to poetry and other creations of the mind and saw it in terms of development. As "the history of man shows us man . . . the history of science is science itself." This thoroughly anti-Kantian notion was accepted and taught systematically by Hegel, who applied it to what he himself called science (*Wissenschaft*), namely philosophy.

One cannot know what one possesses, Goethe goes on to say, "until one knows how to recognize what others have possessed before us." Or as he put it in *Faust:*

> *What from your fathers you received as heir,*
> *Acquire if you would possess it. (682f.)*

This could be the epigraph of Hegel's *Phenomenology* as well as his later philosophy. What Goethe himself has in mind in his preface to the *Farbenlehre* is, of course, above all his *history* of the doctrine of colors, which forms part of his book. But to write that, he says expressly, "was impossible as long as the Newtonian doctrine held the field." It is tempting to add that Goethe had to do away with knowledge to make room for history, but actually he was not all that interested in history. He *was* vitally interested in *development* and opposed to "ossification" (*Verknöcherung*). What he liked in Kant, after Schiller had tried very hard to make him sympathize with Kant, was that in the *Critique of Judgment* art and nature were taken up together. That he found congenial. But in retrospect it seems hard to acquit Kant of having been an apostle of ossification, not merely because he thought that Newton's doctrines were eternal truths but also because he made similar claims for his own doctrines.

A short essay Goethe wrote in 1829 is relevant here though it was published only in 1833, in Volume 10 of Goethe's posthumous works (that is, Volume 50 of the *Ausgabe letzter Hand*). It bears the title *Analyse und Synthese* and begins: "In his third lecture this year [1829] on the history of philosophy, M. Victor Cousin praises the eighteenth century mainly because in its scientific pursuits it concentrated on analysis while bewaring of hasty syntheses, that is of hypotheses." Goethe then goes on to say: "It is not enough to use the analytic method in observing nature . . . we also apply this same analysis to the prevalent syntheses [that is, comprehensive hypotheses] to find out whether people have worked the right way in accordance with true method." And a little further on: "We now turn to another more general observation. A century that concentrates merely on analysis and is, as it were, afraid of synthesis [that is, of hypotheses] is not on the right road; for only both together, like exhaling and inhaling, constitute the life of science."

Hegel had said very similarly that the true philosophical method is "analytic and synthetic at the same time,"[11] and had also associated analysis with empiricism.[12] But what is most interesting is what Goethe said next:

A false hypothesis is better than none at all [*eine falsche Hypothese ist besser als gar keine*]; for that it is false does no harm at all; but when it fortifies itself, when it is

[11] *Werke*, ed. Glockner, vol. 8, p. 449.
[12] *Ibid.*, p. 119.

accepted universally and becomes a kind of creed that nobody may doubt, that nobody may investigate, that is the disaster [*Unheil*] of which centuries suffer.

What could be more anti-Kantian? Kant had been enamored by what he took for "the secure stride of science"; he wanted to make philosophy equally secure; he craved security and certainty or, in one word, had to be sure; and he wanted to expel everything merely hypothetical from philosophy. Goethe does not mention Kant in this connection, but in the very next sentence he indicts those who would not brook any contradiction of Newton's doctrines and continues:

The French especially are to be blamed more than anyone else for the spread and ossification of this doctrine. They should therefore make up for this mistake by favoring in the nineteenth century a fresh analysis of this intricate and ossified [or frozen, or torpid: *erstarrten*] hypothesis.

Goethe was a poet and Kant a philosopher. It does not follow that Goethe, unlike Kant, should not be taken seriously in matters of this sort. Both men were also scientists, and Kant's name is still associated with a theory in astronomy while Goethe made a biological discovery and wrote extensively, in prose as well as poetry, on the metamorphosis of plants. Goethe was basically right about science and contributed a great deal to the discovery of the mind.

13 ▶▶▶ Werner Heisenberg, who won the Nobel Prize for physics for his work on quantum mechanics, has written a very sympathetic essay on "Goethe's Image of Nature" (*Das Naturbild Goethes*). What struck him as most important and revealing in the preface to the *Farbenlehre* is a phrase in the first paragraph of my long quotation: "the abstraction we are afraid of." Heisenberg comments that these words make clear "where Goethe's path must diverge from that of modern natural science [*der geltenden Naturwissenschaft*]."

We can make the point of divergence even more precise. The triumphs of modern physics, from Newton to our time, depend on the ingenious use of mathematics, and Goethe tended to disparage mathematics. What he always wanted, in science as in poetry, was *Anschauung*. There is no exact English equivalent for this German word, which Kant used in an entirely different sense (see Section 22). The verb *anschauen* means to see or contemplate. Goethe's immense lucidity is inseparable from his habit of seeing things instead of relying on pure concepts alone. Kant was *not* a visual person (see Section 30), while Goethe liked to draw and also did delightful watercolors.[13] Although his verbal facility and the power of his language were unsurpassed, he unquestionably agreed with Mephistopheles' sarcastic disparagement of words:

> For just where no ideas are
> The proper word is never far.

Goethe always could find words for what he saw and felt. He mistrusted words that were not backed up by any experience. And he had no need of mathematical certainty. While those who feel most insecure often crave that, Goethe was strong enough to spurn it. In a conversation with F. von Müller, June 18, 1826, he said:

Mathematics has the altogether false reputation of furnishing infallible inferences [*Schlüsse*]. Its whole certainty is nothing more than identity. Two times two is not four, but it is simply two times two, and this we call, abbreviating it, four. Four is by no means something

[13] See Goethe (1821) and (1806–07).

new. And that is how it always is with its deductions [*Und so geht es immerfort bei ihren Folgerungen*], only in the higher formulas we lose sight of the identity.

Goethe failed to recognize the immense usefulness of mathematics for the natural sciences and especially physics and astronomy. This was a serious shortcoming on his part, and in a book on the development of modern physics he might not merit a great deal of attention. But our concern is with the discovery of the mind, and here the hankering for certainty and the model of mathematics have been extremely harmful, while Goethe's approach has proved to be very fruitful. What was needed was attention to the actions and expressions of the mind and the study of their development. And for those whose interest in such a development was not purely theoretical but motivated in some measure by a quest for autonomy, Goethe provided a rich model of that, too.

Newton mathematicized large areas of science. Under his influence mathematical precision and absolute certainty became more than ever part of the very meaning of science. While this view is still dominant among both scientists and laymen, many people, including some scientists, are deeply disturbed by this development, because in one way or another it is so often accompanied by a downgrading of what cannot be measured and quantified. As Goethe's Mephistopheles says in the second scene of the Second Part of *Faust*, speaking to the Chancellor:

> What you can't calculate, you think, cannot be true;
> What you can't weigh, that has no weight for you.

A large part of reality—the part which most engages our feelings and emotions and which one might actually consider the most valuable—is discounted as either inconsequential or even as in some sense unreal.

Championing what cannot be measured or weighed

can be but need not be—and in Goethe's case was not—obscurantist. Some people feel threatened by reason and understanding and seek safety in a plea of incomprehensibility. Goethe was not an apostle of feeling in this sense, and he had no wish to downgrade reason or science. On the contrary, he has his Mephistopheles say in the short monologue that concludes the scene in which he makes his pact with Faust—and Hegel liked to quote this:

> Have but contempt for reason and for science,
> Man's noblest force spurn with defiance,
> Subscribe to magic and illusion,
> The Lord of Lies aids your confusion,
> And, pact or no, I hold you tight.

Far from opposing reason and science, Goethe opposed the notion that all science must be mathematical. For him poetry was not the frosting on an essentially dry and prosaic cake, a make-believe embellishment that covers up the way things truly are. Although some poetry, like some of Faust's effusions, may involve self-deception, Goethe was unwilling to discount either emotion or reason, and he felt that understanding cannot dispense with feeling. I know of no better way to put this point than to say that he pointed the way toward *a poetic science*. In profoundly different ways, Hegel, Nietzsche, and Freud tried to develop a poetic, nonmathematical science.

14 ▶▶▶ In his own country the impact of the greatest poet always exceeds that of any philosopher. Homer, Vergil, Dante, and Shakespeare have no philosophical counterparts; neither does Goethe. He helped to shape the imagination of his people, including millions who never read a line of Kant's. Yet Goethe differs from most other poets in that he also had an immense influence on philosophy and the discovery of the mind.

One might suppose that this was obvious, yet hardly anyone writing about Hegel, Nietzsche, or Freud in English seems to have noticed it. This is due in part to a decline in the knowledge of German. Even philosophy professors in the English-speaking world rarely have enough German to read Goethe for pleasure. If his impact were due to a few short texts, quite a number of scholars would still be able to read those. But as we shall see, Schiller, Hegel, Schopenhauer, Nietzsche, Freud, and Jung were *steeped* in Goethe's life and works. That kind of familiarity is no longer to be found in the English-speaking world outside of departments of German.

In translation, Goethe loses as much as Kant gains. Kant becomes clearer in English. His tapeworm sentences have to be broken up because in languages where nouns have no genders one simply cannot pile up subordinate sentences for one or two pages. In a letter to Goethe, dated December 6, 1825, K. F. Zelter related how one of Kant's old friends from his student days had visited the great philosopher forty years later. Asked whether he had ever felt like reading Kant's books, he replied: "Oh yes, and I'd do it more often but lack enough fingers." Kant did not understand and received this explanation: "Yes, my dear friend, your way of writing is so full of parentheses and conditionals on which I have to keep an eye that I place one finger on this word, and then the second, third, and fourth, and even before I have to turn the page there is no finger left."

People who read Kant in translation rarely realize how badly he wrote and how obscure he is. The lucid simplicity of much of Goethe's best verse, on the other hand, loses in translation. Rilke's often very difficult poems are easier to render into English than Goethe's usually exceptionally clear lines. Those who cannot read Goethe in the original have no way of knowing how great he was.

The situation is made worse by the hypertrophy of specialization. Books on philosophers and psychologists are generally written by philosophers and psychologists who know that it is not their business to write about poets, like Goethe. A philosopher who forgets this or simply does not care is apt to be told by his chairman, without having asked, that while it is wonderful how well his work has been received by highly competent reviewers he ought to know—as I was told at one point—that "your work on Goethe does not count." Although this particular chairman was a renowned humanist and historian of philosophy, he may not have realized that the men who were perhaps the foremost Kant scholars in Germany had written extensively about Goethe; for example, Ernst Cassirer, Georg Simmel, Hans Vaihinger, and Karl Vorländer (see the Bibliography).

For a long time, it was unfashionable for English-speaking philosophers to write about Hegel or Schopenhauer, Nietzsche or Freud, and those who did tried to assimilate them to more fashionable philosophers. It certainly is not surprising that the professors who wrote about these men did not immerse themselves in Goethe as *they* had done. Yet this sort of immersion is precisely what is needed to understand these men better. Without it one simply cannot acquire the necessary feeling for Hegel's, Nietzsche's, or Freud's mentality and universe of discourse. Hegel spoke the truth, not only for himself, when he wrote Goethe on April 24, 1825: "When I survey the course of my spiritual development, I see you woven into it everywhere and would like to call myself one of your sons; my inner nature has . . . set its course by your creations as by signal fires."

Hegel was then in his fifties and at the peak of his career; he did not need anything from Goethe, and he did not pay such extravagant compliments glibly. Yet in the voluminous literature on Hegel this declaration has been largely ignored, along with the abundant evidence that bears it out. Professors trained in analytical philosophy find it almost impossible to believe that Goethe's impact on German philosophy could be comparable to Kant's. After all, Kant had doctrines and offered arguments while Goethe was a poet. It is assumed that literature and philosophy are two totally separate fields. Are they not taught in different departments?

To make matters worse, Goethe's life, though only three years longer than Kant's, was incomparably richer and more interesting, and the body of his writings and letters—143 volumes in the most complete edition—plus his published conversations is so vast that scholars in other fields would much rather not get involved with him. Given that situation, talk of immersion hardly helps. What we need is a bill of particulars, which I shall sum up after recalling how great Goethe's impact actually was.

Lord Byron, who had no small opinion of himself, dedicated his *Sardanapalus* in 1821 "To the Illustrious Goethe" as "the homage of a literary vassal to his liege lord, the first of existing writers, who has created the literature of his own country." Like Hegel in his letter, Byron summed up definitively what a whole generation felt.

Shelley translated into English what were then considered the two most shocking parts of Goethe's *Faust:* the Prologue in Heaven (we have seen how offensive some of Shelley's contemporaries found that) and the Walpurgis Night. Coleridge rendered into English Schiller's *Piccolomini* and *Death of Wallenstein* and, like Schiller, tried to synthesize Kant and Goethe. George Henry Lewes wrote a two-volume *Life and*

Works of Goethe (1855) while George Eliot, who lived with him, translated into English the most important work written by any of Hegel's students, Ludwig Feuerbach's *Essence of Christianity* (1854). Earlier, she had translated the vastly influential *Life of Jesus Critically Examined* by David Friedrich Strauss, who had also been one of Hegel's students (in three volumes, 1846). George Eliot is now remembered as a major novelist, but in those days people in Great Britain knew that German philosophy and literature were not separate realms. Until Thomas Carlyle and Matthew Arnold died in the 1880s, the British educated public could hardly forget that.

Goethe was not a prophet without honor in his own country. Although he was born in 1749, and Kant in 1724, Goethe was admired as the greatest German poet long before Kant established his reputation in 1781 with the publication of his *Critique of Pure Reason*. Kant became famous at the age of fifty-seven. Goethe, who was twenty-five years younger, was acclaimed all over Europe by the time he was twenty-five. His Storm and Stress play, *Götz von Berlichingen* (1773) made him the hero of the younger generation, and a year later his first novel, *Werther*, inspired a wave of suicides not only in Germany but also, for example, in France. When Goethe was twenty-six, three different illicit editions of his collected works appeared, and he had a greater reputation than any German poet had ever had before him. Nor did any other German approximate his fame until he died in his eighties in 1832, or for that matter since then.

His unparalleled impact was due primarily to his poetic genius, to the force of his personality, and to the way he developed over a period of almost sixty years. His influence on philosophy and on the discovery of the mind was not based on a body of doctrines or, least of all, arguments; it was a function of his character and life which were highly visible both directly and in the multicolored reflection of his works. As Goethe's Faust says in the first scene of the Second Part: *"Am farbigen Abglanz haben wir das Leben"* ("In many-hued reflection we have life").

15 ▶▶▶ In sum, Goethe made at least four crucial contributions to the discovery of the mind. First, he provided a model of autonomy that kept his contemporaries from taking seriously Kant's conception of autonomy. Goethe's model may well have been as influential as any since Socrates' and it had a decisive impact not only on generations of writers and artists but also, for example, on Nietzsche, Freud, and existentialism. (Like Kant, Goethe did not consider Jesus a model of autonomy.)

Secondly, Goethe opposed the essentialism of those who considered the mind or soul a ghost in the machine or a spirit that resides behind or above the phenomenal self. Many learned from him that man is his deeds, that mind is what it does, and that the way to discover the mind is not through concept-mongering but through experience. His approach was unusual, and Nietzsche and Freud followed in his footsteps when they taught us to see better.

Thirdly, he saw that the best, if not the only, way to understand the mind and everything spiritual is through its development. He was not a structuralist but an evolutionist.

Finally, he suggested the possibility of a non-mathematical, non-Newtonian science. Whatever one may think of that, the greatest advances in the discovery of the mind were made by men who accepted this idea.

Those greatly influenced by Goethe found three paths open to them. The first involved acceptance of his disparagement of mathematics and an assimilation of nature to mind. This was the path taken by Hegel. He was, however, also deeply influenced by Kant, and felt compelled to affect in all his works a rigor that while not by any means mathematical, was supposed to involve necessity and certainty.

The second path involved a sharp distinction between nature and mind. Wilhelm Dilthey distinguished between *Naturwissenschaften* and *Geisteswissenschaften* and labored his life long to develop some sort of a methodology for the latter. The concept of the "mental sciences" is not as clear as it might be. It certainly embraces the humanities, but one may wonder how the social sciences fit this dichotomy. Yet the fundamental idea was clear enough. It was that mind, or *Geist,* unlike nature, had to be studied in terms of development and history. History was an arch-*Geisteswissenschaft*. In a way, Dilthey's project was more modest than Hegel's; he let go of nature but still tried to work out a method for all the "mental sciences."

The third path was still more modest and fitted in a little better with the growing tendency toward specialization. This was the path chosen by Freud, who concentrated on a single science, psychology. One could also say that he sought to create a new science, a new kind of psychology, namely psychoanalysis.That he advanced the discovery of the mind far more than either Hegel or Dilthey is obvious; but how much all three men owed to Goethe is certainly not a commonplace.

In conclusion, it is remarkable how greatly both Kant and Goethe were influenced by their own type of mind. I hope to show soon how Kant assumed in effect that his mind, which was in many ways exceptional, was the timeless paradigm of the mind. We shall see this in his ethics and aesthetics. Moreover, being afraid of change and guarding rigidly against it in his life, taking heroic measures to prevent it, he naturally failed to note how the mind of an individual, not to speak of the human mind in general, develops. Goethe, on the other hand, was a man who developed more dramatically and quickly than the common run; and seeing that his own mind and his works could not be comprehended except in terms of development, he taught men that the key to comprehension of everything—nature as well as mind—was development.

If one had pointed out to Goethe that this was what he had done, it would hardly have distressed him. He thought that other minds were more or less like his at least in this respect, and that he and the rest were part of nature and not basically different from it. Kant, on the other hand, could not have taken this point in his stride. The extreme obscurity of some philosophers, including Kant, Hegel, and Heidegger, was due in part to an attempt—not conscious, to be sure—to hide something from themselves. They were afraid of something that kept them—even Kierkegaard, who had a wealth of insights—from contributing as much as they might have done to the discovery of the mind. What they were afraid of was the discovery of their own minds.

PART ▶

Influences:
Herder, Lessing, Schiller,
Fichte, Schopenhauer ▶▶▶

16 ▶▶▶ In all the years Kant taught at the University of Königsberg, he had only one student of genius, Johann Gottfried Herder (1744–1803). But when Herder published the first volume of his major work on the philosophy of history in 1784, Kant reviewed it very disparagingly. And in 1799 Herder published a two-volume attack on Kant which he called "A Metacritique on the Critique of Pure Reason." The following year he published a three-volume attack on Kant's aesthetics: *Kalligone.* In Germany, Herder's name is familiar to most educated people, but few are even aware of these polemics, nor are any of Herder's works read widely. What people tend to know about Herder is that he took a pioneering interest in folk poetry and published a collection of his own translations, "Peoples' Voices in Songs" (*Stimmen der Völker in Liedern);* also that in the early 1770s, when he was in his late twenties and Goethe in his early twenties, he made a great impression on Goethe.

None of this would make it necessary to consider Herder in this book, if it had not been suggested in recent years, notably by Isaiah Berlin, that he was the seminal figure who, more than anyone else, brought about some of the changes that I have credited to Goethe's influence. As one reads Sir Isaiah's characteristically erudite study of "Herder and the Enlightenment," one is struck by many interesting quotations from one or another of Herder's essays. But Berlin never considers the case for Goethe, nor does he discuss the attitudes of the German romantics, or of Hegel, Schopenhauer, Nietzsche, or Freud toward either Herder or Goethe. Whoever does that will find that all of them paid overwhelming tribute to Goethe, none of them to Herder. Near the end of his essay Sir Isaiah admits: "The consequences of Herder's doctrines did not make themselves felt immediately" (p. 212). He goes on to say that "the full effect" was not felt until very much later; really only with "the rise of modern antirationalist movements—nationalism, fascism, existentialism, emotivism, and the wars and revolutions made in the name of two among them; that is to say, not until our own time, and perhaps not altogether even today." It is not shown that fascists, existentialists, or emotivists actually were influenced by Herder, or how a force might suddenly act at a distance after the lapse of more than a hundred years.

Charles Taylor made matters worse when he claimed repeatedly in his *Hegel* that Herder had greatly influenced Hegel, without as much as considering any of the rather few passages in Hegel that deal with Herder.[1] As it happens, Hegel was interested in, though probably not much influenced by, Herder's mentor, Johann Georg Hamann, and he disparaged Herder as not being in the same class. He was also interested in Fritz Jacobi, to whom he referred often, and seems to have considered

[1] See also my review article in the London *Times Literary Supplement*.

him far superior to Herder[2] and the most representative figure of what Berlin calls "antirationalist movements." That Herder influenced Hegel would need to be shown, but Taylor produces no evidence at all, and Berlin does not even claim it.

Of Schopenhauer's few passing references to Herder only one is of sufficient interest to be quoted here:

> Yet nothing has true value except what one has thought at first solely *for oneself*. For one can divide thinkers into those who think at first *for themselves* and those who immediately think *for others*. The former are the genuine ones, *self-thinkers* in both senses of that term; they are the real philosophers. For they alone are serious about what is at stake. Moreover, the enjoyment and happiness of their existence consists in thinking. The others are *sophists:* they want to *shine* and seek their happiness in what they hope to gain from others in this way: that is what they are serious about. To which class a person belongs is easily seen from his whole manner. *Lichtenberg* is a model of the first type; *Herder* already belongs to the second.[3]

Nietzsche devoted a section (#118) in *The Wanderer and His Shadow* to Herder. It begins: "Herder is none of all the things that he led others to believe about him (and wished to believe himself): no great thinker and inventor ... " And in Section 125 Nietzsche remarked: "For the subtler and stronger minds (like Lichtenberg) even Herder's main work, for example, his *Ideas for a Philosophy of the History of Mankind,* was dated even when it appeared." There is only one other substantive reference to Herder in Nietzsche's books, in section 3 of *The Case of Wagner:*

> One knows Goethe's fate in moraline-sour, old-maidish Germany. He always seemed offensive to Germans. . . .

[2] See also Hegel's letter to Mehmel, Aug. 26, 1801.
[3] *Parerga & Paralipomena*, vol. II, chap. XXII, sec. 270.

What did they hold against Goethe? The "mount of Venus"; and that he had written *Venetian Epigrams*. Klopstock already felt called upon to deliver a moral sermon to him; there was a time when Herder liked to use the word "Priapus" whenever he spoke of Goethe.

To be sure, Herder sought to oppose Kant's influence, but Goethe, Hegel, and Schopenhauer all found his *Metacritique of Pure Reason* embarrassingly bad, and Hegel compared it very unfavorably with Hamann's earlier short essay with the same title.[4] By the time Herder's work appeared in 1799, the leading spirits in Germany no longer needed to be convinced that something was wrong with Kant, and they agreed that Herder's attempt was utterly inadequate.

Freud cited or discussed Goethe more than a hundred times in his works, and Herder not even once. Goethe's crucial importance for Freud's thought will be taken up in the last volume of this trilogy.

That it was Goethe and not Herder who exerted the decisive anti-Kantian influence on subsequent German thinkers is, I think, undeniable. But that leaves open the question whether Goethe himself was decisively influenced by Herder. Berlin never addresses this question. In 1812, Goethe himself described at length in his autobiography how strongly he had been affected by his encounter with Herder in Strassburg, when he himself was barely over twenty. Ever since, it has been a commonplace of the vast Goethe literature that Herder, who was five years older, opened Goethe's eyes to Gothic architecture and to Shakespeare, and that he stimulated Goethe to collect folk songs. The first major fruit of this encounter, Goethe's *Götz*, thrown into the world immediately afterwards with all the force of an eruption,

---

[4] *Werke*, ed. Glockner, vol. XX, pp. 248. Schopenhauer called it "a bad book" (*World as Will and Idea*, vol. I, sec. 9).

leaves no doubt that it would be exceedingly generous to call Herder a midwife.

Sir Isaiah notes very perceptively that "Herder pleaded for that which he himself conspicuously lacked," that is, "the unity of the human personality." One could say that what he called for was what Goethe had and was. Herder made the young Goethe aware of what was in him and wanted out: that was the secret of Herder's impact on Goethe. But what made history was much less Herder's preaching than Goethe's personality as embodied both in his life and in his work.

Regarding Herder's *"magnum opus, The Ideas for a Philosophy of the History of Mankind,"* it is interesting to note that "in August 1783 Herder and Goethe had come to be on good terms again, and this proved beneficial for the work on the *Ideas.* Herder conceived them in close collaboration and intellectual association with Goethe, though he never allowed himself to become directly dependent on Goethe."[5] By the time his main work appeared in four volumes (1784–91), the age difference between the two men had become immaterial and Herder was no longer the mentor but almost totally overshadowed by Goethe.

Goethe's major creations are nothing if not organic. They do not bear the marks of outside influences, are not forced or fabricated, but convey the feeling that Goethe formulated in Faust's words to Wagner, written when the poet was in his early twenties and found already in the *Urfaust:*

> *What you don't feel, you will not grasp by art,*
> *Unless it wells out of your soul*
> *And with sheer pleasure takes control,*
> *Compelling every listener's heart.*
> *But sit—and sit, and patch and knead,*
> *Cook a ragout, reheat your hashes,*

[5] Kantzenbach (1970), p. 95. For a full discussion of Goethe's influence on Herder see Haym's *Herder,* vol. II, pp. 197-207.

Eine Duplik.

*Contestandi magis gratia, quam aliquid
ex oratione promoturus.*

Dictys Cret.

Braunschweig,
in der Buchhandlung des Fürstl. Waisenhauses.
1 7 7 8.

Blow at the sparks and try to breed
A fire out of piles of ashes!
Children and apes may think it great,
If that should titillate your gum,
But from heart to heart you will never create
If from your heart it does not come (lines 534–45).

17 ▶▶▶ Yet Goethe did have one great predecessor, Gotthold Ephraim Lessing (1729–81), who may even have exerted a decisive influence on *Faust*. In one of Lessing's polemics, *Duplik* ("Rejoinder," 1778), we encounter a famous passage that had an incalculable impact:

> Not the truth in whose possession some human being is or thinks he is, but the honest trouble he has taken to get behind the truth is what constitutes the worth of a human being. For it is not through the possession but through the search for truth that his powers expand, and in this alone consists his ever growing perfection. Possession makes tranquil, indolent, and proud.
> If God held in his closed right hand all truth and in his left hand only the ever live drive for truth, albeit with the addition that I should always and evermore err, and he said to me, Choose! I should humbly grab his left hand, saying: Father, give! Pure truth is after all for you alone!

When this passage first appeared in print, the *Urfaust* was finished, but it did not yet contain the Prologue in Heaven, the pact between Faust and Mephistopheles, or the scene in which Faust is saved in the end. Lessing's magnificent words are taken up in the Prologue when the Lord says, "Man errs as long as he strives," and in the final scene of Part Two in which the angels sing:

> *Who always strives with all his power*
> *We are allowed to save.*

Influences: Herder, Lessing, Schiller, Fichte, Schopenhauer ▶ 65

heit bestehet. — Der Besitz macht ruhig, träge,
stolz —

Wenn Gott in seiner Rechten alle Wahrheit,
und in seiner Linken den einzigen immer regen
Trieb nach Wahrheit, obschon mit dem Zu=
satze, mich immer und ewig zu irren, ver=
schlossen hielte, und spräche zu mir: wähle!
Ich fiele ihm mit Demuth in seine Linke, und
sagte: Vater gieb! die reine Wahrheit ist ja
doch nur für dich allein!

II.

Noch einmal: es ist ledig meine Schuld,
wenn der Ungenannte bis itzt so beträchtlich
nicht scheinet, als er ist. Man lasse ihn diese
fremde Schuld nicht entgelten.

Was kann er dafür, daß ich nur Fragmente
seiner Arbeit fand; und aus Fragmenten gera=
de nur eben diese bekannt machte? Er selbst
würde, um sich in seinem besten Vortheile zu
zeigen, vielleicht ganz andere Proben ausge=
sucht haben; wenn er sich nicht vielmehr alles
Probegeben verbeten hätte.

Denn wie kann man auch von einer weit=
läuftigen zusammengesetzten Maschine, deren
klein=

Moreover, the central notion that tranquility is not desirable is the heart of the pact scene:

> If ever tranquil I lie on a bed of sloth,
> I shall be done for then and there!

Actually, Lessing himself had begun to write a Faust play, and Goethe probably knew something about it before he even finished his own *Urfaust*. Here is a contemporary report about Lessing's project:

> The scene begins with a conference of the spirits of hell, in which the subalterns give an account to the supreme devil of the work they have undertaken and accomplished on earth. . . . The last of the under-devils who comes in reports that he found at least one man on earth at whom one simply cannot get; he has no passion, no weakness . . . only one drive, one inclination, an insatiable thirst for science and knowledge. Hah! cries the supreme devil, then he is mine, forever mine, and more securely mine than if he had any other passion! . . . Now Mephistopheles receives the task and instructions how to go about catching poor Faust. . . . Enough, the hellish hosts think they have accomplished their work; they sing songs of triumph in the fifth act—when an apparition from the higher world interrupts them in the most unexpected and yet most natural . . . way: "Don't be triumphant!" the angel shouts at them; "you have not vanquished humanity and science; the deity did not give man the noblest of all drives in order to make him eternally unhappy; what you saw and think you possess now was nothing but a phantom."

This report by Captain von Blankenburg, dated Leipzig, May 14, 1784, was published in volume 5 of *Litteratur und Völkerkunde* (Dessau and Leipzig, 1784, pages 82–84), and it must have come to the attention of Goethe, who was wondering how he might complete his own *Faust*. That Lessing had been working on a Faust drama was known widely ever since the publication of his seventeenth Letter Concerning the Most Recent Literature, February 16, 1759. At that time many men of letters still considered the subject unsuitable for serious literature, and in a letter to Lessing dated November 19, 1755, Moses Mendelssohn had remarked that the audience was likely to burst into laughter if they heard someone declaim from the stage: "Faustus! Faustus!"

The report of 1784 may well have left its mark on Goethe's conception, and it is doubly noteworthy because Lessing was the first major writer who proposed to save Faust in the end. But in following Lessing, Goethe followed his own genius. It would have been unthinkable for him to consign Faust to hell, and the feeling for striving, becoming, and process was of the essence of the young Goethe and not an alien element that needs to be traced to some outside influence.

18 ▶▶ Goethe's younger contemporaries could hardly fail to follow his development with the keenest interest and excitement. Let us see very briefly how some of them responded. Friedrich Schiller (1759–1805) was the first to try to reconcile Kant and Goethe. He has always been most popular as a dramatist and poet—if possible, even more so than Goethe. He was also a professor of history at the University of Jena, where Fichte was for a while his slightly younger colleague, and his philosophical publications were enormously influential.

Superficially considered, they are contributions to aesthetics. The titles show that: "On Charm and Dignity," "Letters on the Aesthetic Education of the Human Being," "On Naive and Sentimental Poetry," and "On the Sublime." But twentieth-century complaints about "the dreariness of aesthetics" do not apply to Schiller's work. Although the influence of Kant is writ large in his thought, Schiller was no scholastic. He did not deal with aesthetics as one of the accepted branches of philosophy, but wrote about art because it was his life. He felt, to quote from his fifteenth "letter," that a human being "*is wholly human only where he plays.*"

His central concern was with being "wholly human," with freedom and autonomy, and he considered art in this context. When he temporarily "abandoned poetry and drama" from 1789 to 1795, it was, as Julius Elias put it in his article on Schiller in *The Encyclopedia of Philosophy* (1967), to "resolve these problems of the artist's—especially his own vocation." As Elias said directly before that, the problem that was "most crucial for his own development" and had to be resolved most urgently was "the profound inadequacy he felt in himself compared with the effortless felicity of Goethe's Olympian presence."

In Germany it has always been a commonplace both that Schiller was a Kantian of sorts who kept referring to Kant, and that in his aesthetic essays he tried to come to terms with Goethe, who became his close friend in the nineties. What has not been seen so clearly is that Schiller's problem was shared in a way by Schelling, Hegel, and Schopenhauer, as well as many later thinkers, especially in Germany. If one thought about philosophical problems, one could not ignore Kant; but neither could one ignore Goethe if one wished to deal with art, the vocation of man, or autonomy.

Elias concludes his article by saying that Schiller's insights have proved "fruitful in the philosophies of thinkers as diverse as Hegel ... Nietzsche, Dilthey, James, Jung . . . , Marx," and others. In my *Hegel* (1965) I devoted a whole section (7) of more than a dozen pages to an attempt to demonstrate the formative influence of Schiller's "On the Aesthetic Education of Man" on Hegel, who called it "a masterpiece" as soon as it appeared. In a comprehensive study of the discovery of the mind one might well include a chapter on Schiller. Yet the key figures, from Hegel to Nietzsche and Freud, have always felt rightly that, great as Schiller was, Goethe was incomparably greater. And while some of them, notably Hegel, did take much from Schiller, his importance as a theorist was not least that he showed how Goethe was relevant to some of Kant's problems.

In one of his early letters to Goethe, Schiller wrote (January 7, 1795): "So much, however, is certain: the poet is the only true human being, and the best philosopher is only a caricature compared to him." When he wrote this, Schiller did not feel conceited. The poet par excellence was to his mind Goethe, and the best philosopher Kant. A remark about Kant in Schiller's letter to Goethe, December 22, 1798, helps to explain what repelled Schiller: "There is still something about him that, as in Luther's case, brings to mind a monk who, to be sure, has opened his monastery but could not wholly eliminate its traces."

Schiller responded enthusiastically to the most antimonastic and anti-Christian elements in Goethe. Schiller has often been disparaged for being too moralistic, but as soon as he had formed a friendship with Goethe in 1794 he published Goethe's most controversial poems: *Roman Elegies* in 1795, in *Horen,* the journal he edited, and *Venetian Epigrams* in his *Musenalmanach auf das Jahr 1796.* Both of these collections had been finished when Goethe wrote Carl Ludwig von Knebel on January 1, 1791, that he "was not disinclined to publish the former. Herder advised against it . . ." When the old Goethe published a comprehensive edition of his works, he included both the *Elegies* and the *Epigrams* in the first volume, in 1827. By then he was seventy-eight and far from being the stuffed shirt that many people suppose he became in his final period.

In a letter about Schiller's "Aesthetic Education" Goethe wrote (to Wilhelm von Humboldt, December 3,

1795): "He has very felicitous ideas that, once they have been stated, will gain acceptance by and by, however much they will be resisted in the beginning. I fear that first one will contradict him vehemently and in a few years one will copy him without mentioning him."

After Fichte, Schelling, and Hegel, not to speak of their epigones and the whole philosophical tradition that developed in their wake, Schiller's prose strikes us as relatively clear and vivid. But his opponents lavished contempt on his lack of clarity. In the lengthy introduction to their bilingual edition of the "Aesthetic Education" (with the original text and a new English version on facing pages, followed by a commentary and other apparatus) E. M. Wilkinson and L. A. Willoughby deal at length with its "Reception and Repercussions" (p. cxxxiii ff.). In a rather typical long review Schiller was taken to task for his obscurity which had held up the reviewer on every page, his use of technical terms, and the strain involved in adapting his own style to Kant's. In the end the reviewer expressed the hope that someone might "render some piece, whether by Mr. Schiller or his friend Mr. Fichte . . . into German" (p. cxxxv).

Shakespeare makes us sympathize with Coriolanus by giving him such inferior opponents and leads us to feel, as we listen to his detractors, that his faults are hardly faults. Similarly, the shallowness and obtuseness of Schiller's detractors did its share to persuade Hegel and many lesser men that clarity was for dolts. The champions of clarity unfortunately were not in the same league with Kant or Schiller, and in the nineties the lines were drawn, disastrously.

19 ▶▶▶ When this review of Schiller's essay appeared, Johann Gottlieb Fichte (1762–1814) was no longer "his friend." But they had been friends, their concerns were in many ways similar, and the development of German idealism has to be understood against the background of Goethe's work and Schiller's attempt to reconcile Goethe and Kant.

Fichte, though no longer read much today, was for a long time regarded as Kant's most important successor. It was customary to consider Kant, Fichte, Schelling, and Hegel as the great German "Idealists" who had to be studied in this order, and Hegel's death in 1832 was seen as the end of classical German philosophy. One of the disadvantages of this approach was that it made Hegel even more inaccessible than he had to be on account of his difficult style. For Fichte's and Schelling's writings were voluminous and almost equally difficult. Each of these philosophers almost seems to have felt compelled to outdo his predecessors, beginning with Kant—also in obscurity.

That Fichte modeled his philosophical style on Kant's is undeniable. He had been so impressed by Kant's works that he walked to Königsberg to meet his mentor and to show him the manuscript of his first book: *Attempt at a Critique of All Revelation*. Kant persuaded his own publisher to bring it out; the publisher, to Fichte's chagrin, omitted the author's name and preface; and the book was immediately hailed as Kant's own philosophy of religion. When it was revealed that the book was not by Kant but by Fichte, Fichte became famous instantly. Obviously, the book could never have been attributed to Kant by practically everybody, if the style had not been so similar to Kant's.

Three years later, in 1795, Fichte sent Schiller a contribution for the journal Schiller edited, in which the "Aesthetic Education" had begun to appear, and in a letter dated June 24 Schiller turned it down, criticizing not only some of the ideas but also, at some length, the style. Three days later, Fichte replied and first defended his ideas, then attacked Schiller's style—all of this with the most profound respect for Schiller. His own images, he said, came never *"in place* of a concept but *before* or *after* the concept,"* while Schiller's style struck him "as entirely novel. . . . You enthral the imagination, which can only be free, and want to compel it to think. That it cannot do. This is what causes, I think, the exhausting exertion that your philosophical writings impose on me and have imposed on several other people. I first have to translate everything you write before I understand it; and others have the same experience." As for his own long and intricate periods, the trouble is "that the reader does not know how to declaim. If you would hear me read some of my periods. . . . But you are right, our public does not know how to declaim, and one is better advised to proceed accordingly, as Lessing did." Would that he and others had done that!

The tone of Fichte's letter does him credit, but he reaped a very harsh reply. Schiller wrote back:

> . . . I really should have told myself that precisely because you write in this manner and because you think of it as you do, because you are that kind of an individual, you cannot be reached by any reasons that *have their source in me as an individual;* for man's aesthetic drive is the result of his nature, and reasoning may succeed in changing a few kinds of ideas but can never reverse nature. . . . We feel differently, we are different, extremely different natures, and I don't know what can be done about that.

As for Fichte's criticism of Schiller's style and Fichte's claim that the public, while buying and admiring Schiller's philosophical writings, had not yet cited "any opinion, any passage, any result," Schiller replied:

> There is nothing cruder than the taste of the present German public, and to work at changing this wretched taste—not to derive my models from it—is the serious plan of my life.

Schiller's letter was long, but one more passage is extremely relevant here:

> ... The appeal *you* suggest, Goethe, would really please you least of all. But Goethe really cannot do you justice, and his judgment cannot prove anything against you. He is too much of a stranger in the regions of philosophy and hence could not be reconciled to the aesthetic transgressions that he would hold against you. It is odd enough that you have to find out from me how little Goethe is fit to take your side.

And how, Schiller continues, could Fichte fail to know that in aesthetics Goethe deferred to Schiller's judgment even "in his own *manuscripts and writings.*"

Three years later, in 1798, Fichte was charged with atheism and eventually resigned from the University of Jena rather than apologize for his part in the first issue of Volume 8 of the *Philosophisches Journal,* of which he was one of the two editors. Two articles gave offense, the first of them by Fichte himself. The conclusion of Fichte's article is relevant here. "Two excellent poets have expressed this confession of faith of a reasonable and good human being in an inimitably beautiful way." The article ended with a very long quotation from Goethe's *Faust: A Fragment* (1790) and five lines from Schiller's poem, "Words of Faith." Fichte did not name the poets. He did not have to. Everybody knew who they were.

Like Schiller, Fichte sought to reconcile Kant and Goethe. So did Arthur Schopenhauer (1788–1860).

20 ▶▶ Of Schopenhauer's opinion of Fichte one might say that it was unprintable, if Schopenhauer himself had not expressed it in his books again and again and again. Actually, he considered Hegel even worse than Fichte and Schelling, and his comments on Hegel are occasionally as grotesque and downright funny as his notorious diatribe *"Ueber die Weiber"* (On Women) in his *Parerga und Paralipomena* (1851). Like Martin Luther, Schopenhauer was a virtuoso of vituperation. But he was not so coarse and scatological. He was witty, vitriolic, and—in contrast to his ethic—bursting with resentment.

Schopenhauer saw Hegel as the absolute climax of a development that had begun with Fichte and been carried further by Schelling. In the "Critique of the Kantian Philosophy" that Schopenhauer appended to the first volume of his *magnum opus* in 1819 he said of Fichte: "He counted quite rightly on the lack of judgment and the *niaiserie* [inanity] of the public, which accepted bad sophisms, mere hocus-pocus, and nonsensical wishy-washy [Wischiwaschi] for proof." In the first chapter of the second volume, added to the second edition (1844), "Fichte is the father of *pseudophilosophy [Schein-Philosophie]*, of dishonest method."

In the second volume of the *Parerga and Paralipomena,* finally—to summarize material that could easily fill a long chapter—two specific criticisms are of interest:

Something surreptitious that was introduced by *Fichte* and has been habilitated since may be found in the expression *the I* or *ego [das Ich]*. Here the noun and the article in front of it transform that which is essentially and simply subjective into an object; it is the knower as opposed to, and as the condition of, everything known. The wisdom of all languages has expressed this by not treating *I* as a noun, and Fichte therefore had to do violence to language to make his intent prevail. Something still more impudently surreptitious in this same *Fichte* is his impudent abuse of the word *posit* that, instead of having been reproached and exploded, is still in frequent use to this day among all philosophists *[Philosophastern]*, following his example and relying on his authority as a constant aid to sophisms and deceptive doctrines. *Posit, ponere,* from which *propositio* is derived, has been a purely logical expression ever since ancient times and means that in the logical context of a disputation or some other discussion one supposes, presupposes, or affirms something to begin with, granting it logical validity and formal truth for the present, while its reality, material truth, and actuality remain altogether untouched and undecided. *Fichte,* however, gradually gained surreptitiously a real but of course obscure and foggy meaning for this positing, and the ninnies accepted that as valid, and the sophists use it all the time; for since the ego first posited itself and afterwards the non-ego, positing has come to mean creating, producing, or in brief putting into the world, one does not know how; and everything one wants to assume as existing without any reasons and wants to put over and impose on others, is simply *posited,* and there it stands and is there, altogether real. That is the still prevalent method of so-called post-Kantian philosophy and is Fichte's work.[6]

Although *Parerga and Paralipomena* was the work that very belatedly established Schopenhauer's reputation—before the failure of the revolutions of 1848 his pessimism had been exceedingly untimely, and he was ignored—his incisive critique of *positing* was ignored. One kept on "positing," and to this day the legions who write on Hegel as well as Fichte and Schelling are for the most part not bothered by the frequent use of this device.

The ego, *das Ich,* is nowadays associated with Freud, at least by nonphilosophers; but Freud's contrast of ego and id, or *Das Ich und das Es,* to cite the title of his classic of 1923, is not open to Schopenhauer's criticism. What Schopenhauer did object to, on the other hand, was not Fichte's innovation but goes back to Kant. Schopenhauer revered Kant and, although he criticized

[6] End of sec. 28.

Kant at length, refused to see how Kant had been in many ways a disaster. In some ways he himself was corrupted by Kant, even stylistically. But for the fateful notion of the ego and the proliferation of pseudodemonstrations he held Fichte responsible instead of recognizing that it was Kant who had established the affectation of a rigor that, on close inspection, turns out to be an illusion that depends in large part on extreme obscurity.

That Kant's philosophy was his own point of departure, Schopenhauer himself never tired of saying. His own greatest discovery was, as he saw it, that the thing-in-itself was one, not many, and that it was will—blind will. On the face of it—and not only on the face of it—this is a bold anthropomorphism, a projection into ultimate reality of what is first of all experienced as the quintessence of man and, presumably, of the author himself. I suspect that this image of humanity and of himself was influenced by what Schopenhauer once referred to in his *magnum opus* as "the great Goethe" and "his immortal masterpiece, *Faust*."[7] If there is one representative figure in world literature whose quintessence is striving it is surely Goethe's Faust. Incidentally, while Schopenhauer discusses Kant at greater length and in more detail than any other author, there is no writer whom he mentions and quotes more often than Goethe, and the range of the works he cites is most impressive. For our purposes two quotations from Volume 2 of *Parerga und Paralipomena* should suffice.

The first is a critique of Kant in which Goethe is not mentioned but nevertheless provides the countermodel. Here Schopenhauer finds in Kant the source of something for which he often—and also in the continuation of this passage—takes to task Fichte, Schelling, and Hegel:

[7] *Sämmtliche Werke*, Grossherzog Wilhelm Ernst Ausgabe, vol. I, p. 515.

A strange and unworthy definition of philosophy that, however, is found even in *Kant,* is that it is a science *based on mere concepts.* After all, the whole possession of concepts is nothing but what has been deposited in it after having been borrowed and begged from intuited knowledge *[anschaulichen Erkenntnis],* this real and inexhaustible fount of all insight. Hence a true philosophy cannot be spun from mere abstract concepts, but has to be founded on observation and experience, internal as well as external.[8]

Here Schopenhauer speaks as Goethe's, not as Kant's disciple, and the point at issue is obviously of the first importance. Finally, my point that Schopenhauer, like so many others, was in effect trying to reconcile Goethe and Kant, is illustrated neatly by the last sentence of Section 58: "Kant's weak side is that in which Goethe is great; and vice versa."

[8] Sec. 9. See also "The Will in Nature," Introduction: "*Kant,* after theoretical reason is done, lets his categorical imperative, which has been extrapolated *[herausgeklaubten]* out of mere concepts, appear as *deus ex machina* with its absolute ought."

PART ▶

Kant:
The Structure
of the Mind ▶▶▶

21 ▶▶▶ Kant was one of the greatest and most influential philosophers of all time. The range of his publications was exceptionally wide, but if pressed about the nature of his major contributions most philosophers would point to his theory of knowledge and his ethics. Both, as well as much of his comprehensive vision, depend on his model of the human mind. Unfortunately his model of the mind is quite implausible. While few of his successors or admirers have accepted it, many have accepted the need for an essentially unpsychological, unempirical theory of the mind.

He was the first great philosopher since the Middle Ages who was a university professor, and in ever so many ways he is the most representative philosopher of modern times. Few philosophers since Kant have approximated his genius, but many of his shortcomings are widely shared even today, and to some extent at least this is due to his phenomenal influence.

The impact of Kant's *Critique of Pure Reason* was almost incredible. The first edition appeared in 1781 when Kant was not yet known very widely; the second,

Critik

der

reinen Vernunft

von

Immanuel Kant

Profeſſor in Königsberg.

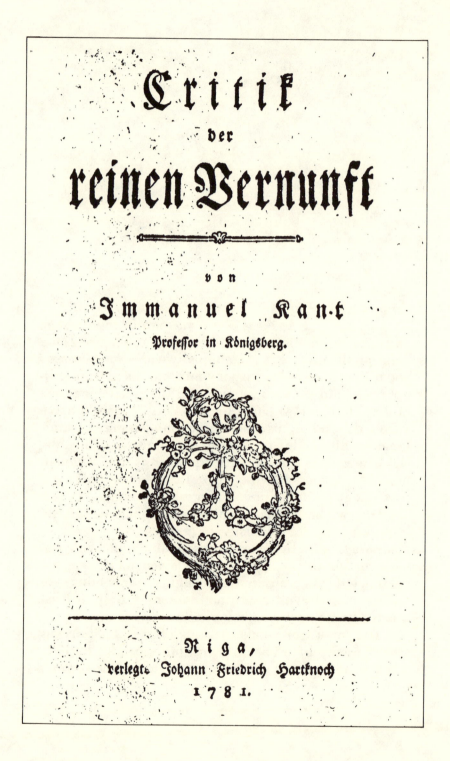

Riga,
verlegts Johann Friedrich Hartknoch
1781.

extensively revised, in 1787; the third, which like all subsequent editions was a reprint of the second, followed in 1790; a fourth edition in 1794; an unauthorized reprint in four volumes a year later; and the fifth edition in 1799. Within roughly ten years of its first appearance, the book was discussed all over Germany, "at Protestant as well as Catholic universities."[1] Soon all of the major German philosophers took their departure from Kant. Fichte, Schelling, Hegel, Fries, and Schopenhauer are only the most famous examples. How are we to explain this stunning success of a book that is so badly written and so difficult to read?

At one blow, Kant had created philosophy in German. There had been a few great German philosophers before him, but none of comparable stature had written in German. Leibniz (1646–1716) had written in French and Latin, and there had been no other German philosopher of even remotely comparable rank since Nicolaus Cusanus (1401–64), who had also written in Latin. So had Albertus Magnus (1193–1280), who taught Thomas Aquinas. Master Eckhart, the great mystic, who died in 1327, had sometimes written in German, but Kant's first *Critique* was the first unquestionably major philosophical book in German. Its appearance in 1781 was comparable to Luther's Reformation in 1517 and almost immediately recognized as the dawn of a new era in German cultural history. By the time Hegel died, exactly fifty years later, Germany could look with pride upon one of the great philosophical traditions of all time, comparable to the Greek and the British.

Neither of those, nor Indian or Chinese philosophy, was ever dominated nearly so much by a single writer, nor did any of them begin so palpably with the publication of a single book. German philosophy was born late but caught up quickly. Descartes had published his *Dis-*

[1] Schultz (1965), p. 112.

cours de la méthode in French in 1637; Hobbes his *Leviathan* in English in 1651. But it was only in 1781 that a German book on philosophy appeared that was at least as great as either. About that there is agreement, but we must still ask what was so great about it.

Like Luther, Kant modified the traditional religious picture of the world and created a new world view that was adapted to the needs of modern man and had immense appeal. David Hume had argued that we cannot really know that every event has a cause. He seemed to have deprived modern science of its foundation. Kant saved human knowledge, including modern science, while at the same time leaving room for God, immortality, and freedom.

What he really believed about God and immortality is arguable, and I shall return to these questions later. But whatever Kant's own feelings may have been, the fact that he made room for belief in both while at the same time accepting the scientific world picture helps to account for the unprecedented impact of his work. Regarding free will, it is as plain as it could be from Kant's writings that he fervently believed in that. This faith was central in his world view, and it is not going too far to suggest that *his most basic problem was: How are autonomy and free will possible in a deterministic Newtonian universe?* It was his ability to solve this problem that persuaded him beyond the shadow of a doubt that his world picture was no mere hypothesis but must be right. At the same time this feat also did its share to persuade others.

Kant's doctrine was designed to reconcile science and religion. The religion in question was not that of Thomas Aquinas, nor that of Luther, who had called reason "the devil's bride" and a "beautiful whore." Here are three more quotations from Luther: "Faith must trample under foot all reason, sense, and understanding, and whatever it sees it must put out of sight, and wish to know nothing but the word of God." "We learn to blind reason when we reach the point where faith begins, and we give her a vacation." "Reason must be deluded, blinded, and destroyed."[2]

The religion Kant tried to reconcile with science was, to cite the title of his book on religion (1793), "religion within the bounds of mere reason alone"—a religion that was cleansed of everything that contradicted reason. In his *Critique of Practical Reason* (1788) Kant offered three "postulates"—of God, free will, and immortality. Under his influence, large numbers of people came to believe that the existence of God, the freedom of the will, and the immortality of the soul were the three most crucial tenets of "religion." One rarely stopped to ask whether the Buddha, the Jina, or Lao-tze had believed in God, whether Moses and the early Hebrew prophets had believed in the immortality of the soul, or whether Luther and Calvin had believed in free will. Kant's doctrines quickly became immensely popular among Protestants, not only in Germany, and became the basis of liberal Protestantism, which is in many ways closer to Kant than to either Luther or Calvin. Liberal Judaism also owes a great deal to Kant.

Kant claimed to have accomplished a Copernican revolution. Actually, his appeal is inseparable from the fact that in his *Critique of Pure Reason* he brought off an *anti-Copernican revolution*. He reversed Copernicus' stunning blow to human self-esteem. Before Copernicus the Western world had believed that man was at the center of the universe and that the sun revolved around our earth. Copernicus' doctrine involved what Freud liked to call a "cosmological mortification" of man's self-love.[3] A generation earlier, Nietzsche had remarked:

[2] For the references and more quotations in the same vein see Kaufmann (1958), sec. 69; for a splendid account of Luther, see Marius (1974).

[3] *Werke*, XII, p. 7 (1917). See also XI, p. 294, and XIV, p. 109.

"Since Copernicus man seems to have got himself on an inclined plane; now he is slipping faster and faster away from the center into—what? into nothingness? into a *penetrating* sense of his nothingness'?"[4] Students of Kant are taught that he sought to counter David Hume's skepticism or positivism—or nihilism. But Kant's immense impact is inseparable from his success in also countering the nihilism that had developed in the wake of Copernicus. He restored man to the center of the world and actually accorded even greater importance to man than the Book of Genesis had done. He tried to prove that it is the human mind that gives nature its laws.[5]

As we shall see, this notion is not as mad as it may sound initially. It depends on Kant's distinction between the phenomenal world and another world that lies beyond it and is unknowable. The conception of two worlds, of appearance and ultimate reality, was old and extremely venerable and thus did not have the earmarks of an *ad hoc* hypothesis. We can trace it back to Plato and beyond him to the Upanishads in India. Plato, like the sages of the Upanishads, denigrated the world of sense experience for the greater glory of an ultimate reality that *could* be known. Like the Indians before him, Plato urged men to turn their back on appearance, to recognize its relative worthlessness, and to strive for knowledge of reality. Indeed, Plato taught that *only* the other world, which was beyond all change and time, could be known, while the realm of appearance, which kept changing, did not permit knowledge but only opinions. The Upanishads had also claimed that time and change were illusory, but unlike Plato they had considered plurality an illusion, insisting that ultimate reality is One. Plato peopled the other world with many timeless Forms or

[4] *Genealogy*, third essay, sec. 25 (1887).
[5] A 125-27 and *Prolegomena*, 36. (See footnote 9 below.)

Ideas. Schopenhauer was the first to make much of the similarities between Kant, Plato, and Indian thought, and it was under Kant's aegis that German scholars in the nineteenth century discovered and explored Indian philosophy.

Max Müller (1823–1900), born in Germany, became a professor at Oxford University and published superb English translations of Kant's *Critique of Pure Reason* and the Buddhist *Dhammapada* (both 1881), the Upanishads (1884), and the Vedas (1891). He also conceived and edited the pioneering and still invaluable fifty-volume series of English translations, *The Sacred Books of the East*.

Paul Deussen (1845–1919), Nietzsche's friend, published a book on Kant's categorical imperative (1891) as well as studies of the Vedanta that are still widely read. His multivolume history of philosophy begins with Indian philosophy and ends with Schopenhauer. By the end of the nineteenth century, Indian philosophers were taking enthusiastically to Kant, to Hegel, and to F. H. Bradley's *Appearance and Reality* (1893).

Kant did *not* denigrate *this* world and was intent on providing a secure basis for science. Indeed, it seemed to some of his successors that he made so little of the thing-in-itself that one might just as well dispense with that and have a full-fledged idealism. But to Kant it seemed essential that there be another world that cannot be known, for to his mind religion and morality depended on that. His religion was quite anticlerical and unorthodox,[6] but he cared deeply about human autonomy and dignity which, he thought, could not be grounded in the Newtonian universe but only in another world.

Kant offered something to almost any taste, and not only philosophical Idealists and liberal Protestants as

[6] See his *Religion Within the Bounds of Mere Reason Alone* (1793).

well as liberal Jews and Hindus found inspiration in his work but also, for example, Ludwig Wittgenstein and Moritz Schlick. A book on Wittgenstein published in 1973 tried to show that Wittgenstein's *Tractatus* was not as Kantian as some earlier interpreters had thought.[7] Yet Kant was the fountainhead of the idea that while science gives us certainty, what is most important lies beyond its reach. The *Tractatus* hints at that near the end (in Section 6.52): "We feel that even when all *possible* scientific questions are answered, the problems of our life have not even begun to be touched." We know from Paul Engelmann's book, *Letters from Ludwig Wittgenstein with a Memoir* (1967), how deeply Wittgenstein felt that the most important issues are not touched by science. In other words, Wittgenstein clearly meant what he said at the end of his short preface. He considered

> the *truth* of the ideas offered here unassailable and definitive. I am thus of the opinion that I have solved the problems in all essentials once and for all. And if I am not wrong about this, then the value of this work consists, secondly, in the fact that it shows how little is accomplished now that these problems are solved.

Moritz Schlick, who was close to Wittgenstein and founded the Vienna Circle of logical positivists, contrasted living experience (*Erleben*) with knowledge or cognition (*Erkennen*) in an article in *Kant-Studien* (1930) that was later reprinted as the first piece in his collected essays (1938).

> About their relative value one may think as one pleases—for me personally it is self-evident that enrichment of living experience always constitutes the higher task, indeed the highest there is—only one should beware of confounding these two sharply divided spheres: if profound living experience is more valuable, this is not

[7] Bartley (1973), pp. 53f., 74f., 161, 170–73.

because it signifies a higher form of knowledge, for it has nothing whatever to do with knowledge . . . (p. 7).

This dubious thesis brings to mind Kant's two-world doctrine. Again, what is most important is held to lie beyond the sphere of knowledge.

Kant himself, however, was as far from agreeing with Schlick or Wittgenstein as he was from German Idealism or Hinduism. He was not prepared to denigrate this world or to give up the other world, and least of all was he willing to surrender the most important problems to unreason in any shape or form. His concept of practical reason is not as clear as it might be and has won few adherents, but its intent is unmistakable. He did *not* accept the position of Wittgenstein's *Tractatus* that "Propositions cannot express anything higher. It is clear that ethics cannot be pronounced [or: articulated] . . . (Ethics and aesthetics are one.)"[8] In the light of the famous conclusion of the *Tractatus*, "Of what one cannot speak, one must remain silent," this meant that a philosopher has nothing to say about ethics and that moral problems must be resolved without the benefit of reason. Kant would have rejected this position as decisively as Schlick's notion that man's highest task is totally divorced from reasoning. Nor did Kant say: As far as we can see, our actions are determined, but I believe nevertheless that the will is free, despite all appearances. He did not mean to champion any license to believe what gives us pleasure or what might have beneficial consequences. Kant never ceased trying to be rational. He was a moral rationalist, meaning that he believed that purely rational procedures could show us what we ought to do, and he also thought that reason can show us how we must act to escape from determinism and to achieve freedom and autonomy.

[8] 6.42 and 6.421.

We shall deal with his *Critique of Pure Reason* first, briefly, to gain some idea of what he was trying to do, and then with his short book on ethics. One of the central ideas of his aesthetics will be considered also because it throws light on the relationship of Kant's mind and temperament to his philosophy.

While the discussion of Kant will stress the ways in which he impeded the discovery of the mind, he was plainly one of the greatest philosophers of all time. There is wide agreement on that point. Kant dealt with many of the most important questions confronting humanity, often with great insight though certainly much more controversially than he himself realized. His manner was usually "scholastic" and at times approximated a parody of the academic style, but he also had a distinctive and comprehensive vision that embraced metaphysical views as well as a theory of knowledge, ethics no less than aesthetics, philosophy of religion, of right, and of science; he published books on anthropology and logic; and he had an intricate theory about the mind. He clearly felt that his views were coherent and supported each other, and this was, in fact, one of the main reasons why he felt that his philosophy must be true. He did not merely sketch his vision in large strokes but worked it out in stunning detail, providing ample nourishment both for people in search of a reasoned world view and for professional philosophers, who have never tired of examining his arguments and of discussing what appear to be some interesting inconsistencies.

On top of all that he also embodied ever so many traits that are encountered on a lesser scale in many others, including large numbers of twentieth-century philosophers. Plato suggested near the beginning of his *Republic* (368) that it would be helpful to study what justice means in a state, instead of beginning with the individual, because it is easier to read large characters.

For this reason also it is rewarding to deal at length with Kant. Although he was a very small man physically, in other ways he was more than life-size.

22 ▶▶▶ Kant himself felt that he had discovered the structure of the mind, and that this was the crux of his achievement. In the preface to the second edition of his major work, the *Critique of Pure Reason* (p. xvif.), he explained the nature of what ever since has been called his Copernican Revolution:

> It is just as it was with . . . *Copernicus* who, when one could not get on with the explanation of the heavenly motions as long as one supposed that the whole army of stars revolved around the spectator, tried whether things would not go better when he made the spectator revolve while leaving the stars in peace. In metaphysics one can try something similar regarding the *intuition* of objects. If our intuition had to depend on the structure of the objects, I do not see how one could have any *a priori* knowledge of them; but if the object (as an object of the senses) depends on the structure of our faculty of intuition, then I can imagine this possibility very well.

Kant assumed that both Euclidean geometry and Newtonian science offered us absolutely certain knowledge, and he formulated his problem: "How is pure mathematics possible? How is science possible?"[9] His solution was that absolutely certain knowledge of the world would be impossible if the world we know were not constituted by the human mind. But if the world we know derived its form from our mind, then the discovery of the structure of our mind would allow us to make apodictic claims about the world. In his *Critique of Pure*

[9] B 20. (B identifies page references to the second edition of *Critique of Pure Reason*; A, those to the first.)

Reason Kant tried to show *what the mind had to be like* to make the certainty of Euclidean geometry and Newtonian science possible.

He called this search for necessary presuppositions his "transcendental method." This is one of his many unhappy coinages. He loved "transcendent" and "transcendental," sometimes distinguishing them and sometimes not, and ever since "transcendental" has been used by others in a multitude of different senses, and more often than not those who use the term fail to specify what precisely they mean.

"Transcendent" usually means "beyond experience" or "outside the world" and is contrasted with "immanent." When Kant distinguished "transcendent" and "transcendental" he said:

> I call transcendental all knowledge that concerns itself not with objects but with our way of knowing objects insofar as such knowledge is supposed to be possible *a priori*. A system of such concepts [note that grammatically "such concepts" hangs in the air] would be called *transcendental philosophy* (B 25).

"Transcendental," Kant says in his *Prolegomena,* in the third footnote from the end, "does not refer to what transcends all experience but to what precedes it (*a priori*) without having any other function than to make possible knowledge by experience. When these concepts transcend knowledge, then their use is called transcendent . . ."

Kant frequently forgot the distinctions he made so laboriously, and Norman Kemp Smith remarks in *A Commentary to Kant's "Critique of Pure Reason"* "that Kant flatly contradicts himself in almost every chapter; and that there is hardly a technical term which is not employed by him in a variety of different and conflicting senses. As a writer, he is the least exact of all the great thinkers" (p. xx).

Although Norman Kemp Smith's translation of Kant's *Critique of Pure Reason* is by far the most widely used English version, his commentary is more widely respected than read, and the image of Kant as a model of intellectual rigor and probity persists. Few philosophers indeed would agree that "he is the least exact of all the great thinkers," and some English-speaking philosophers still seem to think that of all the major German philosophers Kant was, except perhaps for Leibniz, the most exact. *The crucial point about Kant's lack of rigor,* however, is not whether he was more or less exact than Fichte, Hegel, or Heidegger; it *is* rather *that he went to enormous lengths to affect a rigor that turns out on closer inspection to be mere pretense (though he himself was evidently taken in),* and that his successors, including Fichte, Hegel, and Heidegger, followed his example. Heidegger's distinction of *existenzial* and *existenziell* furnishes a close parallel to Kant's distinction of *tranzendent* and *tranzendental:* now it is made emphatically and serves as a shibboleth that instantly reveals as outsiders those who fail to heed it, and then Heidegger himself confuses the two.

When Norman Kemp Smith called Kant "the least exact of all the great thinkers," many philosophers still took for granted that Nietzsche was so inexact that he could not be considered a great thinker at all. Having tried to show in my studies of Nietzsche and in my translations and commentaries that he was a very great thinker indeed, I should not want to be misunderstood about Kant's manner of writing. Unquestionably, careful commentators can show, and have shown, how some inconsistencies are merely superficial and how some arguments that are faulty as they stand can be amended or reconstructed. Often different commentators propose different emendations and reconstructions, but that does not go to show that Kant could not have been a great philosopher. In fact, he was one of the greatest philosophers of all time—despite his spurious rigor. He was not the first philosopher who made a great point of being rigorous when he actually was not. Perhaps this is a vice characteristic of scholastic philosophers, great as well as small, and *in this respect* Spinoza in his *Ethics* and Kant in one major work after another were scholastics. My reason for stressing this aspect of Kant is that he was the first great philosopher of modern times who was a professor, while Nietzsche was almost the last great philosopher who never was a philosophy professor (he was a professor of classical philosophy but gave up his chair before writing his major works)—and modern philosophy has followed Kant's example, not Nietzsche's, Spinoza's, Goethe's, or Plato's. Kant had a comprehensive vision that he tried to spell out; he found it difficult to do this step by step; and he never understood the inadequacies of his presentation. Fichte and Schelling, Hegel and Schopenhauer were unquestionably corrupted by Kant, while many lesser men down to our own time, including a great many who have no distinctive vision at all, have little in common with Kant except for a spurious rigor. In their writings as in his, the multiplication of unhelpful coinages and distinctions serves mainly to obscure the fact that some of the most crucial issues are evaded. It would be unfair to hold Kant responsible for the shortcomings of many analytical philosophers who in this way follow in his footsteps, but it may be salutary to see such shortcomings on a large scale in a major thinker—and we shall therefore return to this theme.

Kant further distinguished *a priori* judgments which are, by definition, universally and necessarily true and not based on experience, from empirical or *a posteriori* judgments which are based on experience and cannot be said to be universally and necessarily true. He also distinguished analytical judgments, which are true by definition (for example, all circles are round), from synthetic judgments, which are not (for example, some houses are round). Then he claimed that mathematics and science offer us synthetic judgments *a priori,* such as "five plus seven is twelve" or "every event has a cause," and he asked: "How are synthetic judgments *a priori* possible?" (B 19).

To answer this question, Kant offered an anatomy of the mind, distinguishing "sensibility," understanding, and reason, and dealing at length with each of these. Time and space, he argued, are the forms of the human "sensibility" through which we experience or "intuit" things.

Kant's word for what is virtually always translated as "intuition" is *Anschauung* which, like the verb *anschauen* ("intuit"), literally means "view." But Kant, unlike Goethe, had very little sensitivity for words, and his terms are frequently misleading. In this instance, the visual image is as inappropriate as the English "intuition." What Kant meant was neither vision nor hunches but sense experience in which he included not only the five senses but also what he called "the inner sense," by which he meant something like introspection. But he never bothered to spell out what precisely he meant either by "the inner sense" or by *Sinnlichkeit,* rendered as "sensibility" by virtually all of his translators and commentators.

Actually, even some excellent German-English dictionaries do not give "sensibility" as one of the meanings of *Sinnlichkeit.* What the German word means is either sensuality or sensuousness, and those who read Kant in English can hardly have any idea of what it is like to read him in German. While finishing my dissertation at Harvard, I assisted Professor C. I. Lewis in a course in which I had to read more than fifty weekly summaries of installments of Kant's *Critique of Pure Reason.* All but one discussed "sensibility," but the German-born son of the foremost living German playwright kept referring to "sensuality." I wrote "sensibility" on the margin and was informed in the next summary: "If whoever read this knew any German, he would know that *Sinnlichkeit* means sensuality." This is true, but in Kant it does not. What Kant meant to suggest was that all experience comes to us via the senses, and that its forms are space and time, except that what comes to us through the internal sense is in time but not in space. But Kant does not enumerate the senses, nor does he discuss proprioception or hard cases.

The twelve categories—three each of quantity, quality, relation, and modality—are the forms of the human understanding in terms of which we understand things. Specifically, they are unity, plurality, and totality; reality, negation, and limitation; substance and accident, cause and effect, and reciprocity between agent and patient; and finally possibility/impossibility, existence/nonexistence, and necessity/contingency. Unlike Goethe, Kant was not in the least afraid of abstractions. On the contrary, he felt at home among concepts and did not bother to define all of them, much less to give concrete examples.

His *Critique of Pure Reason* is so complex that it would be only too easy to lose the thread if we stopped to substantiate these criticisms. It will be far better to press them a little later on in connection with Kant's short book on ethics and his enormously influential remarks about aesthetics. In fact, for our purposes we can ignore Kant's intricate "deduction of the categories," which is different in the first edition (A 64–130) and the second (B 89–169) and has probably been discussed more in British and American seminars on Kant than any other subject in his philosophy. People go into philosophy for different reasons, and this "deduction" has held an endless fascination for the many graduate students and professors who love trying to solve puzzles. Practically nobody accepts Kant's table of twelve categories, and there is virtual agreement that his various attempts to "deduce" these categories are not tenable as they stand. Nevertheless many a course on Kant bogs down in this swamp and never reaches the far more compelling refutations of the traditional arguments for God's existence (A 590–642, B 618–70). H. J. Paton's scholarly and impressive two-volume work, *Kant's Metaphysics of Experience* is aptly subtitled: *A Commentary on the First Half of the Kritik der reinen Vernunft*. More than 270 pages of the first volume are devoted to the deduction of the categories.

If our concern here were with puzzle-solving, we might concentrate on the short but baffling section "On the Schematism of the Pure Concepts of Understanding," which immediately follows the so-called "deduction" and is crucial for Kant's theory (A 137–47, B 176–87). We could then try to determine whether Norman Kemp Smith is right when he says about Kant's discussion (p. 334): "No such explanation can be accepted. For if category and sensuous intuition are really heterogeneous, no subsumption is possible; and if they are not really heterogeneous, no such problem as Kant here refers to will exist." Or is Paton's sixty-page defense of Kant's ten pages successful? We can dispense with this intricate controversy. Our main concern here is with the ways in which Kant impeded the discovery of the mind. But before we criticize him, we must try to gain some understanding of what he tried to accomplish in his *Critique of Pure Reason*. It is only too easy to lose sight of that.

Since we are concerned with Kant's influence, we must take note of a fateful comment he offered on his own table of twelve categories: "Regarding this table of categories one could bring forth some neat considerations [*artige Betrachtungen*] that could perhaps have striking consequences for the scientific form of all rational knowledge," he said prophetically in the second edition (B 109); and the second of his neat points was that there were three categories in each class and that "the third category always comes into being through the connection of the second with the first in its class."

This hint was not lost on his successors. Of course, they also knew the footnote at the end of Kant's long preface to his *Critique of Judgment* (1790), which most modern writers on dialectic have ignored:

> It has been considered odd that the way I divide things up in pure philosophy is almost always tripartite. But that is due to the nature of the material. If such a division is to be *a priori*, it will either be *analytical,* in accordance with the principle of contradiction, and in that case it will always be dichotomous . . . or it will be *synthetic;* and if in the latter case it is to be derived from *concepts a priori* (and not, as in mathematics, from intuition which corresponds *a priori* to the concept), then the division must necessarily be a trichotomy in line with what is needed for a synthetic unity, namely (1) a condition, (2) something conditioned, and (3) the concept that issues from the union of the conditioned with its condition.

There is no need here to analyze this difficult note in detail, but its influence on Fichte, Schelling, Hegel, and the whole development of modern dialectic meets the eye. Although Kant himself used the term "dialectic" for what he criticized in his *Critique of Pure Reason* and not for what he himself taught, there is a sense in which one could say that, like Plato before him, he led men to turn their back on experience and to engage in dialectic instead.

So far we have not come to grips with the title of the book. What is the point of Kant's "Critique"?

In his discussion of time (A 35, B 52) Kant pointed out that he taught the "empirical reality of time, that is its objective validity regarding all objects that may ever be given to our senses," while "we deny to time any claim to absolute reality." In the same vein Kant's doctrine could be called empirical realism but transcendental idealism, and the latter name for it is not uncommon, although Kant said in his *Prolegomena* (1783)[10] that he rather regretted "that I myself have given my theory the name of transcendental idealism" (notably A 490f.); he now preferred to "withdraw" it in favor of "critical" idealism. The name does not matter greatly, but the point at issue is crucial. The things *we know* are *really* spatiotemporal; and arithmetic, Euclidean geometry, and Newtonian science give us absolutely certain knowledge of them. We need have no fear whatsoever that some experience or other tomorrow will suddenly disprove Euclid or Newton. It will be noted that Kant implicitly assumes—incidentally, without any argument whatsoever—that the human mind cannot change in any fundamental way. He does not only believe that his model of it is right but also that the mind always has been and will be the same. Yet he admits emphatically that we cannot know what the world is like apart from human experience or, as some might like to say, what it is "really" like. We can have no knowledge about what Kant calls the thing in itself (*das Ding an sich*). What we know are phenomena.

The "critique of pure reason" consists in showing how reason comes to grief when it tries to give us knowledge that transcends the phenomenal world. In particular, Kant seeks to demolish what he calls rational psychology, rational cosmology, and rational theology. No claims to offer us rational knowledge of the soul, the world as a whole, or God are tenable.

In an eye-catching manner he expounds four "antinomies" on more than thirty facing pages, the four "theses" and their "proofs" on left-hand pages, the four "antitheses" and their "proofs" on the facing right-hand

[10] Sec. 13, note 3.

pages. The theses assert: "The world has a beginning in time" and is spatially finite; "Every compound substance in the world consists of simple parts, and nothing exists anywhere but the simple, or what is composed of it"; "Causality, according to the laws of nature, is not the only causality from which all the phenomena of the world can be deduced. In order to account for these phenomena it is necessary also to admit another causality, that of freedom"; and finally "There exists an absolutely necessary being belonging to the world, either as a part or a cause of it." The antitheses assert: "The world has no beginning and no limits in space" but is spatially as well as temporally infinite; "No compound thing in the world consists of simple parts, and there exists nowhere in the world anything simple"; "There is no freedom, but everything in the world takes place entirely according to the laws of nature"; and "There nowhere exists an absolutely necessary being, either within or without the world, as the cause of it."

Perhaps there is nothing in the whole history of philosophy between Plato and Nietzsche that matches the drama of these pages which culminate in a section entitled "Transcendental Idealism as the Key to the Solution of the Cosmological Dialectic" (A 490). In the following section the solution is summed up concisely:

> If the world is a whole existing by itself, it is either finite or infinite. Now the former as well as the latter proposition is false, as has been shown by the proofs given in the antithesis on one and in the thesis on the other side. It is false, therefore, that the world (the sum total of all phenomena) is a whole existing by itself. Hence it follows that phenomena in general are nothing outside our representations, which was what we meant by their transcendental ideality (A 506f.).

The antinomies and their resolution would seem to be a hard act to follow, but Kant goes on to offer a devastating critique of the traditional proofs for God's existence, and this had quite as much to do with the impact of the book as the antinomies. Yet in the Preface to the second edition in 1787 (B xxx) Kant explained: "I had to do away with knowledge to make room for faith." He had left room for God and freedom beyond the world of appearance, in that realm of which no knowledge is possible.

A year later, in 1788, Kant argued rather unconvincingly in his *Critique of Practical Reason* that practical reason—or as we might say, our moral sense, which Kant considers rational—demands that God should exist, that the soul should be immortal, and that the will should be free in that other realm, beyond phenomena. The arguments supporting these three "postulates," as Kant himself called them, have never won wide acceptance, and the impact of Kant's second *Critique* has never been comparable to that of the first.

23 ▸▸▸ The short book on ethics which Kant published in 1785, three years before the *Critique of Practical Reason,* occupies a unique place among his works. It was here that he first developed his conception of autonomy and his moral rationalism. Its impact rivals that of the *Critique of Pure Reason,* and the volume is second to none of Kant's major works in brevity, elegance, and readability. It also illuminates the relation of Kant's own mind to his philosophy and specifically to his influential doctrines about the human mind.

Grundlegung zur Metaphysik der Sitten has been translated under various titles, including "Foundation," "Fundamental Principles," and "Groundwork of the Metaphysics of Morals." The German word suggests an activity on Kant's part and means literally "laying the ground." "Laying the Foundations for the Metaphysics of Morals" would be an accurate rendering.

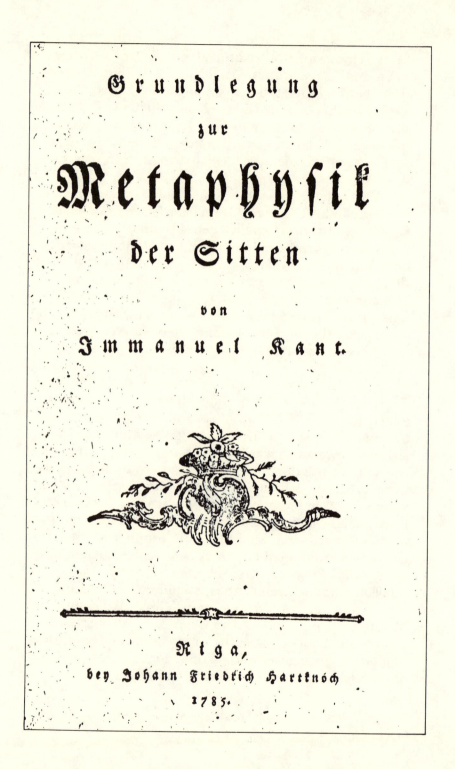

Grundlegung

zur

Metaphysik

der Sitten

von

Immanuel Kant.

Riga,
bey Johann Friedrich Hartknoch
1785.

The original German edition comprised less than 150 small pages, Lewis Beck's scholarly translation barely over eighty. To say that none of Kant's major works is more readable is not to deny that the book bristles with difficulties. At the lowest level, there is an abundance of sentences that run on for nearly a whole page. One beginning in the middle of the sixth paragraph of the Preface actually continues for a page and a half in the original edition and is immediately followed by half a dozen competitors that do not quite equal that record. The tenth paragraph of the second chapter consists of a single sentence that almost fills two whole pages. These serpentine sentences often cannot be construed, and different German editors have proposed different emendations. One can hardly help wondering at times whether a philosopher who writes that way could possibly be motivated by some fear of clarity. Another problem contributes to this quandary.

Kant tries to work out his position in Gothic, not to say, baroque, detail, using a highly intricate scholastic terminology. Among his key terms are maxims and principles, motives and inducements, and pathological and practical interests. There is no good reason for not making clear at the outset what precisely is meant by each of these six terms. The resultant gain in the clarity of the whole argument would have been immense, and one seems entitled to expect no less from a professor who said repeatedly that he spurned literary elegance for the sake of rigor.

In the preface to the second edition of the *Critique of Pure Reason,* for example, Kant reassured the government that his critique "can never become popular," but

This is the only way to cut off the roots of *materialism, fatalism, atheism,* free-spiriting *unbelief, fanciful enthusiasm* [*Schwärmerei*], and *superstition,* which can become generally harmful, and finally also *idealism* and *skepticism* which are more dangerous for the schools and less likely to spread to the public. If governments consider it a good idea to occupy themselves with the affairs of scholars, it would be much more in keeping with their wise concern for the sciences and for human beings to favor the freedom of such a critique, which alone can provide a firm footing for rational work, than to support the ridiculous despotism of the schools which raise a loud clamor about the public danger when one tears their spider webs of which the public has never taken any notice and whose loss therefore it can never feel (B xxxivf.).

Kant went on to oppose "the garrulous shallowness under the assumed name of popularity" and insisted that he opposed skepticism: what he wanted must be done "necessarily dogmatically and systematically according to the most rigorous demands, and thus scholastically [*schulgerecht*] (not popularly) . . . " (xxxvi).

Demanding academic freedom for his enterprise, Kant assured the government that his book could never become popular; but at the same time he suggested—and this is a theme that runs through his work—that so-called popular philosophy was shallow while his own was so extremely rigorous that for that reason it could not hope to be readable by the general public. What I am saying is that what makes Kant so difficult to read and often so hopelessly obscure is not at all exemplary rigor but rather his appalling *lack* of rigor.

Some philosophers meet any such criticism of the *Critique of Pure Reason* by saying that what Kant tried to do was so profound that it is Philistine to suppose that he could have achieved clarity. After all, Kant struck out in an entirely new direction. His short book on ethics, however, makes it as clear as can be that Kant's lack of rigor was not due to his profundity. Rather, it covers up difficulties that he should have faced.

Against his will, Kant's towering example taught

German philosophers the hollow affectation of a rigor that on close examination is not there. In the *Grundlegung* one certainly gets the feeling that Kant wanted clarity—up to a point. He specifies that point, attaching some importance to the mystery that begins there. But the whole thrust of his argument is that there is nothing mysterious about what human beings ought to do. On the contrary, reason tells us clearly—so clearly that even a highly sympathetic reader may be led to wonder whether Kant must not be wrong because he leaves no room for moral quandaries. However maddening his style may be, one does not have the feeling that Kant is an obscurantist. Yet the web he spins out of concepts hangs in the air and is out of touch with life.

The word *Prinzip* (principle) is used by Kant throughout the book on almost every other page without ever being defined. But Section 1 of the *Critique of Practical Reason,* published three years later, opens with a definition of *Praktische Grundsätze* and of maxims, and Section 2 begins: *"Alle praktische Prinzipien . . . "* It turns out that he uses *Grundsätze* and *Prinzipien* interchangeably and that his definition in Section 1 illuminates his earlier book.

> Practical *principles* are propositions that contain a general determination of the will that subsumes several practical rules. They are subjective, or *maxims*, when the subject considers the condition valid only for his own will; they are objective, or practical *laws*, when it is recognized as objective, that is valid for the will of every rational being.

Kant immediately adds in a note on Section 1: "If we assume that pure reason can contain a practical ground sufficient to determine the will, then there are practical laws; if not, then all practical principles will be mere maxims." All of this is consistent with the *Grundlegung* and helps us to understand Kant. In the *Grundlegung* maxims are defined twice. In the first footnote of Chapter 1 he says: "*Maxim* is the subjective principle of willing." In the seventh footnote of Chapter 2: "*Maxim* is the subjective principle to act." In the original edition, these two definitions are thirty-six pages apart, and considering that Kant's whole argument revolves around maxims and principles it is something of a scandal that he does not state clearly what he means, giving a few examples of maxims.

To be sure, very soon after the second footnote definition Kant does try to make his argument more concrete by giving four examples, but they have elicited a large literature because they seem to make nonsense of his arguments. In *The Autonomy of Reason: A Commentary on Kant's Groundwork of the Metaphysic of Morals* (1973), Robert Paul Wolff, who is full of admiration for Kant, says nevertheless: "Two of the examples are simply no good at all, a third fails, although in an interesting manner, and only one . . . can be salvaged by appropriate alterations" (p. 161f.). I do not agree entirely with this verdict and shall present my own view in Sections 26 and 27 where the four examples will be considered at some length; but Wolff's painstaking commentary is overwhelmingly sympathetic to Kant.

Kant was not the kind of thinker who begins by reflecting on concrete instances in the moral life and then attempts to distil from them generalizations that eventually are tested by being applied to other concrete cases. *He felt at home among abstractions, and as soon as he gave concrete examples it turned out that his conceptual scheme did not fit them.* At that point one would expect a scientist to reconsider and perhaps revise his theories. But Kant never even noticed that his scheme did not fit the cases he adduced!

Actually, this way of putting the matter is still too kind: Kant thought in terms of *words*, not concepts. He lacked any clear concept of a maxim, and his definitions ("the subjective principle of willing" and "the subjective principle to act") cover up a lack of clarity and bring to mind the words of Goethe's Mephistopheles cited near the end of Section 10 above:

> Yes, stick to words at any rate;
> There never was a surer gate
> Into the temple, Certainty. . . .
> For just where no ideas are
> The proper word is never far.
> With words a dispute can be won,
> With words a system can be spun,
> In words one can believe unshaken . . .

Kant scholars are still debating what exactly a "schema" might be, but there is no need here to stir up this hornets' nest. We can leave the *Critique of Pure Reason* with its endless complexities to the specialists and concentrate on Kant's little volume on ethics. Here the whole argument—and indeed Kant's moral philosophy—depends on "maxims," but Kant did not have any very clear idea of what a maxim is. This should become evident when we examine the four examples he gives, but since he did not start out from concrete cases, we first need to reconstruct his line of thought.

24 ▶▶ We noted earlier that Kant's most fundamental problem was: How are autonomy and free will possible in a deterministic Newtonian universe? The crux of Kant's attempt to lay the foundation for ethics is his answer to this question. As long as our actions are prompted by our inclinations, they are causally determined and we are not free. But Kant argued that we escape from determinism when our actions are not prompted by any inclination but solely by respect for reason.

As long as we make it a rule, or for that matter a

habit, to follow our inclinations, sleep as long as we like, smoke as much as we like, and do whatever we like, curbed only by enlightened self-interest or, in one word, prudence, our lives are governed by what Kant called pathological interests and hypothetical imperatives. ("Pathological interests" will be discussed at length in Section 28.) A hypothetical imperative commands: If you want this, do that. When I obey it, I am the slave of my inclination or, as Kant also says, of the object I desire. The only way to escape from psychological determinism is to adopt a maxim that is not tainted by any pathological interest whatsoever and to obey an imperative that is not hypothetical but categorical. There is, says Kant, only one categorical imperative, but he goes on to show that there are three widely different formulations of it, and some commentators claim that there are really five. If one accepts Kant's own count, one has to admit that the first formulation has two variants which Kant offers on the same page, between the footnote in which he defines maxims, and the famous four examples.

> The categorical imperative is thus only one, namely this: *Act only according to that maxim through which you can will at the same time that it should become a universal law.* . . . Thus the universal imperative of duty could also be formulated: *Act as if the maxim of your action should become through your will a universal natural law.*

The primary idea of Kant's *Grundlegung* is that I am free when I act without any irrational motive, solely out of respect for reason. The question why and how one would act if one had no motive in the phenomenal world is secondary for Kant, and he insists again and again that it involves an unfathomable mystery although his *Critique of Pure Reason* has shown that it is not impossible. In a way, every noumenal self performs miracles as God did according to the tradition. The mystery, however, concerns only what we might call the metaphysical aspect of freedom. The content of the categorical imperative as the sole alternative to hypothetical imperatives is, according to Kant, as clear as can be. He himself does not give the following example, but it might have helped more to illuminate this point than the examples he did give.

When I do mathematics and make no mistake, my work is in no way vitiated by my irrational nature. I obtain results that every rational being would reach.[11] My procedure is prompted solely by respect for reason—and I am free. In the moral realm I must similarly divest myself of all irrationality. As long as I desire particular objects, I have failed to do this. But when I discover maxims that can be universalized and contain nothing personal or subjective, I may be assured that when I act on them, prompted solely by respect for reason, I am free. Kant assumes that universality is the mark of rationality, while the particular and subjective are irrational. As long as I have a will of my own, I am not free!

Thus freedom and autonomy à la Kant involve emancipation from our individuality and subjectivity. At this point the similarity to Martin Luther's *Exegesis of the Lord's Prayer for Simple Lay Folk* (1519) is striking. Here are some of Luther's observations on "Thy will be done . . .":

> People say: But God has given us a free will. Answer: Indeed, he has given you a free will. Why then do you want to make of it a will of your own instead of leaving it free? When you do with it what you will, it is not free but your own. But God gave neither you nor anyone else a will of your own; for a will of one's own comes from the devil and Adam, who received their free will from God

[11] Mathematical discoveries need not concern us here. Suffice it to mention that David Hilbert, the great German mathematician (1862–1943), once said of a student who had given up mathematics to become a novelist: "It is just as well. He did not have any imagination."

and made it their own. A truly free will is one that wills nothing of its own but only sees to God's will and thus also remains free, getting attached and stuck to nothing [*nirgend anhangend oder anklebend*].

And a few pages earlier Luther says:

Man should train to have an overwill [*Ueberwillen*] against his will and never to feel more insecure than when he feels that only one will is in him instead of two wills opposed to each other, and he should thus become used to following the overwill against his will. For whoever has and does his own will is certainly against God's will.[12]

At first glance, the only major difference between Kant and the early Luther may seem to be that Kant does not speak of a will of one's own but of the inclinations, and not of an overwill but of reason. But Kant considered fear of God incompatible with autonomy and actually a prime example of "heteronomy," that is, obedience to a law given by someone else. Autonomy means to Kant that I obey a law I have given myself. This notion is derived from Rousseau's *Social Contract* (1762); and it is noteworthy that there were no pictures in Kant's house except for a portrait of Rousseau in his living room.[13]

Luther's conception of freedom, quoted above, is likely to strike modern readers as paradoxical and utterly implausible, if not as a piece of theological casuistry. As

---

[12] *Auslegung des Vater-Unsers für die einfältigen Laien* (1519) in *Sämmtliche Schriften*, ed. Johann Georg Walch, vol. 7, col. 1132 and 1126; in the St. Louis reprint of 1891, col. 786 and 781. For Luther's later views on free will see *De servo arbitrio* (1526) and *Sämmtliche Werke*, ed. J. K. Irmischer, vol. 58 (*Tischreden*, vol. 2), pp. 214–39.

[13] "Obedience to a law one has prescribed to oneself is freedom" (*Social Contract*, bk. I, chap. VIII). For Kant's relation to Rousseau see Cassirer (1918), pp. 92–95, Vorländer (1924), I, pp. 148–51, Cassirer (1945), and Beck (1969), pp. 489–91. More on the portrait in sec. 30 below.

long as I do what I wish I am not free; it is only when I do not follow my own will that my will is free. Yet few readers note how similar Kant's position is, and many approach his notion of autonomy with credulous if somewhat puzzled awe.

This is probably due in large part to the fact that after giving his famous four examples, and before giving his account of autonomy, Kant expounds another formulation of the categorical imperative which is very impressive indeed. *"Act so that you treat humanity both in your own person and in every other person always as an end also and never as a means only."* This formulation establishes Kant as one of the greatest moral teachers of mankind, but it is usually misquoted and reduced to nonsense by the omission of two crucial words: *also* and *only*. We cannot help using others as a means to various ends, and there is nothing immoral in that, as Kant recognized. What Kant exhorted us not to do is to treat human beings as mere things. It is in this context that he then introduces autonomy before distinguishing between price and dignity, the point being that things have a market price while human beings have no price but a unique dignity.

All of this is very attractive and humane, and many a reader comes away with the impression that Kant somehow proves this ethic, even if it is difficult to follow or reconstruct his argument. In fact, the argument *can* be reconstructed and falls very far short of any proof. It is merely an inveterate academic prejudice that obscurity and density warrant a presumption of rigor.

The deduction of Kant's beautiful and concise formulation of an ethic derived from Moses and the prophets is actually contained in two sentences that total a dozen lines, just two pages before the means/end formulation of the categorical imperative.

Suppose, however, that there were something *whose existence in itself* had an absolute value, something that as an *end in itself* could be a ground of definite laws, then the ground of a possible categorical imperative, that is practical law, would lie in this and in this alone.

Now I say: Human beings and altogether all rational beings *exist* as ends in themselves, *not as a means only* for any arbitrary use by this or that will, and must be considered in all their actions, whether directed toward themselves or to other rational beings, always *as ends also*.

Plainly, this is no proof. What Kant asserts in the second paragraph is his faith—part of the faith on which he was raised. And he then proceeds to put his cards on the table. If there were "nothing that had *absolute value*" and "if all value were conditional," then all imperatives would be hypothetical and there would be no categorical imperative. If there is to be an unconditional imperative, something must have unconditional value, and Kant says that humanity does or that all rational beings do. It is doubtful whether in 1785 he thought that there actually were rational beings besides man, but his point is that human beings have absolute value and dignity and must never be treated as means only, because they are rational and not on account of any other property.

This principle of humanity and every rational being in general *as an end in itself* . . . is not derived from experience, first of all because of its universality, as it extends to all rational beings in general, and no experience could be sufficient to determine something about that; secondly, because humanity is here represented not as an end for man (subjectively), that is as an object that one really adopts as an end for oneself, but as an objective end that, whatever ends we may choose to adopt, is supposed to constitute as a law the supreme limiting condition of all subjective ends, thus must originate from pure reason.

That Kant's principle is not derived from experience and not based on psychology or any kind of empirical generalization is obvious. He seems to conclude that his principle therefore "must originate from pure reason," although this final clause hangs in the air, syntactically, and different Kant scholars have offered slightly different conjectures as to how it might be integrated grammatically.[14] But while a universal proposition about all rational beings and a supreme law that restricts all ends we might wish to adopt cannot be based on experience, it clearly does not follow that they "must originate from pure reason." After all, they might be derived from a religious tradition, and they might not be well founded at all. Yet by the end of that paragraph Kant offers us what is sometimes considered his third formulation of the categorical imperative, this time at the end of a long and involved sentence and not at all in the form of an imperative: "now from this follows the third practical principle of the will as the supreme condition of the agreement of the will with the universal practical reason, the idea *of the will of every rational being as a will that legislates universally.*"

Essentially, Kant tells people what a great many of them want to hear. He offers them a drastically liberalized biblical ethic, stripped of all references to the supernatural, and he manages to create the impression that his procedure is rational and rigorous and that this ethic is founded on reason or demanded by reason. Actually, Kant's procedure is not at all rigorous and his ethic is neither founded on reason nor demanded by it. Where he writes, "Now I say: human beings and altogether all rational beings *exist* as ends in themselves, *not as a means only,*" another philosopher might say:

14 See Karl Vorländer's ed. of the *Grundlegung* (1906), p. 56. Proposals for emendations abound throughout this little book.

"All *living* beings are ends in themselves and not mere means only." His ethic would encompass animals and would presumably be vegetarian. Yet another philosopher might agree with Kant that a categorical imperative depends on there being something that has absolute value, and go on to say that hence at least one being must have absolute value and—in the words employed by Thomas Aquinas in his five proofs of God's existence—"this everyone understands to be God." Still another philosopher might agree that if there is to be an unconditional imperative, something must have absolute value, but conclude that nothing has absolute value and there is no categorical imperative.

Kant's misguided transcendental method always begins with what he wants to accept as absolutely certain—Euclidean geometry, Newtonian science, the categorical imperative, the notion that by virtue of their reason all human beings have a unique dignity—and then he asks what must be the case for these things to be absolutely certain. Nietzsche had a point when he said in *The Gay Science* (Section 193): "Kant wanted to prove, in a way that would dumbfound the common man, that the common man was right." To put the point still more concisely: Kant was a virtuoso of rationalization.

What makes him so unusual is that by the time he published his *magnum opus* in 1781 he had a comprehensive vision in which everything fell into place. As a corrective of a charge often raised against Nietzsche and of the prejudice that density and opaqueness bespeak rigor, I appreciate Robert Paul Wolff's claim in his commentary on the *Grundlegung* (p. 4): "Of all the great philosophers, there is none so rich in insights and so plagued by inconsistency as Kant." Actually, Nietzsche was far richer in insights, but it is noteworthy that Wolff, after analyzing closely first "Kant's Theory of Mental Activity" (in a book with that title, in 1963) and then the *Grundlegung*, should find so little substance in the myth of Kant's scrupulous rigor. As we have seen, Norman Kemp Smith, who translated Kant's *Critique of Pure Reason* into English, voiced the same view in his commentary a generation earlier. But what kept persuading Kant that he must be right was not one or another supposedly rigorous demonstration but rather the way in which all the pieces seemed to him to fit together.

25 ▶▶▶ To understand Kant's mentality as well as several crucial passages in his works we must realize that the religious inspiration of his ethic is to be found in Moses. In his *Religion Within the Bounds of Mere Reason* (1793) Kant had counted himself among the "rigorists"—"a name that is meant to be opprobrious but actually is laudatory" (p. 9). Later in the same year Friedrich Schiller published a remarkable essay "On Charm and Dignity" (*Ueber Anmut und Würde*) in which he included some reflections on "the immortal author of the *Critique*," whose rigorism he found excessive:

> In Kant's moral philosophy the idea of *duty* is presented with such harshness that all the graces are frightened away and a poor intellect might easily be tempted to seek moral perfection on the way of gloomy and monastic asceticism. Although the great sage of the world has tried to guard against any such misinterpretation, than which nothing could be more outrageous for his cheerful and free spirit, he himself has nevertheless, it seems to me, provoked it . . .[15]

Schiller, who impressed upon his younger contemporaries the need to reconcile Kant with Goethe, made it easy for Kant to mitigate his rigorism. In the second edition of his book on religion (1794) Kant added a very

[15] In the tenth paragraph before the subheading "Dignity."

gracious footnote about the criticism offered by "Herr Prof. Schiller" in his essay, "written with a master's hand"; but he refused to walk over the bridge Schiller had built for him. He really *had* to refuse because according to his view freedom depended on the absence of any psychological motive, which would entangle us, of necessity, in the web of psychological determinism. This is overlooked, along with the passages at issue, by interpreters who still insist that Kant was *not* a rigorist.

It is noteworthy *how* Kant refused. He did not merely reiterate what he had said in the text above and in the *Grundlegung* but also said:

> I confess gladly that I cannot allow *charm* to accompany the *concept of duty*, precisely owing to its dignity. For it contains unconditional necessitation which stands in flat contradiction against charm. The majesty of the law (like that on Sinai) evokes reverence . . . which arouses the *respect* of the subordinate for his commander, but in this case, since the commander is to be found within ourselves, a *feeling of the sublimity* of our own calling, which enraptures us more than anything beautiful.

Schiller's discussion of feeling led Kant to reveal something of his own feelings. The moral law within him had for him all the majesty of the Mosaic law on Sinai and enraptured him. The celebrated opening of the "Conclusion" of the *Critique of Practical Reason* comes to mind: "Two things fill the mind [*Gemüt*] with ever new and increasing admiration and reverence, the more often and continuously we reflect on them: *the starry heavens above me and the moral law within me.*"

There is reason to believe that he associated both with his mother, who had died when he was thirteen.[16] In all of the three biographies of Kant that appeared in 1804, immediately after his death, much is made of

[16] Beck (1960), p. 282, shares this view.

Kant's deep feelings for his mother and her lasting influence on him.

"When the great man spoke of his mother his heart was moved, his eyes shone, and every one of his words expressed cordial and childlike reverence," says Jachmann before going on to tell us "that Kant once did not speak to his sisters for twenty-five years although he lived in the same town with them" (p. 163). His mother was a woman who had made something of herself, could write and spell passably—"for her station and time that was much and rare," according to Wasianski (p. 251)—and while her own religious feeling was "genuine and by no means effusive [*schwärmerisch*]" (*ibid.*), she demanded nothing less than "*holiness*" of her son. Borowski, who stresses this point (p. 13), is worth quoting at greater length:

> The father demanded work and honesty, especially avoidance of all lies; the mother also *holiness*. Thus K. grew up before her eyes, and what I have just said of his mother may have had the effect of establishing in his ethic an inexorable strictness, as is quite proper, and to raise up so high the principle of holiness that, on account of its unattainability, assures us of the certainty of another world. This demand of his pure practical reason to be holy had been at a very early age the demand his good mother had made on him.

Borowski adds in a footnote: "I should emphasize that K. did not change anything in this passage in my manuscript, nor made any comment on it, and consequently approved of it. It sheds a surely not insignificant light on the rigorism of his ethic."

Kant had indeed based his postulate of immortality, in his *Critique of Practical Reason* (1788) on the claim that practical reason demands that the achievement of holiness should be possible. Since it is not possible in this life, "it therefore can be encountered only in a *pro-*

gressus ad infinitum," and this "is possible only if we presuppose an infinitely enduring *existence* and personality of the same rational being (which one calls the immortality of the soul)" (p. 219f.).

This argument clearly implies the separate existence of many different moral personalities beyond the phenomenal world—one for each person encountered in the phenomenal world. The objection that Kant is here applying the categories of quantity (unity and plurality) beyond the phenomenal world, in defiance of his own teaching in the first *Critique,* he might have met by saying that he is only offering a postulate and not certain knowledge, and that the doctrine of the first *Critique* does not rule out the possibility that there might be a large number of moral selves in the beyond. The objection that the *progressus ad infinitum* presupposes the reality of time beyond the phenomenal world might be met in the same way. But over what transphenomenal imperfections does the immortal soul continue to triumph on and on and on? Is Kant also postulating transphenomenal inclinations?

This postulate is clearly inspired neither by Moses nor by Jesus—unless one should say that it represents an attempt to bring the Christian faith in the immortality of the soul as close as possible to Moses' categorical "You shall be holy" and to his agnosticism about the hereafter. Kant agrees that we can know nothing about the hereafter, and he allows no place at all for salvation through faith or the sacraments. Some people would call this a—or even *the*—Protestant ethic. Luther, a master of invective, would have found it difficult to find words for such a flagrant misnomer, and Calvin, who had Servetus burnt for rejecting belief in the Trinity, would scarcely have been satisfied with a milder punishment for Kant.

One of the last sections of Kant's book on religion bears the title "The Moral Principle of [a] Religion That Stands Opposed to the Religious Delusion" and begins:

"First I posit the following sentence as a principle that requires no proof: *Whatever man supposes he can do to please God apart from leading a good life is mere religious delusion and a perverted service of God [Afterdienst Gottes].*" This principle is printed in large type and elaborated at great length in the following pages. Thus Kant says three pages later: "As soon as man departs however slightly from the above maxim, the perverted service of God (superstition) no longer has any bounds." And another half a dozen pages later:

Between a Tungusic *shaman* and a European *prelate* . . . between the entirely sensuous *Mongol* who in the morning places the claw of a bear skin on his head with the brief prayer, "Don't slay me!" to the sublimated *puritan* and independent in *Connecticut* there is, to be sure, a powerful difference in *manners* but not in the principle of believing; for regarding that they all, without exception, belong to one and the same class—the class of those whose service of God stresses what in itself does not constitute a better human being, (like believing certain statutory propositions or engaging in various arbitrary observances).

Considering how often Kant has been linked with pietism, which was his own religious background, it is noteworthy that at the end of the last long footnote in Section 3 he goes out of his way to identify pietism with "a *slavish* bent of mind [*Gemütsart*]." Obviously, Kant did not care for the more than six hundred commandments and prohibitions in the Five Books of Moses, or for the traditional Christian dogmas and articles of faith, or for Paul's theology, or for the insistence on faith and sacraments in the Gospels. He was much closer to Micah's disparagement of sacrifices, which culminates in the words:

You have been told, man, what is good,
and what does the Lord demand of you

but to do justice and love kindness
and to walk humbly with your god? (6.8)

It is doubly remarkable that Kant nevertheless spoke of "the majesty of the law (like that on Sinai)." Plainly, this was the association that led him to use again and again the term "law"—in spite of Paul and Luther, who had filled their writings with polemics against "the law."

The three biographers who had known Kant well did not only agree on the importance of his mother for his moral education, they also related that she had occasionally taken him outside the town to instill in him awe for God's works, and it seems likely, though they do not say so, that she directed his gaze to the starry heavens. Whether Kant also associated the starry heavens with Abraham and Genesis 15.5, we do not know, but the archetype of the categorical imperative is certainly the refrain of the Mosaic law: "You shall." And the commandment "You shall be holy" is found in Leviticus 19, directly before the commandment to revere mother and father (in that order). The same chapter abounds in categorical demands, including some of the Ten Commandments as well as "You shall love your neighbor as yourself" and "The stranger who sojourns with you shall be to you as the native among you, and you shall love him as yourself."

The commandment to be holy is found elsewhere, too, in the Law of Moses: Leviticus 11.44–45, 20.7, and 26. It is not found in the Gospels and really as distinctively Mosaic as the challenge in Exodus 19, in the chapter preceding the Ten Commandments: "You shall be to me a kingdom of priests and a holy people." In the ancient Near East only priests were literate and educated, and the demand that all should be as priests was revolutionary.

What is called for is a transformation. We must cease being as we are. We are summoned to rise to a higher state. Instead of being content with, or resigned to, our lot, we are told to make something of ourselves. This is one of the most revolutionary ideas of the Five Books of Moses.[17]

Actually, Jesus may have quoted the commandment "You shall be holy," but Matthew (5.48) rendered it in Greek "You shall be perfect," and Luke (6.36) "You shall be merciful."[18] For Kant's postulate of the immortality of the soul, "perfect" would actually have been a little more suitable than "holy," which makes it doubly remarkable that Kant used the Mosaic word instead of alluding to the Sermon on the Mount. It clearly harks back to his mother's demand.

There are two reasons why the impact of Moses on Kant has not become a commonplace long ago. The primary reason is that Kant did not pay tribute to Moses or Judaism. Like most of the great Germans of his time— Lessing was the outstanding exception—Kant never entirely overcame the prejudices on which he was raised. He revered Moses Mendelssohn, with whom he had a most interesting correspondence, and the friend whom he favored with the most fascinating letters was his confidant and former student Marcus Herz. His favorite students included some other Jews as well, and after reading Solomon Maimon's sympathetic critique of his philosophy he wrote Herz (May 26, 1789), "none of my opponents has understood me and the main question so well." Kant could have said truthfully: "Some of my best friends are Jews." Yet he did not think of them as Jews even though it was common knowledge that they were. They were enlightened human beings and did not fit the

---

[17] See sec. 22–26 in Kaufmann, *What Is Man?*

[18] The Hebrew word is *q'doshim, heilig* in German, and the two Greek words are *teleioi* and *oiktirmones, vollkommen* and *barmherzig* in German. Strack and Billerbeck (1922 and 1924) do not associate the two verses in the Gospels with "You shall be holy," and there are Hebrew equivalents for the two Greek adjectives: *tamim* (or *shalem*) and *rahum*.

stereotype on which he had been raised and which he never quite outgrew.

In the second volume of his *Immanuel Kant* (1924), which is the best intellectual biography we have of Kant, Karl Vorländer, one of the leading Kant scholars of all time, devoted a section of eight pages (73–80) to Kant's attitudes toward Judaism and Jews. There are a few contemporary reports of anti-Semitic remarks he is said to have made in conversation. Those Vorländer sees no reason to doubt include a scurrilous comment at a dinner in his house, June 14, 1798, when Kant was seventy-four, as well as a strange reaction to Lessing's great play, *Nathan der Weise,* which Johann Georg Hamann related in a letter to Herder, May 6, 1779. Hamann, though "inclined toward anti-Semitism" and hence, according to Vorländer, reliable in this context, liked the play, while Kant was, according to Hamann, "averse to any hero coming from this people. That is how divinely strict our philosophy is in its prejudices despite all its tolerance and impartiality." The dinner remark, which Vorländer quotes as the "strongest" or "most virulent" thing (*Das Stärkste*) Kant *said* about the Jews, was reported by "the thoroughly reliable" Abegg: "As long as the Jews—are Jews and circumcised, they will never become more useful than harmful in civil society. Now they are vampires in society" (p. 73f.).

Vorländer says very reasonably that we should "not attach any value to all these private reports if similarly unfavorable judgments were not to be found also in his *writings*"—albeit only in the 1790s when Kant was well past his prime. In fact, it was only in 1798 when he was seventy-four and his powers were failing that he published some truly embarrassing and unworthy remarks in his *Anthropology,* in a long footnote.[19]

[19] First ed. (Warda #195) at the end of sec. 36; second ed. (1800, Warda #198), end of sec. 43; *Akademie* (allegedly based on second edition), sec. 46.

The Palestinians living among us have acquired since their exile . . . the not unfounded reputation of deceit. . . . Now it seems strange to think of a *nation* of deceivers, but after all it is just as strange to think of a nation of nothing but merchants whose by far largest part is held together by an ancient superstition that is recognized by the state in which they live, seeks no civic honor but tries to substitute for this loss the advantages of outwitting the people among whom they find protection and even each other. Now this cannot be any different, given a whole nation of nothing but merchants as nonproducing members of society (e.g., the Jews in Poland). . . . Instead of the vain plan to moralize this people regarding the point of deceit and honesty, I would rather explain my surmise regarding the origin of this peculiar constitution (namely, of a people of nothing but merchants). . . . Hence their dispersion through the whole world with their religious and linguistic ties should not be charged to a *curse* pronounced over this nation but seen rather as a *blessing*, the more so because their wealth, when one considers individuals, probably exceeds that of every other nation with the same number of members.

Like most of his contemporaries and many eminent writers after him, Kant was simply unable to see any continuity between the Jewish people of his time, of whom he lacked firsthand knowledge and whom he therefore saw through the glasses of prejudice, and either the lofty passages in the Bible that had formed his own moral sense or the Jews whom he knew personally and cherished as friends. He applauded Moses Mendelssohn's brilliant defense "of *unconditional freedom of conscience*" in *Jerusalem* (1783), which also made a profound impression on Hegel a few years later, but neither of them seems to have taken seriously Mendelssohn's claim that this position was characteristic of Judaism. Kant saw Judaism as a "mess of observances" (in his book on religion he spoke of a *Wust von Observanzen*). Speaking more soberly, one might say that he associated Judaism with statutory laws. Vorländer suggests that Kant's "dislike of the Old Testament" was due in part to his reaction to the pietism of his upbringing. Nevertheless it seems important to note how some elements of his moral education had come from the Old Testament, left their mark on him, and became central in his moral philosophy. That also helps to account for the great attraction of his philosophy to so many Jews in his own time and, much later, to Hermann Cohen who did so much to renew interest in Kant during the last thirty years of the nineteenth century. For Cohen, like Mendelssohn, took his Judaism very seriously.

There is another reason why the importance of the Old Testament for Kant's ethic has been insufficiently appreciated. After his ethic had become part of the common sense of Liberal Protestantism, Protestant theologians began to argue that the morality of the Old Testament was a morality of rewards (*Lohnmoral*) while that of the New Testament, being far superior, was not. Proceeding from their own unquestioned faith in the superiority of Kant's nonprudential ethic, generations of Protestant writers varied the theme that was finally carried to the absurd by Reinhold Niebuhr when he spoke of "the full rigorism and the nonprudential character of Jesus' ethic," ignoring the Gospels' constant appeal to rewards and punishments.[20] But as long as one assimilates Jesus to Kant and Kant to Jesus, while assuming that Kant stands diametrically opposed to the law given on Sinai, one bars any adequate understanding of Kant.

First of all, Kant had no use whatsoever for the central eschatological concern that permeates the Gospels as well as Paul's epistles. The recurring appeals to the end of the world, the day of judgment, hellfire, wailing and gnashing of teeth, and rewards in heaven are

---

[20] Niebuhr (1935, 1956), 55. For a detailed refutation see Kaufmann (1958), sec. 68 and 55.

diametrically opposed to Kant's rigorous agnosticism about all that lies beyond the world of science. Nor were Paul's lengthy polemics against "the law" congenial to Kant.

Then, Kant had no sooner offered his impressive ends/means formulation of the categorical imperative than he added a footnote that was clearly meant to disparage Jesus' "Golden Rule."

> Let no one suppose for a moment that the trivial *quod tibi non vis fueri*, etc. [what you do not want to happen to you, do not do unto others], could here serve as a guideline or principle. For it is merely derived from that [the categorical imperative], albeit with various limitations; it cannot be a universal law, for it does not contain the ground of the duties toward oneself nor of the duties of love toward others (for many a person would gladly agree that others should not benefit him if only he could be relieved of being their benefactor), nor of the duties we owe each other; for a criminal might argue on these grounds against the judges punishing him, etc.

To be sure, the Latin adage is negative, while the "Golden Rule" has been extolled by many Christians as far superior because it is positive and says: "Whatever you wish men to do to you, do to them."[21] Now it is actually arguable that the positive version is greatly inferior to the negative one,[22] but here it is quite sufficient to note that Kant's strictures apply to the Golden Rule as well, if not more so, and this seems to have been his real target. After Kant published his book on religion in 1793, the King of Prussia, Friedrich Wilhelm II, wrote him:

> Our Most High Person has noted for a long time with displeasure how you are misusing your philosophy to distort and denigrate some of the main and fundamental

[21] Matthew 7.12; Luke 6.31.
[22] Kaufmann, *The Faith of a Heretic*, p. 212.

doctrines of Holy Scripture and Christianity; how you have done this especially in your book *Religion Within the Bounds of Mere Reason* and no less in other small essays.

The king had gone on to warn Kant never to let this happen again, and after quoting this letter in the preface to his *Quarrel among the Faculties* (1798) Kant also quoted his reply in which he promised never to do it again, as well as his reasons for believing that now that the king had died the promise no longer held because he had given it "as your royal majesty's most faithful subject," and "this expression I chose with caution so that I would not renounce the freedom of my judgment in this religious matter *forever* but only as long as his majesty might live."[23]

This passage in the preface of Kant's last major work shows how some of his contemporaries saw him, and it also helps to illuminate his mentality. Kant made a point of the fact that neither the king's letter nor his own reply had ever reached the ears of the public, and there was no need for him to publicize them now had he not felt the urge to show his readers how clever he had been!

26 ▶▶▶ We are ready now to understand Kant's notorious four examples in the *Grundlegung*. At crucial points Moses holds the key to them.

We noted earlier, in Section 24, that Kant offers two slightly different formulations of the categorical imperative on a single page. It may be well to recall the second version: "Act as if the maxim of your action should become through your will a universal natural law." Kant then goes on:

---

[23] This is doubly odd in view of the fact that the king was twenty years younger than Kant. Had Kant really counted on outliving him?

Now let us enumerate a few duties, in accordance with the customary division of duties into duties to ourselves and duties to others, perfect and imperfect duties.

1. One who, on account of a series of ills that has grown to the point of hopelessness, feels weary of life still has sufficient command of his reason to be able to ask himself whether it may not be contrary to his duty to himself to take his own life. Now he makes the test whether the maxim of his action could become a universal natural law. His maxim, however, is: from self-love I adopt the principle that when life, if prolonged, threatens more ills than it promises agreeable things, I shall shorten it. [This sentence is ungrammatical in the original and cannot be construed though its meaning is clear.] The only question that remains is whether this principle of self-love could become a universal natural law. But then one sees soon that a nature whose law it would be to destroy life itself by means of the same feeling whose purpose [*Bestimmung*] it is to advance the promotion of life, would contradict itself and thus could not persist as nature, and thus this maxim could not possibly have a place as a universal natural law and consequently is wholly at odds with the supreme principle of all duty.

Here we have an example of a maxim. But it remains unclear whether Kant is trying to show that suicide is always immoral or only that this particular maxim is morally unjustifiable. He seems to think that he is establishing the stronger claim, although in fact his argument does not even establish the weaker claim.

Regarding the stronger claim, that suicide is always immoral, Kant never stops to ask whether some maxims that a person considering suicide might well adopt could not perhaps be universalized. Life and literature are full of pertinent examples, beginning at least with the first suicide in the Bible: Samson's. The Bible does not censure his suicide any more than any of the other suicides in the Bible, but comments admiringly: "The dead he slew dying exceeded those he had slain living." Surely,

Kant's introduction of self-love is gratuitous, and it is not difficult to think of examples in which suicide is motivated by love of others. One might be afraid that under torture one would give away others, and hence might kill oneself to protect them. Or one might prefer suicide to becoming a wretched burden for others, physically, emotionally, and financially.

Even the weaker claim, that the maxim of the person he imagines cannot be universalized, Kant fails to prove. The alleged contradiction depends on the gratuitous assumption that self-love has been implanted in us for a purpose (to advance the promotion of life). The suicide Kant imagines is motivated by self-love in a way that conflicts with this purpose. Without realizing what he is doing, Kant is actually appealing to an assumed purpose of nature that is derived from Moses' categorical demand: "Choose life!" (Deuteronomy 30.19). The whole machinery of universalizing maxims is a smoke screen: the suicide violates Moses' commandment, at least as Kant understands it.

Now I have said earlier that Kant really lacked any clear concept of a maxim. Kant's definitions no less than the first example which we have just considered leave open the question whether all of us have maxims whenever we act, or at least when we act deliberately. If it is the case—and I think it is—that many people and perhaps even most people make choices and decisions and act without entertaining any maxims, then Kant's attempt to lay the foundations for ethics fails. But on one understanding of the word "maxim" it is simply a fact that many people much of the time, if not most people most of the time, act without maxims—that is, without invoking general, albeit subjective, principles or rules that govern their conduct.

Now Kant might say, as in fact he does not, that we ought to formulate maxims and submit them to his test.

But with a little ingenuity one should be able to formulate maxims that would pass the test—unless all particulars drop away when the maxim becomes a universal law. In that case, the introduction of self-love no less than the references to ills and agreeable things are all entirely beside the point, and what matters is simply that suicide cannot be made a universal natural law because nature (alias Moses) commands us to choose life. It remains unclear what a maxim is, and Kant's conceptual definitions do not help as concrete examples might. Kant liked to eat a roast for dinner and evidently did not feel that butchers were immoral *ex officio*. What would be a butcher's maxim? Kill sheep, pigs, and steers? Surely, not simply: Kill! And even when submitted to Kant's test and universalized it would not become: Kill!

Of course, there are people, notably including Kant himself, who formulate a lot of maxims for themselves. When we turn to Kant's biography (in Section 31) we shall find no dearth of examples. And Kant evidently assumed that the minds of other people were like his own although in fact his was in ever so many ways quite exceptional. When people who do not share this habit want to find out whether an action they are considering is moral and, having read Kant, wish to test their maxim, how can they discover their maxim? Is it by introspection? Must they try to discover what really motivates them? Or is the intellect free to devise a maxim—and if that fails the test, to try again?

There is a sense in which it is clear enough what a maxim is: a rule that we adopt for our conduct. In ordinary discourse it might be overly fastidious to press for greater precision. But when a philosopher spurns good, clear prose, insisting repeatedly that he is so extremely rigorous that for that reason he cannot make any concessions to "popularity," and when he bases his whole moral philosophy on the demand that we must univer-

salize our maxims, then it is worth pointing out that proceeding "scholastically (not popularly)" and being
"rigorous" are two very different things.

"With words a system can be spun," and, as a matter
of psychological fact, there may be no surer gate to certainty than reliance on words. But abstract nouns, in
which Kant revels, are no substitute for concrete examples. And just as the lucidity of Lessing, Goethe, Heine,
Nietzsche, and Freud was inseparable from their ability
to see what they wrote about, the extraordinary obscurity
of Kant and some other philosophers, notably including
Heidegger, is due to their excessive reliance on words
and their inability to deal with concrete instances. Kant
was neither the first nor the last philosopher to deceive
himself and his public about this crippling incapacity by
claiming that it was dictated by "the most rigorous demands."

27 ▶▶▶ In fairness to Kant, we still
have to consider his other three examples. The second is
the best of the lot, but most readers have failed to get its
point because Kant confused the issue. A man in distress
wants to borrow money, realizes that he will be unable
to pay it back, but also realizes that nobody will lend him
money unless he promises to pay it back. He wonders
whether it would be immoral to make a promise under
these circumstances.

> Supposing that he decided to promise nevertheless, then
> his maxim of action would run as follows: When I believe
> myself to be in financial need, I will borrow money and
> promise to pay it back even though I know that this will
> never happen. Now this principle of self-love ... is
> perhaps compatible with my whole future well-being,
> but the question remains whether it is right. Hence, I
> transform the demand of self-love into a universal law
> and formulate the question thus: how would it be if my

maxim became a universal law? Then I see at once that it could never be a valid universal natural law that agrees with itself but must necessarily contradict itself. For the universality of a law that everybody who believes himself to be in distress could promise whatever he pleases, with the intention of not keeping it [the sentence is once again ungrammatical, but the meaning is clear], would make promising and its purpose impossible since nobody would believe that something had been promised but would laugh at all such utterances as vain pretense.

First, one may wonder again whether the man's maxim would *have* to run like that or whether he might not be able to formulate a better maxim. Secondly, one should ask where self-love comes from so suddenly. Kant introduced it also, even as part of the maxim, in his first example. But just as one might commit suicide for the sake of others, one might decide to borrow money and make a promise that one knows one probably cannot keep, not from self-love but, say, in order to buy medicine for a child who without it would die. The details do not matter as long as it is understood that it might well be impossible to obtain the medicine without dishonesty.

Self-love seems to be beside the point Kant wants to make.[24] His central point is clearly that a person who breaks a promise is inconsistent. His action contradicts his words. And if he says in his heart, I will not keep this promise, even while his lips say that he will, then he contradicts himself then and there. The machinery of universalizing the maxim is merely designed to bring out into the open this contradiction.

[24] In a short article "On a Supposed Right to Lie out of Love of Humanity" (1797) Kant said, but certainly did not prove, that "It is a holy commandment of reason that commands us unconditionally and cannot be limited by any conveniences, to be *truthful* (honest) in all declarations" (*Akademie*, vol. 8, p. 429). Kant insisted specifically that if a murderer should ask me whether his intended victim is in my house, I must not lie.

Kant assumes that the essence of immorality is making an exception in one's own behalf. When I make a promise, I bank on the assumption that promises are kept. That is part of the definition of "promise." When I plan all along to break it, I say in effect: I depend on promises being kept, but I am an exception. And when Kant points out that this maxim cannot be universalized because promises would disappear if it were understood that they need not be kept, his point is not, as has often been alleged, that he did not like this result because he was fond of promises. He did not appeal to our likes, dislikes, or inclinations.

The first example does not work as well as this one unless it is assumed, and Kant does assume, that it is a universally accepted law that we must choose life. Assuming that, the man considering suicide would once again make an exception in his own behalf.

The third example closely resembles the first. Here Kant no longer bothers to formulate any maxim, but he argues that we must develop our talents and capacities. Kant admits that nature could exist

> even though man (like the native of the South Seas) allowed his talents to rust and concentrated only on leisure, pleasure, procreation, or in one word enjoyment; yet he cannot possibly *will* that this should become a universal law of nature or should be implanted in us as such by a natural instinct. For as a rational being he wills necessarily that all his capacities should be developed because after all they serve him [and are given to him] for all sorts of purposes.

Again, this is quite unpersuasive, but it should be noted that Kant's appeal is not to our inclinations, not to whether we would like the consequences, but rather to the purpose for which (as he puts it in the phrase I have placed in brackets because it was added only in the second edition) our talents were "given" to us. Kant's reference to the South Sea islanders might have suggested even to him that his conception was culturally conditioned. Some people speak of the Protestant ethic in this connection, but it certainly comes from Sinai and distinguished the Jews long before there was any Protestantism. It was only when the Reformers acquainted their followers with the Old Testament that the ancient challenge to become holy and to make something of oneself came to be heeded by large numbers of people in Europe.

Kant's last example is probably the worst of the four. He pictures a person who has no wish to help others.

> What is it to me? Let everyone be as happy as it pleases heaven or as he can make himself; I shall not take anything away from him nor even envy him; only I do not feel like contributing anything to his well-being or his assistance in distress. . . . Although it is possible that according to this maxim a universal law of nature could exist, it is nevertheless impossible to *will* that such a principle should be universally valid as a law of nature. For a will resolving that would contradict itself [if Kant could show that, he would be home free] since cases could arise after all in which he would need the love and concern of others and where by such a natural law that owed its origin to his own will he would deprive himself of all hope of the help that he desires for himself.

End of the examples.

Kant's fourth and last case depends on the assumption that by virtue of our rationality we cannot help willing that when we are in dire need others should help us. Once that implausible premise is granted, it follows once again that the person who makes the decision of which Kant disapproves is making an exception in his own favor. But picture an Asian ascetic in meditation who is starving himself to death! Kant assumes throughout that life and self-improvement ought to continue, and it is revealing that two of his four examples, though they do not fit well into their immediate context, deal specifically with life (versus suicide) and self-improvement (versus allowing one's talents to rust). And the categorical commandments to choose life and make something of oneself come from Moses no less than the notion that we are obliged to help those in need.

That Kant was very selective in what he took from the Old Testament as well as the New should be obvious. It would serve no purpose here to fill pages with lists of ideas that he did *not* accept. But one general point is worth making. Vorländer made it in three words when he entitled a section of his *Immanuel Kant*[25] "*Geringschätzung des Geschichtlichen*": Kant held the historical in low esteem. In religion he associated it with the compulsion to believe something on authority instead of deferring only to one's own reason. In a note found among his papers and published posthumously he attributed to Jesus a "moral" and "soul-improving" religion of reason, contrasting it with the historical religion that "consists of the worship of this Jesus" and is thus a religion "received secondhand."[26] In Kant's books Jesus is scarcely mentioned, but Kant has recourse to a multitude of circumlocutions, such as *Heiliger des Evangelii* (the holy man of the evangel or gospel). In the notes that he himself did not publish we find occasional references to "Christ"; for example, "That Christ had and taught a religion, is clear; but not that he should have wished to be an object to religion."[27] Kant's antihistorical bias naturally closed much of the Old Testament to him, too, and may be considered a fatal flaw of his whole philosophy.

At this point it may seem as if Kant had after all taken very little from the Old Testament. It may be well

[25] Vol. II, pp. 164–67.
[26] *Ibid.*, p. 174; cf. *Akademie*, vol. XV, p. 608f.
[27] *Ibid.*, p. 173f.

to sum up the main points he accepted. First, it was from "Sinai" that he derived his concept of law. Morality had to his mind the form of a majestic law, and he kept stressing this term, in spite of Paul's and Luther's polemics against "the law."

Secondly, the content of the law was also derived from Moses. The gist of it is that humanity has a unique dignity that raises it above the rest of nature, and that no human being may be treated as a mere thing. The First Book of Moses suggests that man was created in the image of God and that all human beings are descended from a single couple, while Kant seeks the sanction for man's dignity in his possession of reason and occasionally speaks of all rational beings. In the 1750s Kant covered a book published in 1752 with marginal comments for use in his lecture, and one of his comments was that all angels are rational.[28] Even his conception of rational beings owed something to the Bible.

Thirdly, it is important to note that for Kant the sanction of the moral law was not mere reason. Critics of his *Grundlegung* and especially of the famous four examples given by Kant have always come to grief when they have overlooked this; they have simply been unable to make sense of Kant's examples. The examples appeal to a purpose of nature, and this is not suddenly pulled out of a hat but introduced early in the first chapter of the book—in the fifth paragraph, to be precise. Here Kant speaks expressly of the "purpose of nature," arguing that it cannot be man's happiness, as "instinct" would be far better suited to bring that about, while humanity has been endowed with reason and will. We are called upon to will the good, and to will it not because we happen to like it or it gives us pleasure but because it is what we are commanded to do, our duty. It is our duty to choose life and to become holy. Both the appeal to a

[28] *Ibid.*, p. 156.

purpose that transcends us and the content of the purpose are inspired by Moses.

Kant translated the ancient historical drama of the emergence from slavery into freedom under law into a timeless morality play that each of us ought to enact. But since he disliked the historical element in religion, he failed to realize that this was what he was doing, and it never occurred to him that his ethic as well as his theory of knowledge and the rest of his philosophy might be a product of history and bear the traces of cultural conditioning. This gives his philosophy a certain flatness that does not seem to bother philosophers who also lack a historical sense and are open to the same charges.

28 ▶▶▶ What is lacking in Kant's model of the mind and in his conception of autonomy is by no means only a sense of history and some understanding of his own place in it and his own conditioning. If history put him off because it was so irrational, he had even less time for psychology. And to say that his model of the mind and his conception of autonomy are therefore rather flat would be excessively polite.

Kant wrote an article entitled "Idea for a Universal History with Cosmopolitan Intent" in which he made a brilliant suggestion that helped to inspire Hegel's and Marx's interpretations of history. Kant proposed that the moving force of human history was what he called *Antagonism* and that eventually it would lead men to peace on earth. The essay, published in 1784, a year before the *Grundlegung,* begins with the "purpose of nature," and in his "fourth axiom" Kant explains: "Man wants concord; but nature knows better what is good for his species; she wants discord." And in the seventh section he elaborates:

Nature has used the unsociability of man, and even of . . . large states . . . as a means . . . by wars, by the overstrained and unrelenting armament for these, by the need which every state must thus feel in the end, even in the midst of peace, she drives first to imperfect attempts and eventually after many devastations . . . to that which their reason might have told them even without so many sad experiences—namely to leave the lawless level of the savages and to enter into a League of Nations [*Völkerbund*] in which every state, even the smallest one, may expect its security and rights not from its own power . . . but alone from this great *League of Nations.*

Here is the idea that Hegel later called "the cunning of reason" (*die List der Vernunft*). Reason, or nature, employs the irrational to bring about rational aims in the long run. The essay shows once again how deeply Kant was influenced by Old Testament notions—history has a purpose, and in the end "nation shall not lift up sword against nation, neither shall they learn war any more."[29] His belief in a purpose of nature was a crucial element of his thought.

The demythologizing of the biblical idea of a divine purpose is encountered eight years earlier in Adam Smith's *Inquiry Into the Nature and Causes of the Wealth of Nations* (1776). The individual, says Smith in the ninth paragraph of Book IV, Chapter II,

neither intends to promote the public interest, nor knows how much he is promoting it. By preferring the support of domestic to that of foreign industry, he intends only his own security; and by directing that industry in such a manner as its produce may be of the greatest value, he intends only his own gain, and he is in this, as in many other cases, led by an invisible hand to promote an end which was no part of his intention.

Kant did not merely voice the same idea. The purpose he finds in nature is biblical and messianic, and Hegel and Marx followed him rather than Smith.

[29] Isaiah 2.4 and Micah 4.3.

In the psychological realm Kant showed no comparable appreciation of the irrational. Here he was a rigorist who believed that freedom depended on our acting from respect for reason without being motivated by any inclination. The absence of what he called "pathological interest" seemed to him essential.

Kant thought in terms of sharp conceptual dichotomies of which he often thought quite mistakenly that they represented exhaustive alternatives. The most famous example is the contrast between phenomena and noumena, or the things that appear to us and the unknowable things-in-themselves. Plainly, this is not an exhaustive dichotomy. Different eyes and sense organs, including those of different animals, perceive the same scene differently, and a perspectivist might question whether in the end it still makes any sense to ask what something is "really" like without specifying a particular perspective or universe of discourse.

Kant's ethic, his model of the moral mind, and his conception of autonomy are based on a series of even more dubious dichotomies. They can be arranged in pairs, though Kant never noted this, and will then be seen to correspond to the dichotomy of Kant's two worlds, this world and the other world. The terms in question are defined here and there, often with an appearance of scholastic exactitude, but then they are defined again in a slightly different way, Kant having quite evidently forgotten that he has already introduced the distinction he needs. Everything would have been much clearer if he had introduced nine pairs of terms near the beginning.

phenomenal world	noumenal world
determinism	freedom
subjective principles	objective principles
maxims	universal laws
motives (*Triebfedern*)	inducements (*Bewegungsgründe*)
pathological interests	practical or moral interest

inclinations   reason
hypothetical imperatives   categorical imperative
heteronomy   autonomy

Everyone of these pairs merits critical reflection. Does freedom really consist in the performance of actions that have no cause in the phenomenal world? Am I free when my acts bear no relation to my phenomenal self, my individuality?[30] Is there not ample ground between maxims that are valid for me only and laws that are applicable to all rational beings? And must an imperative appeal either to prudence, pleasure, and self-love or be categorical?

Here it will suffice to take a closer look at two pairs of terms: motives (*Triebfeder* means literally "driving spring") and inducements (*Bewegungsgrund* is literally ground of motion), and the two kinds of interest that Kant distinguishes. Although Kant speaks of motives again and again, he is not interested in motives but in the possibility of actions that are not caused by any motive. He is not interested in psychology but in the possibility of actions about which psychology would be unable to say anything. He admits:

> It is indeed altogether impossible to single out with complete certainty by means of experience a single case in which the maxim of an otherwise dutiful action has been based solely on moral grounds and on the representation of one's duty. For although it is the case now and then that in the course of the most severe self-examination we encounter nothing apart from the moral ground of duty that could have been powerful enough to move one to this or that good action and such a great sacrifice, we cannot infer from that with any certainty that there really was no secret impulse [*Antrieb*] of self-

[30] For a contrary view see, for example, F. Bergmann, *On Being Free* (1977).

love that under the pretense of this idea was the really determining cause of the will. We like to flatter ourselves with a false presumed nobler inducement, but in fact even the most rigorous examination can never penetrate completely behind our secret motives; for when it is the moral value that is at stake, what matters are not the actions one sees but the inner principles one does not see.

This is the second paragraph of the second chapter of the *Grundlegung*. But Kant adds in the next paragraph:

> ... Even if there should never have been any actions that sprang from such pure sources, what is at stake here is not at all whether this or that happens, but reason should command by itself and independently of all phenomena what ought to happen, so that actions of which the world has perhaps never yet given any example and whose feasibility anyone who bases everything on experience might doubt very much, should nevertheless be commanded relentlessly by reason, and that, for example, pure honesty in friendship could be demanded of every human being not one whit less even if up to this point there should never have been any honest friend. ...

Psychology is for Kant beside the point, and discrimination among motives does not concern him. Motives are by definition "sensuous" and irrational, and what reason demands, according to Kant, are actions prompted solely by respect for the moral law. In the last long footnote of Chapter I we are told: "Although respect is a feeling, it is nevertheless not a feeling *received* through some influence but one *self-caused* by a concept of reason." And this footnote ends: "All moral so-called *interest* consists solely of *respect* for the law."

A dozen pages later, in the third footnote of the second chapter, Kant returns to the subject of interest:

The dependence of the will on principles of reason is called an *interest*. . . . But even the human will can *take an interest* in something without therefore acting out of interest. The former signifies a *practical* interest in the action, the second the *pathological* interest in the object of the action.[31]

For about twenty pages after that, Kant dispenses with the conception of interest, and when he introduces it again he has plainly forgotten the distinction between two kinds of interest. He now rules out "any admixture or any kind of interest as a motive"; he speaks of "the renunciation of all interest when one wills from duty"; and *"grounded in no interest"* and "no interest whatsoever" become his refrain.

After that "interest" is referred to occasionally, always in the sense of "pathological" interest, until a section early in the last chapter suddenly bears the title "On the interest that adheres to the ideas of morality." Here Kant says at one point: "I will concede that no interest *impels* [*treibt*] me to do this, for this would not furnish a categorical imperative; but I must nevertheless necessarily *take* an interest in this."

Another dozen pages later, in the final footnote of the book, Kant, having evidently forgotten his earlier definition of interest as well as his distinction between two kinds of interest, offers another definition and labors hard to establish a similar distinction, without however recalling the terms "practical" and "pathological." To add to the confusion, "practical" interest is also sometimes referred to more felicitously as "moral interest."

In sum, Kant's remarks on interest in his short book on ethics fall very far short of the rigor he opposed to

[31] In the second edition of his *Critique of Pure Reason* (1787) we find this definition: "affected pathologically (moved by causes of the sensibility [*Bewegungsursachen der Sinnlichkeit*])."

Critik

der

Urtheilskraft

von

Immanuel Kant.

Berlin, und Libau,
bey Lagarde und Friederich
1790.

"popular" writing. And if he had been a little more rigorous he would also have been clearer. But that is not all that needs to be said about Kant's comments on interest. *His lack of rigor and clarity concealed from him and from his readers the absurdity of some of his views.* To show this it will be best to consider his immensely influential remarks about interest in his *Critique of Judgment* (1790).

29 ▶▶▶ In the second section of Kant's *Critique of Judgment* interest is defined as "that approbation [*Wohlgefallen*] which we connect with the representation of the existence of an object." As such, interest is necessarily connected with the faculty of desire. "The judgment about beauty that is colored in the least by interest is very partial and no pure aesthetic judgment. One must not in the least favor the existence of an object but must be entirely indifferent in this respect to be the judge in matters of taste."

Now one might expect Kant to introduce, if only eventually, a special kind of interest—say, "aesthetic" interest—either to establish a parallel to "practical" or "moral" interest or to escape from the apparent absurdity of his position. But he insists emphatically that approbation of the beautiful occurs without interest of *any* kind—*ohne alles Interesse;* he labors the point for several pages and eventually repeats this phrase, emphasizing it in print, at the end of Section 5. There are three kinds of approbation that he recognizes: that of the beautiful, which is marked by the absence of *all* interest, that of the agreeable, which "is connected with interest," and that of the good, which "is connected with interest." In Section 2, moreover, Kant says expressly that "there are no more kinds of interest than those which shall now be named," and then goes on to discuss in turn the interest in the agreeable and that in the good, and in his discussion of the latter he refers not only to pathological interest but also to moral interest, the "highest interest" that we take in moral goodness.

Later in the book, Kant suddenly recognizes an "empirical interest in the beautiful" (Section 41) and an "intellectual interest in the beautiful" (Section 42), but he still insists that the judgment of taste must not be determined or colored by any interest. It is only after an object has been judged to be beautiful that one may take an empirical interest in it, which is not only pathological but, according to Kant, restricted to the social sphere. Isolated from society, nobody would take an empirical interest in the beautiful! And this interest is "of no importance to us here." Of the interest in beauty that flourishes in solitude he had no inkling.

"Intellectual interest" in beauty has no affinity with moral interest, is restricted to the beauty of nature, comes only after totally disinterested approbation, and is due to the fact that natural beauty supports our moral sense by holding out the hope that it may have objective validity. As for works of art, Kant recognizes only two possibilities: "They are either such imitations of nature that they achieve deception and then have the effect of—supposed—natural beauty; or they are arts that intentionally and visibly aim at our approbation." But art "in itself can never arouse interest."

All this is really quite extraordinary. One may applaud Kant's distinction between the agreeable and the beautiful, but what is one to make of his outrageous claim that the experience of beautiful works of art is devoid of any interest? When I look at some Buddha images, some Rembrandt self-portraits, or one of van Gogh's paintings of his room, I am profoundly interested in what I see, and my aesthetic judgments are and should be informed by this interest. Nor is this interest by any means merely a result of my value judgment and something I would not feel if isolated from society. The interest might run every bit as deep in solitude, and through this interest I may discover more and more that will and should influence further aesthetic judgments.

Kant and the aestheticians who follow in his footsteps fail to ask what actually happens when we encounter a work of art. In one of his *Maxims and Reflections,* written in 1821, Goethe offered a pertinent comment:

> It used to happen and still happens to me that a work of art displeases me when I first see it because I am not up to it. But if I sense that it has some merit, I try to get at it, and there is no lack of the most delightful discoveries: I become aware of new qualities in the objects and of new capacities in myself.[32]

Those who find beautiful only what in their childhood they were told to find beautiful are hardly fit to play "the judge in matters of taste." To be a judge worth listening to one must not only reconsider the aesthetic judgments one accepted or absorbed as a child but also explore what one was not trained to find beautiful and even what one was taught to find ugly.

In *A History of Fine Art in India and Ceylon from the Earliest Times to the Present Day* (1911), Vincent A. Smith, after quoting Goethe's maxim on page 3, says later on (p. 252), speaking of a celebrated bronze:

> If it could be freed from the horrible deformity of the extra arms, it might receive almost unqualified praise, but the monstrosity of the second left arm drawn across the breast, and calling for the surgeon's amputating knife to remove the diseased growth, spoils an otherwise elegant and admirable work.

It never occurred to this distinguished art historian that the wings of Simone Martini's or Fra Angelico's

[32] *Werke*, ed. Beutler, vol. 9, p. 514; *Propyläen-Ausgabe*, vol. 35, p. 109.

angels or of the "Victory of Samothrace" in the Louvre were monstrosities, and that paintings and sculptures of this kind might be improved by the surgeon's knife or by painting over "the diseased growth." What is at stake here is not so much iconographical research that might determine the symbolical meaning of the extra arms, although that need not be irrelevant either, as it is sufficient interest to look at a sculpture from many angles, to imagine it without various parts, to compare it with other sculptures, to inquire what people who do find it beautiful like about it, and to see whether increased interest leads us to find it more or less beautiful than we did at first.

30 ▶▶▶ Kant is plainly wrong about interest in aesthetics, and he is also wrong, if not quite so obviously, about interest in the moral sphere. *His fundamental mistakes are essentially the same everywhere.* He relies on dichotomies and classifications that he takes to be exhaustive; he plays with concepts and an elaborate terminology while spurning any close examination of moral or aesthetic experience; and he takes his own highly unusual mind as the model of the human mind without asking whether his own mind might be psychologically or historically conditioned and perhaps only one type among many.

His own mind became for Kant the norm, and he treated it as men usually treat what they endow with authority: he did not ask how it had become the way it was, and he did not compare it with alternative models. Of course, his mind had developed like anyone else's; indeed, much more than most men's minds. But he did not care to know how it had changed and in what respects it had remained relatively unchanged since his boyhood. Near the beginning of his *Prolegomena* (1783, p. 13) he said—and this phrase has often been quoted—

that David Hume had "many years ago first interrupted my dogmatic slumber and given my investigations in the field of speculative philosophy an altogether different direction." This is a very neat and memorable construction and in some ways the opposite of a developmental approach. It is a way of dividing one's life into two chapters: before and after. I was benighted, but then I saw the light; I did not know, but now I do. Lewis White Beck has contested this construction in a truly delightful manner: *The dogmatic slumber from which he was aroused by Hume was a nap which did not begin until after 1766"* (1969, p. 439). The details of Kant's development need not concern us here. What is important is that Kant did not care to know how his mind had become the way it was, how it might have been influenced by his upbringing or his situation in eighteenth century Königsberg, or how it differed from the mind of, say, Goethe.

While Kant's mind was in many ways unusual, his extreme insensitivity to art probably was not as exceptional as I would like to believe. Many, if not most, people, including professors in many fields and even aestheticians, share this insensitivity. Even as Plato taught philosophers that one could write about tragedy without ever stopping to consider a single tragedy, Kant gave writers on aesthetics a good conscience when they disregarded the experiences of those who create as well as those who are deeply moved by works of art. Even today some aestheticians still echo Kant on interest without asking what would prompt anyone to create or pay much attention to works of art if not some interest.

Kant's remarks on the lack of interest in aesthetic experience are so implausible that one might be tempted to reinterpret them if at all possible; but he clearly meant what he said. Borowski reports in his memoir of 1804 (p. 81):

To paintings and engravings, even if they were out-standing, he never seemed to pay attention. I have never seen him look at such things even in places where universally admired collections were displayed in halls or rooms. . . . Apart from an engraving of J. J. Rousseau in his living room, nothing of the sort was to be found in his whole house—and even this was surely a present from a friend, and he must have felt that he owed it to him as a duty imposed on him to keep it.

In other words, the fact that there was one picture in Kant's house required an explanation! The reason must have been moral!

In a footnote, the biographer adds that a person to whom he read this passage assured him that the engraving had indeed been a present from Ruffmann—"this noble and splendid man whom all of his friends still remember with emotion and longing."

In 1764, when Kant was hoping very much for a professorship, the chair for poetry fell vacant and he was asked whether he would like it, but he declined because he felt that this would hardly be the right field for him (p. 19). Nevertheless, one may agree with R. B. Jachmann when he says in the tenth letter of his memoir of 1804 that Kant had more feeling for poetry and eloquence than for any of the other arts; after all he himself wrote some verses on departed colleagues, duly published in the great *Akademie* edition. There is no need to comment on these verses, but his views, as recorded by Jachmann, are certainly worth quoting.

Easy versification was for him, next to the poetic contents, a chief requirement of a beautiful poem. Nor did he consider anything a poem if it was not rhymed or at least metrical. Rhymeless poetry he called prose gone mad and could not find it at all to his taste.

As it happens, some of the most remarkable German poetry of the eighteenth century was unrhymed. The most eminent German poet around the middle of the century, Friedrich Gottlieb Klopstock, who was born the same year as Kant and died one year before him, attracted a great deal of attention with his unrhymed epic, *The Messiah*, which appeared in four volumes between 1751 and 1773. The impact of Johann Heinrich Voss' unrhymed translation of Homer's *Odyssey* (1781) was even greater, and the appropriation of Greek poetry, which was unrhymed, was among the most significant literary developments in Germany during the last quarter of the eighteenth century.

In the 1770s Goethe emerged as the greatest German poet and has never ceased to be regarded as such to this day. Goethe's poems "Prometheus" and "Noble let man be/helpful and good . . ."—both written in free verse—had been included by F. G. Jacobi in his book *On the Doctrine of Spinoza, in Letters to Herr Moses Mendelssohn* (1785), which created a storm of controversy and came to Kant's attention, and it was partly in response to various requests that he take a stand that Kant published an article in 1786, "What Does It Mean: To Orient Oneself in Thinking?" In 1789 Jacobi's book appeared in a second, expanded edition. The second poem was duly credited and might have been expected to appeal to Kant on account of its contents. The author of "Prometheus" was not named, but it is arguable that no better poem had ever been published in German up to that time. But for Kant rhymeless verse was "prose gone mad." He never took the least notice of Goethe in his works or even in his letters. When one considers the range of Goethe's publications through, say, 1797, which included *Faust: A Fragment* (1790), and their immense impact throughout Germany, if not Europe, this is scarcely credible.

Schiller fared no better as a poet, although we have seen that Kant responded in a footnote to a criticism Schiller had offered. Lessing's *Nathan*, whose enlightened attitudes one might have expected Kant to approve with some enthusiasm, he did not like, as we have seen. Matthias Claudius he never mentioned. For Homer he had little feeling.[33] In sum, he lived during the greatest period of German literature but had no organ for it whatsoever. It should be added that Kant was a voracious reader who surprised visitors from other countries by knowing their cities, solely from books, better than they did.

Kant also lived through the greatest period of German music if not the world's music. Bach died in 1750, Handel in 1759, Mozart in 1791. Haydn was eight years younger than Kant and died five years after him. (Beethoven did not come into his own until the early nineteenth century.) Yet in Kant's works and letters none of them is ever mentioned. Kant wrote two books on aesthetics, but if ever there was a "man that hath no music in himself" that man was Kant. Borowski reports:

> Music he considered an innocent sensuous pleasure. He very cordially admonished me when I was fifteen, and also several other students at that time, not to get involved in it, as it required much time to learn anything and still more to practice before one could attain a passable level—always at the expense of other more serious sciences.

He also felt that "if one took the trouble to lend an ear to this art, one could at least expect to be rewarded by being cheered up and made glad." The phrasing here is beautiful: *wenn man schon sein Ohr dieser Kunst hingebe* . . . (p. 81). Jachmann's report in his tenth letter is very similar. Of all the arts Kant "had the least sense for music, although he did occasionally attend concerts by great masters." Vorländer says (I, p. 388f.) that

[33] Vorländer, vol. I, 372f. A whole chapter, pp. 370–405, deals with "Kant and Art."

"people in Königsberg had frequent opportunities to hear good music. There were a large number of fine virtuosos in the city." Operas were performed as well as plays. But the only music Kant seems to have enjoyed moderately was military marches.

Kant's lack of any organ for art cannot be explained away by assuming that in Königsberg he simply had no opportunity to see or hear great works. The Keyserlings, in whose house Kant was "one of the most frequent and preferred guests," had a large collection of paintings, including a Rembrandt, and over a thousand engravings of works of art;[34] and another one of Kant's friends possessed several hundred paintings, including a Dürer, three Cranachs, and a Van Dyck. Yet another acquaintance had a collection of 250 paintings, including a portrait of an old man by Rembrandt as well as many other Dutch masters.[35] Nor will it do to admit that great men, too, have their limitations, and that Kant's lack of any sense for the visual arts, music, and poetry is simply a personal shortcoming that has no bearing on his eminence as a philosopher. Kant's *Critique of Judgment*, one of his acknowledged masterpieces which many of his admirers rank with his first *Critique* and his ethics, was vitiated by an utterly untenable model of the mind at which Kant had arrived by assuming that the human mind was naturally and always like his own.

This is so obvious in relation to art, music, and poetry that it seemed best to consider them first; but now the question arises whether the case is not essentially similar regarding Kant's dichotomy of pathological interest and moral interest, which consists of respect for the moral law. Are there not interests that are never dreamed of in Kant's philosophy?

Plato, whose attitude toward the arts also leaves

[34] Vorländer, vol. I, p. 198f.
[35] *Ibid.*, p. 387.

much to be desired, can help us at this point. For all his censoriousness regarding music, poetry, and the visual arts, he associated beauty with love, and love with a longing for immortality. Here is an interest worth distinguishing from the narrowly hedonistic self-interest that dominates Kant's conception of pathological interests. To suppose that the only alternatives to that kind of utilitarian interest are either moral interest or no interest whatsoever is simply an egregious error.

John Dewey once noted that valuation is prompted by "some need, lack, or privation."[36] Many such needs, lacks, and privations have been insufficiently appreciated by other moralists and aestheticians besides Kant; for example, our experience of sickness, old age, and death, of infirmity and finitude, of cosmic solitude or lostness, of falling short of our own ideals—or in brief our sense of imperfection. For Kant, holiness represented a commandment. For many other human beings, perfection is the object of a profound interest. In Plato's *Symposium* (207) we read that "love is a longing for immortality," but it would be better to say—and Plato meant this also—that *love is a longing for perfection.* That definition would encompass Aristophanes' great myth in the *Symposium* where love is pictured as the search for our other half. We were whole once but were then divided and now long to become complete again. My definition would also encompass both the serpent's promise "You will be as God" and God's commandment "You shall be holy." It would include the Buddha's promise of a triumph over old age, suffering, and death. And it illuminates, I think, both our moral experience and our experience of beauty.

In some works of art we sense a perfection that is lacking in our own existence. That is true in different ways of some Buddha images and some Rembrandts, of

[36] 1939, p. 34.

Bach's music and Mozart's, of Sophocles and Shakespeare. (Lessing, incidentally, wrote a whole book on Sophocles; Kant never even mentioned him.) The longing for perfection is also central in the *moral* experience of many people, and Kant's dichotomy of interests as well as his whole analysis of the foundations of ethics misses the mark as far as human beings of this type are concerned. Kant analyzed only one particular type of morality, which Hegel later called *Moralität* and contrasted with *Sittlichkeit*.

Schopenhauer adopted and adapted Kant's insistence that the aesthetic experience is devoid of all interest. He helped this strange error to survive. But in other respects he realized as clearly as any of Kant's major successors that Kant's model of the mind simply would not do, and Schopenhauer admired Goethe as much as anybody did.

Surely, the interests Kant overlooked and implicitly ruled out of court are far more important for an understanding of the human mind than his implausible division of the mind into reason, understanding, sensibility, and judgment, or his dichotomies of theoretical and practical reason and of reason and inclination. His fundamental fault is that instead of starting from an exploration of moral or aesthetic experience he always starts out from abstractions, concepts, or rather, as we have seen, words. One crucial example still needs to be added: the notorious thesis that ought implies can, from which Kant in his *Philosophy of Right* deduces the extraordinary claim that "a collision of duties is therefore unthinkable."

A philosopher who takes experience more seriously than the web one can spin out of words might conclude that any thesis entailing such an incredible conclusion must be wrong. Indeed, such a philosopher might ask, if only he felt committed to Kant's "transcendental method": what must the human mind be like to experience again and again collisions of duties or, if you prefer, conflicts of values? Hegel tried to reconcile Goethe and Kant at this point, too, by allowing for collisions but only as rare exceptions that occurred in periods of world historical transitions from one era to another. Even Kierkegaard was still sufficiently under the spell of Kant to consider such conflicts extraordinary exceptions that could occur when God addresses some individual directly as he did Abraham. Nietzsche was sufficiently emancipated from Kant to recognize that conflicts of values are of the very essence of human life.

Finally, it is noteworthy that Kant's untenable model of the human mind has no place at all for love, unless it is assimilated to "pathological interests." Kant never showed how much that passes as love is really no more than a configuration of pathological interests. He simply failed to consider love. The reason seems clear: In his own adult experience he found no love, and he assumed that his own mind was typical. But the discovery of the mind requires some understanding of love and art.

PART ▶ IV

Kant:
Autonomy,
Style, and Certainty ▶▶▶

31 ▶▶▶ Kant's conception of autonomy brings to mind George Orwell's *Nineteen Eighty-Four:* "WAR IS PEACE, FREEDOM IS SLAVERY, IGNORANCE IS STRENGTH." As long as I do what I feel like doing, I am not free. One should suppose that following one's inclinations was a necessary although not sufficient condition of autonomy. But according to Kant it is incompatible with autonomy because for him freedom and autonomy meant escape from psychological determinism, and he assumed that respect for "the moral law" was not psychologically conditioned.

At this point his lack of historical sense and psychological sophistication became crucial. It simply did not occur to him that the type of mind he had was as much the result of historical and psychological conditioning as any other. This is most easily seen by looking at Kant's self-interpretation—at the way he practiced his own ethic.

In his sixth letter, Jachmann emphasized in print the sentence: *"Kant lived as he taught!"* Jachmann, as Vorländer agrees, seems eminently trustworthy, and it is as clear as can be that Kant *meant* to live as he taught, that this was a matter of pride and integrity for him. Hence his moral life may be considered as a self-interpretation of the greatest weight—a self-interpretation sustained over many years that cannot be disposed of as a momentary aberration.

The end of Jachmann's sixth letter is interesting, too. In connection with Kant's immense regard for truth we are told: "He himself never wanted to appear any different from the way he was." He intensely disliked all affectations in speech; and "he strictly adhered to the orthography that had been customary and generally accepted during his youth and disapproved of all affected changes in it as an unnecessary imposition on the reader." What is revealing and characteristic is that Kant considered the norms to which he had to conform in his childhood as natural and right, feeling that everybody should accept them. It did not occur to him that they, too, were historically conditioned and the result of many changes.

The seventh letter is the most important for our purposes, for it is here that Jachmann aims to show "that Kant was a man of maxims" who lived according to his own ethic. Actually, the conclusion of the immediately preceding paragraph sets the stage by showing us how very much Kant was a child of his time, how sheltered a life he lived—how remote from the realities of the twentieth century. "With a calm and joyous heart I could always shout, 'Come in!' when someone knocked at my door—the excellent man used to say often—for I could be certain that no creditor stood outside." Thus he felt that he had purchased total security simply by never borrowing money. That a person who did not owe anybody any money might nevertheless be overcome by terror at the sound of a knock at the door, simply did not occur to him. His universe was Newtonian, governed by rational law and order, and worlds removed from the

Inquisition or from Kafka's universe and the horrors that make Kafka seem prophetic. To Kant himself his own ethic was anything but eccentric; it was a way of living, as the Stoics might have said, in accordance with nature, approximating the lawfulness and regularity of nature.

Almost everything became for him "an occasion to devise a maxim for himself which he henceforth followed with the most unshakable firmness. In this way his whole life had gradually become a chain of maxims that eventually formed a firm system of character." Two of Jachmann's examples help to show what this meant.

Kant was chronically constipated. Jachmann relates how for many years Kant took a daily pill to help him. When the condition got worse, Jachmann's brother, who was a physician in Königsberg, persuaded him to double the number of pills.

> But no sooner had this happened than Kant reflected that this increase would have no end, and he adopted the maxim never to take, as long as he lived, more than two pills a day; nor would he depart from this maxim even in his last years when, according to his physicians' judgment, an increased dosage would have been very beneficial for him.

Here we have Kant's conception of autonomy in action. The advice proffered by his doctors consisted only of hypothetical imperatives and appealed to his inclinations. As long as one heeds such appeals one is caught in a web of cause and effect and not free. Jachmann continues:

> In the same way he had formulated a maxim for himself regarding the smoking of tobacco, which was perhaps his supreme sensuous pleasure [poor man!], to smoke only one full clay pipe a day because he did not see where he should stop otherwise. . . . In this way he had eventually tied his whole way of thinking and living to rules of reason to which he remained as loyal in the smallest cir-

cumstances as in the most important matters. Since his dominion over his inclinations and drives was unconditional, nothing in the world could lead him to depart from his duty once he had recognized it. He did nothing that he did not want to do, and his will was free, for it depended on his law of reason. All attempts by others to subdue his will and guide it differently were in vain; he adhered firmly to what he had resolved after some rational reflection, and even when inclinations and permissible purposes counseled him to act differently, he persisted in the duty that he had imposed on himself.

Socrates, in Plato's *Symposium*, could take or leave alcohol. He was neither addicted to it, nor did he require a maxim to stop after the second cup. When the wine and above all the conversation were good, he went on talking and drinking until the last person had passed out, left at dawn, took a bath, and spent the day as if nothing had happened. Although Socrates did not speak of autonomy, the model of autonomy that he provided is incomparably more plausible than Kant's. What little plausibility Kant's model has depends entirely on the loaded alternative of the person who is unable to stop when he has had enough. Kant assumes in effect that there are only these two possibilities: the profligate and himself.

Kant would have left the symposium early, for he had made it an iron rule for himself to be in bed from ten to five. He was proud, and often asked his servant to bear witness, that he had never failed to get up at five when his servant entered the room, shouting: *Es ist Zeit!* (It is time!) And he always retired early, even when he was invited out, to make sure that he would be in his bed by ten. His schedule was not subject to fleeting inclinations or to hypothetical imperatives presented to him by other people. He followed rules he had imposed on himself. But one does not have to accept any particular theory about the compulsive or obsessional type, let alone the anal character, to feel that this kind of rigidity is not a

sign of freedom or autonomy. The contrast with Socrates lends powerful confirmation to this feeling. And Kant's contemporaries had no need to look that far back. They associated autonomy with Goethe, and the development of thought after Kant cannot be understood very well without taking account of Goethe and his influence.

It would make good sense to speak of a Goethean imperative which is rather different from Kant's categorical imperative and yet not hypothetical or prudential. Creative people ought not to take on so many obligations that are not rooted in their heart or soul that they have insufficient time or energy to do what only they can do. To be sure, Goethe himself was so versatile and did so many different things that a German cartoon once showed one officer saying to another: "There's one thing I don't understand about von Goethe: how can a minister of state find time to write so many poems?" But on the whole Goethe spent his life doing what he felt like doing. More importantly, it is worth pointing out how much of his time and energy Kant spent on doing what only he could do, and how one of the four examples in his short book on ethics involves the maxim that we ought to develop our talents. Yet it is not only a historical fact that the immense influence of Kant's ethics has been inseparable from "duty" and from what is not personal or individual, but Kant himself went to heroic lengths in writing about ethics to dissociate it from inclination, heart, and soul. It is not easy to put the decisive point very precisely. Yet there are two words that bring out why there is something so dead in Kant and in Kantian ethics and in much academic philosophy and why Goethe, like other major poets and artists, radiates aliveness: spontaneity and enthusiasm. To proscribe spontaneity and enthusiasm is to prescribe deadness.

The four dots in the last long quotation mark the omission of a sentence about Kant's inflexible maxim "to smoke only one full clay pipe a day because he did not see where he should stop otherwise." The generally rather worshipful Jachmann continues: "If there had been some kind of clay pipe as large as several small ones, he would surely have used that because this would not have conflicted with his maxim; but he could not be persuaded by any means to use a different pipe bowl." To switch to a bowl not made of clay would have violated his maxim! So much depended on the precise formulation! So close was Kant to the religious mentality of countless Jesuits, orthodox rabbis, and other casuists. That the rules are made by oneself in the first place is clearly not enough to guarantee that, when one's whole life becomes "a chain of maxims," one does not become a prisoner. As spontaneity is ruled out, freedom gradually becomes a function of casuistic ingenuity.

For Friedrich Schiller and the German philosophers who were impressed by Goethe, this aspect of Kant's philosophy proved unacceptable. But for some twentieth-century philosophers to whom Goethe means nothing, this element in Kant is attractive.

As philosophy becomes more and more scholastic and prizes ingenuity while being deeply suspicious of spontaneity and individuality, so-called rational reconstructions of Kant's ethic have become popular. But what is nowadays called a rational reconstruction sometimes brings to mind the exegetical approaches of scholastics of bygone ages. With a bland disregard for history and context, not to speak of the original author's mentality, one reads ideas of one's own into a celebrated text. This is hardly a symptom of autonomy, but it is part of the charm of Kant that he allows the heteronomous to feel they are autonomous. "FREEDOM IS SLAVERY," and slavery parades as freedom.

Kant, of course, was not merely a man who made a point of being in bed from ten to five or of writing every morning, even if he himself felt that these habits were of the essence of his autonomy. A critic who feels that in these respects he was unfree and a creature of routine may feel nevertheless that Kant *was* a relatively free spirit and demonstrated a measure of autonomy in *what* he wrote within this compulsive framework. He was not as free a spirit or as autonomous as Goethe, but obviously did display considerable independence. And some of those who have greatly admired him have responded to this quality.

Kant himself, to be sure, thought in terms of sharp dichotomies: according to him, one is either autonomous or heteronomous. My conception of autonomy, which is developed in *Without Guilt and Justice: From Decidophobia to Autonomy* (1973), is different and admits of degrees. Even as some are more courageous than others and some have higher standards of honesty than others, and it is simplistic to think merely in terms of courage and cowardice, honesty and dishonesty, it is also misleading to suppose that one either is or is not autonomous.

32 ▶▶▶ Style is the mirror of a mind. Kant's is anything but a harmless eccentricity. It is a contagious disease for which it would be hard to find a more descriptive name than pernicious anemia. What is pernicious about its bloodlessness, its lack of vitality and spontaneity, is that it is the language of self-deception. Needing nothing less than absolute certainty, the writer foregoes the excitement of living dangerously with probabilities or bold hypotheses; but his sense of certainty is spurious and depends on the obscurity of his style, which does not allow him to see clearly.

Kant's is not the language of a free spirit like Lessing, who preferred the ceaseless fight for truth to the possession of it and who had the strength to live without absolute truth.[1] Kant, too, was a man of courage, and 200 years later we are apt to overlook how much daring it took to set limits to knowledge as he did, smashing the "rational" psychology, cosmology, and theology of some of his predecessors. Yet he depended heavily on equivocation. He pictured himself as another Copernicus while he tried to undo the damage that Copernicus had done to human self-esteem. Kant did away with knowledge—to make room for faith, a supposedly rational faith; he argued that practical reason demanded that the ideas on which he had been raised in childhood must be true. Kant's message was not either/or, *aut aut* in Latin, but *et et*, both; you can eat your cake and have it, too.

Kant could not get himself to let go. His language is the language of a constipated casuist who is afraid of letting go of a sentence; he goes on and on, adding clauses, often past the point where they can be construed. This scandalous style was meant to be, and soon became, the paradigm of serious philosophic writing. Whatever was not written more or less like this was presumed not to be serious philosophy. Yet as soon as Kant becomes a little clearer, as he does in the four examples in his short book on ethics, it becomes apparent to everyone who makes a serious effort to follow him that Kant's lack of rigor is staggering.

Kant himself suggested, and it has been widely believed, that his language was the price he paid for being scientific, but in fact it cloaks a lack of rigor. It really is a cloak, a veil of concepts that comes between the thinker and experience and allows him to ignore experience. The language is the language of scholasticism that spurns any description or analysis of our experience, looks down its nose at psychology and history, and juggles concepts, setting up dichotomies and trichotomies

[1] See sec. 17 above.

with the aid of curious terms, without stopping or stooping to ask whether what is most important has not been left out. Kant's language is a scandal not only stylistically but also methodologically. It kept him and others from seeing what he was doing.

In *A Commentary on Kant's Critique of Practical Reason* (1960), Lewis White Beck, the foremost American Kant scholar, whose graciousness matches his erudition, offers a detailed analysis of Kant's postulate of the immortality of the soul and asks in the end: "What, then, is left of the postulate? Only a hope. . . . Kant has given no very good reason why one should believe in it" (p. 270). That is an extraordinarily polite way of stating an inescapable conclusion. And two pages earlier: "I hesitate to suggest what seems to me to be the only reason, as it is almost incredible that Kant could have made such a mistake." But that is what we find at every step. The forbidding language does not eliminate incredible mistakes; it keeps Kant as well as readers who do not read him very, very closely from discovering them.

Kant's language has been as influential as any part of his work. Few have accepted his postulates, and I therefore have not even bothered to dissect his postulate of God's existence; but in Germany and in most places where philosophers are generally professors, Kant has become a model philosopher: even if one could not approximate his genius one could at least try to write like him.

Kant could write with some grace, and "The new style emerges for the first time in his main work, the *Critique of Pure Reason.*"[2] From that point on the style of Kant's major works is scandalous. Yet admiration for Kant has blinded some interpreters to the facts. Thus Ernst Cassirer, whose reputation as a philosopher is considerable, said in his German book on Kant's life and

[2] Vorländer, vol. II, p. 99.

doctrine (1918), speaking of Kant's *Grundlegung:*

> In none of the major works expounding his critical
> philosophy is Kant's personality so immediately present,
> in none is the rigor of the deduction [!] so perfectly fused
> with such a free agility of thought, and ethical strength
> and greatness with a sense for psychological detail [!],
> and sharpness in the definition of concepts [!] with the
> noble matter-of-factness of a popular language that
> abounds in felicitous images and examples (p. 253f.).

Cassirer's lack of incisiveness is often frustrating in
his other books, too, and Vorländer's two-volume biography of Kant is much richer in materials; but this passage defies belief. For Cassirer makes no attempt to
show how the notorious four examples can be defended
against the most obvious criticisms or why he considers
them "felicitous." Here is what *Vorländer* says about
Kant's mature style:

> We have no wish to gloss over the weaknesses of Kant's
> style any more than his other imperfections. They are to
> be found in abundance not only in the three *Critiques*
> but, taking their color from them, also in other writings of
> the "critical" period. Above all the piling up of three,
> four, five, six, and at one point actually seven subordinate
> sentences that are fitted into each other within a single
> long sentence; but also pleonasms, displacements of
> words that make for a lack of clarity, ponderous circum-
> locutions, anacolutha, unnecessary repetitions of the
> same expression or construction—for example, on a
> single page, 262, of the *Critique of Pure Reason*
> (Kehrbach ['s edition = A295f. = B351f.]) we find no less
> than eighteen relative clauses that have been squeezed
> into a mere three sentences, and on p. xixf. of the second
> preface we find five not especially disturbing genetives
> one right after the other. And what is worse, he uses even
> important philosophical concepts, like transcendental,
> subjective, objective, etc., not always in the same sense.
> Add to this the frequently confusing arrangement of the

material in which one rarely senses anything resembling symmetry. Just read the table of contents of the *Critique of Pure Reason* with all its Parts, Sections, Divisions, Books, Main Segments, General Notes, and Appendices—what Schopenhauer called the Gothic style. Or construct for yourself a table of contents for the *Critique of Practical Reason* which was published without one, and note how the first main part has 168 pages and the second only 13, and the rest of the arrangement is also as confusing and asymmetrical as possible. To all this, finally, add the often wearisome verbosity, prolixity, and obscurity of the presentation . . . (p. 101f.).

Let nobody suppose that Kant's long sentences are carefully crafted like the involved periods of classical orators. Anacolutha are inconsistencies in logic and syntax—sudden shifts from one construction to another, which are common in ordinary speech and in streams of consciousness. And the second edition of the *Critique of Pure Reason*, revised to make things clearer, also lacked a table of contents, just like the second *Critique* which appeared a year later.

Oddly, the first edition of 1781 had a table of contents—which was woefully brief and incredibly asymmetrical. This is worth mentioning because one might suppose that the whole structure was clear at least to Kant's own mind, and that he had written his masterpiece on the basis of a detailed outline. But he obviously had not.

Roman I comprises almost 700 pages, Roman II, which in the table of contents is divided only into four Main Segments, 150. Roman I is divided into Part One, which consists of two "Sections," and Part Two, which consists of two "Divisions." That is all the breakdown offered us for a book of almost 900 pages. The smallest units range in length from eight pages to over four hundred! One gets the impression that when Kant had finished writing the book, he did not take the time to look back to see what exactly he had got and how it all fitted together. And the third edition, like the second, offered no table of contents at all.

Of course, all this may strike some readers as irrelevant, merely external, and of no inherent interest or importance. In fact, it has a bearing on the question of Kant's rigor, his method, and his mentality. He was not half as rigorous and scientific as he thought he was, and the model he provided was disastrous.

33 ▶▶▶ Kant impeded the discovery of the mind by (1) establishing a misguided "transcendental" method, by (2) providing an untenable model of the mind as well as (3) a grotesque notion of autonomy, by (4) persuading generations of philosophers that serious and important studies must be written like the *Critique of Pure Reason,* and finally (5) by insisting that in philosophical analyses of the mind hypotheses are illegitimate and certainty and necessity are requirements. The last two points still require discussion, and both need to be related to Kant's own mind or mentality.

The *Critique of Pure Reason* is such a stylistic atrocity that one must ask—and scholars have long asked—how it came to be written the way it was. Surely, nobody could have decided deliberately that the book ought to be written that way! And yet it quickly became a model for others.

One of the most eminent German Kant scholars, Hans Vaihinger, proposed the so-called patchwork theory, and Norman Kemp Smith propagated it in his immensely interesting commentary. In brief, the theory is that Kant accumulated many bits and pieces for more than a decade and then patched them together, more or less figuratively speaking, with scissors and paste. This is held to account for the many inconsistencies in the book and for its poor organization.

This theory was developed when the so-called Higher Criticism of the Bible was flourishing in Germany, and it was widely believed—and some Bible scholars still believe—that the five Books of Moses are patchwork. The orthodox Mosaic theory was countered with a mosaic theory that held quite literally that verses and even half verses in Genesis, for example, could be assigned confidently to one or another written source; first, either the Jahvist or the Elohist or a "priestly author," and a little later on, as more people had to make scholarly contributions, to J_1, J_2, E_1, E_2, P_1, P_2, etc., etc. Instead of playing on the word "Mosaic" one could also speak of a materialistic theory of literary creation. It was supposed that the greatest book ever written, Genesis, was composed of particles that its creator had simply fitted together.[3]

Kant's *Critique,* of course, differs from Genesis in a multitude of ways and is assuredly not a masterpiece of literature whose poetic beauty has never been surpassed. Those who are interested in the details of the controversy about the patchwork theory have to read Vaihinger (1902), Smith's commentary, H. J. Paton (1930 and 1936, Volume I, p. 38ff.), and Beck (1969, p. 468f.). Among the things that speak against the patchwork theory are Kant's own words, which will be quoted soon. But even as it is clear that the writer of Genesis drew on more than one tradition, it is unquestionable that when Kant wrote the *Critique of Pure Reason* he had accumulated notes for more than ten years. The book did not come into being all at once, out of nothing. In addition to Kant's own words, the inconsistencies in the *Grundlegung* are also highly relevant. Here is a short book that the proponents of the patchwork theory do not explain as a mosaic, and yet we encounter practically the

[3] For a more detailed critique, see Kaufmann (1958), secs. 87–89.

same problems. Both books, as well as the *Critique of Practical Reason*, are creations of the same singular mind.

34 ▶▶▶ When the *Critique of Pure Reason* appeared, Kant was fifty-seven. Berkeley and Hume published their masterpieces in their twenties; Schopenhauer his at thirty-one. Kierkegaard died at forty-two, Nietzsche stopped writing at forty-four, Spinoza died at forty-five, and Hegel, who was a late bloomer, published his first book at thirty-six and his last at fifty-one. But if Kant had died at fifty-six, hardly anyone would have heard of him. Actually, he had published his first book in his twenties, and he had followed it up with many other publications, not yet in his later style. But in his fifties he felt that all he had published so far was beneath comparison with "the system" that was gradually taking shape in his head. And after his brief inaugural dissertation of 1770, when he finally became a professor, he published hardly anything until the *Critique* appeared in 1781.

As early as June 7, 1771, Kant wrote Herz that he was at work on a book with the title "The Limits of Sensibility and Reason" and, after having gone over all the materials and weighing and fitting together everything, had recently finished the whole plan. The title, *Die Grenzen der Sinnlichkeit und der Vernunft*,[4] was probably inspired by Lessing's *Laokoon oder über die*

---

[4] *Sinnlichkeit* cannot mean *sense* in the sense of what is "intelligible" or not "empty of meaning," although readers of P. F. Strawson's preface to his book, *The Bounds of Sense: An Essay on Kant's Critique of Pure Reason* (1966) might be led to assume that Kant had once considered a title of that sort.

Grenzen der Malerei und Poesie (1766), "Laocoon or on the Limits of Painting and Poetry."[5]

Eight and a half months later, Kant had forgotten what he had written Herz and told him in another letter, February 21, 1772, how he had planned a book that "might perhaps have the title 'The Limits of Sensibility and Reason.' " The first part was to be "theoretical" and was to have "two sections, (1) phenomenology in general, and (2) metaphysics, but dealing only with its nature and method. The second part would also be in two sections, (1) general principles of feeling, taste, and sensuous desire, and (2) the first principles of morals." After going into the details at some length, Kant reported that he was "now in a position to bring out a 'Critique of Pure Reason,' dealing with the nature of theoretical as well as practical knowledge, insofar as the latter is purely intellectual," that the first part would "deal with the sources of metaphysics, its methods and limits"—and that he would "publish the first part within about three months"! That was nine years before the *Critique* actually appeared. But even then Kant knew that "after that I will work out the pure principles of ethics."

More than three months had passed, indeed almost two years, when Kant wrote Herz late in 1773 that he was "still hoping sometimes to have the book published by Easter 1774," and "Even when I take into account the frequent indispositions that always cause interruptions, I can still almost certainly promise to have it ready a little after Easter"! He was greatly looking forward to getting his "transcendental philosophy" out of the way, as that would enable him to turn "to metaphysics, which

[5] Emil Arnoldt's laborious attempt to refute this suggestion in his very erudite and long-winded essay on "The external genesis and the time it took to write the *Critique of Pure Reason*" (1894), pp. 111–13, is quite unconvincing. I accept Vaihinger's suggestion, the more so because Arnoldt himself argues for Kant's knowledge of *Laokoon* (p. 193f.).

has only two parts, the metaphysics of nature and the metaphysics of morals, of which I shall publish the latter first."

It is not excessively unkind to charge Kant with self-deception. For almost ten years he kept thinking that he would publish his *magnum opus* in roughly three months' time and felt so sure of this that he could promise it "almost certainly"—and perhaps said so in writing to increase the pressure on himself. In retrospect these expectations seem incredible unless we assume that in those days Kant pictured the *Critique* as a far shorter book than it turned out to be.

More than three and a half years after the Easter promise and the reference to "frequent indispositions," Kant wrote Herz on August 20, 1777, both about his physical problems and about what was holding up the book. He singled out one of his chronic indispositions that interfered with his work, hoping that Herz, as a physician, might be able to help with a prescription. "Although I am not really plagued by obstructions, I nevertheless have every morning such laborious and generally inadequate exoneration that the feces which remains behind and accumulates becomes, as far as I can judge, the cause of a foggy head as well as flatulence." As for the book, "What I am *calling* the *Critique of Pure Reason* lies in the way of the completion of all other works like a stone, and I am now occupied solely with its removal and hope to be finished with it entirely this winter," which would have meant publication by Easter 1778. The only remaining problem was, he claimed, to present "everything in it with total clarity."

Emil Arnoldt relates that when Kant wrote this letter, and indeed throughout 1777, he definitely was not yet ready to prepare any final version. In addition to the problems mentioned, he had not yet "overcome all the difficulties of the transcendental dialectic," and moreover J. N. Tetens published a two-volume work that

year which, no doubt, delayed Kant's project. Tetens'
*Philosophical Attempts Concerning Human Nature and
Its Development* comprised more than 1,600 pages, and
Arnoldt (p. 147f.) agrees with Hermann Cohen that it
greatly influenced Kant in a number of ways, although
Kant never once referred to Tetens either in his *Critique*
or in any of his other books. Yet Kant complained in
several letters after the publication of his book that Tetens had disappointed him by not doing anything to
promote the *Critique!*

In April 1778 Kant wrote Herz that the rumor then
circulating in Berlin to the effect that parts of his book
had by now come off the printer's presses

> has been spread too hastily. Since I do not want to exact
> anything from myself by force (because I would like to go
> on working in the world a little longer), many other proj-
> ects are coming in between. But it is progressing and, I
> hope, will be finished this summer. The causes for this
> delay of an essay that, as far as length goes, won't amount
> to much [!], you will grant some day, I hope, to have been
> valid, considering the nature of the case and of the proj-
> ect itself. *Tetens,* in his lengthy work on human nature,
> has said much that is acute; but, without a doubt, he let it
> be printed, or at least stand, just as he wrote it.

Kant went on to say that if his health should be tolerable
during the summer he hoped to be able then "to communicate the promised little work [*Werkchen*] to the
public."

There is no adequate English word for *Werkchen.*
The diminutive suffix suggests the Latin *opusculum* and
a minor as well as small work. Yet there are few works in
the whole history of philosophy that one would be less
inclined to call a *Werkchen* than Kant's *Critique of Pure
Reason,* and it is plain that he was not being humorous.
After all, he had said only a few lines before that the
work would not amount to much in length (*die an*

Bogenzahl nicht viel austragen wird), which makes it as clear as can be that as late as 1778 Kant's whole conception of his *Critique* was still utterly different from the work of almost 900 pages that he finally published in 1781.

The actual writing of the book we know remains shrouded in mystery. Emil Arnoldt's lengthy investigation of it sometimes reads like a parody of Kant and of Teutonic scholarship. It comprises about ninety pages, followed by an "Appendix" of 462 pages, which is divided into six parts, of which "No. 4 & No. 5" form one part with subdivisions down to 3.c.delta, while No. 6 comprises a single page, described in the Table of Contents as "Explanation about the exclusion of the announced No. 6 of the Appendix from the series of the discussions presented here." Regarding the actual writing of the *Critique* we read on page 169: "Hence, I believe, the *assertion* can almost be risked: Around the middle of December 1778 Kant had begun to attack the task of writing down for the printer the, or some version of the, *Critique of Pure Reason*." Again the English cannot match the flavor of the German: *die oder eine Niederschrift der Kritik der reinen Vernunft für den Druck in Angriff genommen.* But while "assertion" is emphasized in print, this claim can only be risked "almost." And there is the question of how much weight should be given to Hamann's letter to Herder, May 17, 1779, in which we read: *Kant arbeitet frisch darauf los an seiner Moral der reinen Vernunft,* which means that "Kant is working briskly on his Morality [!] of Pure Reason."

Arnoldt thinks that Kant composed a detailed draft of his *Critique* between April or May and August or September 1779, including a great many concrete examples and explications that he eliminated when he prepared the book for the printer from about December 1779 to October or November 1780. But this is certainly dubious and would seem to call into question Kant's honesty in his fascinating letters to Christian Garve on August 7, 1783, and to Moses Mendelssohn on August 16, 1783. The way he put it to Mendelssohn has often been quoted rather freely. Here is a literal translation:

> ... For the product of reflection extending over a period of at least twelve years I had set afoot [*zu Stande gebracht*] within four to five months, in flight as it were [!], to be sure with the greatest attention to the contents but with less industry regarding the presentation and furtherance of easy understanding by the reader—a resolve that I still do not regret because without that and given a longer delay for the sake of introducing popularity, the work would probably have remained undone altogether because the latter fault can be remedied by and by, once the product is there in a rough version.

Kant is here trying to explain why the book apparently did not appeal to Mendelssohn, and in context the suggestion is clearly that the exposition might still be improved—which is what Kant actually tried to accomplish in the second edition, in 1787. What he is saying is certainly *not* that it took between four and five months to write a first draft with lots of examples that were designed to make things easier for a larger public, and that he then had allowed the draft to rest three months before he returned to it and spent almost another year to revise it for the printer.

I should not attach much weight to Hamann's remark about the "Morality of Pure Reason" but find Kant's own account of the actual writing of the *Critique* fascinating because it is so utterly at odds with the received image of Kant. Who would ever have supposed that the book was written "in flight as it were" by an author who never took the time to look back at what he had written?

How different prejudices are from facts! Many professors think that Nietzsche wrote that way, and that there is no difference to speak of between Nietzsche's notes, published posthumously, and the so-called aphorisms in his books. But on December 8, 1888, less than a month before his final breakdown, Nietzsche wrote Heinrich Köselitz (*alias* Peter Gast) that he had returned the manuscript of *Ecce Homo* to the printer "after laying it once more on the gold scales from the first to the last word to set my conscience finally at rest." The beauty of Nietzsche's style is due in no small measure to the fact that he usually weighed every word. Professors who write badly often think that serious books that are written well must have been written with great ease and little care and therefore are not truly serious. Kant's style became the model of serious philosophy. Actually, good writing is usually the result of rigorous self-criticism and repeated rewriting, and it is arguable that the lack of such self-criticism is deeply unscientific.

Kant wrote Christian Garve:

> . . . I set it afoot in about four to five months, fearing that such a complicated business would eventually become, if I delayed it any longer, a burden for me and my increasing years (as I am already in my sixtieth) and might in the end make it impossible for me, while right now I still have the whole system in my head.

One gets the sense that after such long obstruction Kant had come to feel frightened of waiting any longer and could see no other solution than to get it all out at once in a single tremendous explosion. And if he told Mendelssohn and Garve the truth, he must have written his *Critique* quite literally *almost as fast as it would take anyone to copy it.*

From Wasianski's memoir of 1804 and above all from Jachmann's fifteenth letter, we know Kant's daily schedule, which does not seem to have varied even slightly during his productive years. After rising at five,

Kant had breakfast, which consisted of two cups of very weak tea and one pipe, and then worked on his lectures until seven. From seven to nine he lectured, and *from nine to 12:45 he wrote*, in his bathrobe and slippers, wearing a nightcap. Many professors feel exhausted after two consecutive lectures, and very few get up at five. But Kant did his writing after two hours of teaching, devoting three hours and forty-five minutes to this task, day after day. (Wasianski related [p. 239] that Kant loved his watch so much "that he said now and then: if he were in dire distress, it would be the last thing he would sell.")

At this point it is interesting to digress briefly to see how Kant arranged the rest of his day. From one to four he had luncheon, which could last until six when he had many guests. He ate only once a day and never ate or drank anything after lunch except water. He liked the smell of coffee and at parties felt tempted by it but never drank coffee because he considered the oil harmful. The luncheons took so long because Kant relished conversation. This is actually an instance of Jachmann's dictum that Kant lived as he taught. In 1798 Kant himself published his lectures on anthropology, which show how gracefully he could write and lecture, and in the final section (78) of the First Part he dealt at length with meals, saying among other things:

> Eating *alone* (*solipsimus convictorii*) is unhealthy for a *philosophizing* scholar and is not restoration but (especially when it amounts to solitary *gluttony*) exhaustion, fatiguing work and not animating play of ideas. . . . At a festive table, when the multitude of courses is designed solely to keep the guests together for a long time (*coenam ducere*), the conversation usually moves through three stages: 1. *narration*, 2. *argumentation*, and 3. *joking.*—A. The news of the day, first domestic and then also foreign, that have come in through private letters and newspapers.—B. When this first appetite has been satisfied, the company becomes more vivacious; for in the

course of reasoning, differences of judgment about one and the same subject that has been started can scarcely be avoided, and nobody has the worst opinion of his own; and this gives rise to a dispute that stimulates the appetite for the main dish and bottle and, according to the intensity of the dispute and the participation in it, also aids the digestion.—C. But because reasoning always is a kind of work and . . . this eventually becomes burdensome, the conversation naturally moves on to the mere play of wit, partly also in order to please the woman who is present . . . and thus the meal ends with *laughter*. . . .

The transition from 1, 2, 3 to A, B, C is a typical inconsistency, but what is more striking is the lack of spontaneity even in conversation.

At Kant's house the first course was soup with some meat in it and usually also noodles, and the second was dried fruit or fish, cod being Kant's favorite. The third course was a roast, which Kant ate with mustard; he sucked the juice from the meat and then put the rest back on his plate. Everybody had a quarter of a bottle of wine in front of his place, usually Médoc, with no seconds. The fourth course was bread and cheese, which Kant ate with lots of butter; and when there were many guests the meal ended with cake. Afterwards, Kant would not sit lest he fall asleep, and he soon went for a walk for at least an hour—a little longer when the weather was good. He walked alone, slowly to avoid sweating, and took notes. On his return home he either read or received visitors but did not write, and by ten he was in bed.

To return to the *Critique*, if he wrote it in four months, working five days a week, he averaged ten printed pages a day; if it took him five months and he worked six days a week, he would have averaged a little more than six and a half printed pages a day. It seems reasonable to assume that he averaged about eight. And he had to provide clean copy for the printer without the help of a typewriter or a secretary. In other words, the

Critique of Pure Reason was written so fast that there was no time to weigh words or to reconsider long and involved sentences or arguments.

This accounts for an otherwise puzzling phrase at the end of Kant's preface to the second edition:

> Even apparent contradictions can be picked out of any written work, especially if it proceeds as free speech, if one compares individual passages that have been torn from their context; and in the eyes of those who rely on the judgment of others they cast a disadvantageous light on the work, but anyone who has mastered the idea of the whole finds it very easy to dissolve them.

Of course, it is precisely the commentators and scholars who do not rely on secondary sources but wrestle with the text who are bothered by Kant's frequent contradictions. As Lewis Beck once put it (1969, p. 468), "The difficulties a reader experiences tend to increase with the number of readings he gives it." But what at first glance seems almost incomprehensible is Kant's claim that the style of the book is that of free speech (*vornehmlich als freye Rede fortgehenden Schrift*). It may be objected: Surely, we have never met anyone who talks the way Kant writes! Yet Kant knew that what he had put on paper and not taken the time to revise carefully was his stream of consciousness. And the many sentences that cannot be construed invite comparison with the transcription of a tape. Kant did not prevaricate when he claimed that the book was "set afoot within four to five months, in flight as it were."

Kant had published one book in the 1740s and several in the fifties and sixties, but almost nothing in the seventies. With the publication of his *magnum opus,* however, it was as if a dike had broken. Two years later, in 1783, Kant published his *Prolegomena,* a book of over 200 pages in which he tried to present the ideas of his *Critique* in more accessible form. Another two years later, he published his short book on ethics, the *Grundlegung*, which also gives the impression of having been written "in flight as it were." The following year he published his *Metaphysical First Principles of Natural Science*, and in 1787 the second edition, very extensively revised, of his *Critique of Pure Reason*, now well over 900 pages long. In 1788 his *Critique of Practical Reason* appeared, in 1790 his *Critique of Judgment*, in 1793 *Religion Within the Bounds of Mere Reason*, in 1795 his essay "On Eternal Peace," another two years later a two-volume work entitled *The Metaphysics of Ethics*, and in 1798 his *Anthropology*. These are merely the highlights of a vast productivity that includes quite a number of other books as well as many essays and articles.

Kant occasionally wrote almost with some grace, but his major works, and especially the second and the third *Critiques*, were modeled on the first *Critique*. The *Critiques* became the model without peer of rigorous German philosophy. One could write an occasional essay in a more popular style, but works that aspired to the significance of Kant's three *Critiques* had better be written in that style!

This may sound like an exaggeration, but we have already seen how Fichte's first book was stylistically, too, so close to Kant that it was actually taken to be Kant's. Fichte occasionally tried to write in a more popular vein, but these efforts only added to the spreading sense that really important "scientific" works had to be written in the style of Kant's *Critique*, or at least not in ordinary German. It was widely felt that something was extremely odd about Kant's style, but he somehow persuaded the Germans that *philosophy required a special language*.

In time, Hegel and then, roughly a hundred years later, Heidegger tried purposefully to create such a language. Descartes had provided a very different model for

French philosophers, and Bacon and Hobbes for the British. Nevertheless, some twentieth-century French philosophers succumbed to the fatal example of Kant, Hegel, and Heidegger, to the point of translating Kant's, Hegel's, or Heidegger's terms into French.

We shall see later how Hegel's *Phenomenology* was written in very much the same way as Kant's *Critique of Pure Reason*. Sartre's often beautifully written literary works are the product of continual revisions, while his "philosophical manuscripts are written in longhand, with almost no crossings out or erasures"—and very much the worse for that—and his *Critique de la raison dialectique*, which he considers his philosophical *magnum opus*, was written like Kant's *Critique*, as fast as the author could write. "I worked on it ten hours a day, taking Corydrane [that is, "Speed"]—in the end I was taking twenty pills a day—and I really felt that this book had to be finished. The amphetamines gave me a quickness of thought and writing that was at least three times my normal rhythm, and I wanted to go fast." Not only has Simone de Beauvoir recorded in her autobiography (1963) how Sartre almost killed himself in the process, but he himself has related how he reached the point where he "was scribbling illegibly rather than writing: I wrote sentences absolutely devoid of meaning, without relation to the play [*Altona*], which frightened Simone de Beauvoir."[6] In the case of the play, of course, Sartre caught himself because he kept going over his literary creations. But writing his *Critique* during the same period was another matter, for here it was evidently a virtue if the result resembled Kant's *Critique* and was scarcely readable.

Among the great German philosophers Scho-

[6] "Sartre at Seventy: An Interview [with Michel Contat]" in *The New York Review*, Aug. 7, 1975. Reprinted with minor stylistic differences in Sartre, *Life/Situations* (1977), pp. 7, 18, 19.

penhauer was plainly influenced as much by Goethe as by Kant, even in his style, while Nietzsche was the only major figure who resolutely refused to follow Kant's example. The price he had to pay for that was that some philosophy professors thought for a while that he could not really be a serious philosopher. Actually, he broke not only with Kant's impossible style but also with his misguided method, his untenable model of the mind, and his grotesque notion of autonomy.[7] And no philosopher contributed more than Nietzsche to the discovery of the mind.

35 ▶▶▶ In the preface to the first edition of the *Critique of Pure Reason* Kant said:

> Regarding certainty I have pronounced this sentence on myself: in this kind of consideration it is in no way permissible to *opine* and everything that as much as resembles a hypothesis is forbidden goods that may not be offered even for the least price, but as soon as it is discovered it must be confiscated (A ix).

No doubt, he recalled Newton's celebrated dictum, in the General Scholium to *Principia: Hypotheses non fingo* (I do not invent hypotheses). But we should also recall Goethe's polemics against the Newtonians: "A false hypothesis is better than none at all" (Section 12, above).

In addition to absolute certainty Kant also demands and claims to have attained "completeness" and necessity. He actually says:

> The perfect unity of knowledge of this kind that consists of nothing but pure concepts so that no element of expe-

---

[7] Wilcox (1974), chap. IV, "Kant, the Thing-in-Itself, and Nietzsche's Skepticism," has shown how even Nietzsche was influenced a little by Kant.

rience . . . can have any influence on it and expand or augment it makes this unconditional completeness not only feasible but also necessary (A xiv).

To be sure, the dream of absolute certainty is older than Kant and can be traced back to Descartes, to Plato, and even to Parmenides, but it was Kant who impressed this trinity of certainty, completeness, and necessity on his successors, especially in Germany.

It is astonishing that a philosopher with Kant's deep need for certainty who also had the conviction as well as the reputation that he had attained certainty should actually be so elusive regarding some, if not most, of his fundamental ideas. Or is it astonishing? A conjecture can be formulated crisply; a hypothesis is of no use if it is not stated clearly; but if one makes bold to lay down certainties for all time without admitting even the possibility that in the light of further developments—if only one's own development—one may be led to change one's mind, a lack of clarity is all too understandable.

Take Kant's doctrine of the thing-in-itself. This is the cornerstone of the whole system and the point where Fichte, Schelling, Hegel, and Schopenhauer attempted revisions of the master's philosophy. There is no need here to survey all the controversies about this doctrine; it will suffice to mention the basic problem that almost any student of Kant is bound to notice. Kant insists that traditional metaphysicians have made the egregious mistake of applying the twelve categories to what lies beyond all possible experience. But "In numerous passages Kant applies the categories (such as unity, plurality, reality, causality, existence) to the things in themselves" and he often "claims that our ego is affected by the things in themselves, thus turning them into the ultimate cause of our representations; in this capacity they are altogether indispensable in the 'critical' system."[8]

Our concern here is preeminently with the discovery of the mind, and the problem just mentioned has a direct bearing on Kant's conception of the mind. What is the status of the mind or spirit, self or soul? Is it a phenomenon or not? Erich Adickes, one of the greatest German Kant scholars, whom I have just quoted, comes to the conclusion that according to Kant "one and the same ego is on the one hand in and for itself timeless and hence unknowable, while on the other hand it is experienced and known by me, which is to say by itself, in my empirical consciousness in the form of time and thus as an appearance" (p. 156f.). In our discussion of Kant's postulate of the immortality of the soul we saw that Kant postulated the immortality of one soul per person, that he applied the categories to these souls, and that the whole point of the postulate was that each soul would continue eternally to become holier and holier—which would seem to mean that each of them prevails more and ever more over transphenomenal inclinations.

Kant's agnosticism, his insistence that we cannot *know* anything at all about the soul, is easy enough to understand and sympathize with, but when he claims that the point of doing away with knowledge is to make room for faith, and when he argues that the faith in question is not irrational but on the contrary what reason demands, it does not seem unreasonable to inquire what precisely it is that reason demands.

Friedrich Nicolovius, who published Kant's books during the 1790s, remarked in 1798 that Kant's recent books had led "many Kantians" to "suppose that he did not agree with himself." His students in Königsberg thought that he did not really believe in immortality.

[8] Adickes (1924), p. 157.

Johann Brahl, who often dined with Kant, said: "Although he postulates a god, he himself does not believe in it, and he also pays no heed to the future insofar as it can grant a continued existence."[9] Jachmann, whose reliability is beyond question and whom Kant himself had asked to write his biography, promising to furnish the necessary materials, relates in the eleventh letter of his beautiful memoir what Kant had said to him about immortality. Kant began by asking him

> what a rational person . . . should choose if before the end of life an angel from heaven . . . appeared to him and presented him with the irrevocable choice . . . whether he wished to exist for all eternity or to cease altogether to exist when his life ended. And he [Kant] was of the opinion that it would be rather foolhardy to opt for a totally unknown state that would last eternally, thus surrendering freely to an uncertain fate that, regardless of all remorse over one's choice, regardless of all disgust with the endless monotony, and regardless of all longing for a change, would still be inexorable and eternal.

Jachmann goes on to point out that these remarks do not contradict Kant's postulate, for Kant could have believed that practical reason demanded something that was not at all desirable from the point of view of our inclinations. One might add that the immortality he postulated was characterized by ceaseless self-improvement—a singularly strenuous kind of monotony.

My prime concern here is not with the immortality of the soul but with Kant's conception of scientific philosophy. If he had simply taken either the line that there is much that we can never know or the line that an honest man must sometimes allow, as Socrates did at the end of the *Apology*, that more than one hypothesis is available and that we have no way of telling which is

[9] Vorländer, vol. II, p. 181.

best, I should be satisfied. But Kant insisted on excluding from his "critical" philosophy all mere hypotheses; he aimed and claimed to provide certainty, and *he concealed his own uncertainties, confusions, and changes of mind behind an absurd way of writing*—and this practice no less than his style was soon copied widely, and still is to this day.

We have seen how in 1778 Kant still thought of his *Critique of Pure Reason* as a *Werkchen* that "would not amount to much in length," which means that much of the argument of the book of almost 900 pages published three years later must have come to Kant more or less at the last moment if not actually while writing the work "in flight as it were." In the same vein, some of the arguments of the *Critique of Practical Reason* can be shown to have occurred to Kant only as he was writing that book. In his commentary on it (p. 267), Lewis Beck cites a passage written just a little earlier and says:

> This seems to be an intimation of the moral argument that is to follow in a few months; but it is so much an *obiter dictum* . . . that it may not be justified to see more than an obscure germ of the later argument in it.

And what, it might be asked, is wrong with that? Absolutely nothing. But a writer who publishes ideas and arguments as they come to him should offer them tentatively as attempts, suggestions, or hypotheses. I venture the conjecture that Kant's insistence on his certainty is related closely to his obscurity. What is stated clearly and concisely invites objections and alternative hypotheses. To preclude both, Kant avoids being clear and concise.[10] Deliberately? Of course not. What is at work here is the same timidity that demands certainty in the first place.

In German, there is a single word that can mean

[10] Cf. Kaufmann (1958), sec. 51: "The ambiguity of dogma."

certainty or security: *Sicherheit.* It is revealing that the adjective, *sicher,* is encountered in the very first sentence of the second edition of the *Critique of Pure Reason* where Kant speaks of *den sicheren Gang einer Wissenschaft,* and this same phrase is repeated a dozen times in his preface. The phrase has been translated as "the secure stride of a science," and Kant himself contrasts it with groping or fumbling about. Kant wants to be sure and is afraid of uncertainty as well as insecurity.

When Kant was offered a professorship in Erlangen in 1769, while he was still waiting for a chair in Königsberg, he turned it down. Some writers suppose that he did this because the move might have interfered with his work on the *Critique of Pure Reason* which, as we have seen, he did not start writing until ten years later. But Kant's letter to Erlangen voices his great timidity, his fear of "changes that would seem small to others." This timidity contrasts with the boldness of his attack on traditional metaphysics and theology, but even that daring had drastic limits, and I have tried to show how Kant sought security in obscurity and equivocations.

The paradox of Kant's boldness and timidity might be put this way: Kant was afraid of recognizing his own courage. As a soldier may risk his life, feeling that he has no choice at all and is merely doing his duty, Kant felt that his audacious hypotheses were not the creations of his intrepid imagination but pieces of secure knowledge. He did not allow himself to think that he risked being wrong, and he concealed his daring from himself by assuring himself and his readers again and again that he was emulating "the secure stride of a science." One of the boldest thinkers of all time kept deceiving himself about his own audacity, as Hegel did after him. Kant was like a man who walks a ridge, totally unaware of the precipices on both sides, feeling sure that he is perfectly safe.

Kant's admirers have often stressed his high regard for truth and honesty, and he unquestionably went to heroic extremes in denying the "supposed right to lie" to prevent a murder (see footnote 24 above). Yet we have seen how he boasted a year later, in 1798, how he had outwitted the King of Prussia (text for footnote 23). In a letter to Mendelssohn, April 8, 1766, Kant said: "To be sure, there is much I think with the clearest conviction possible and to my own great satisfaction that I shall never have the courage to say; but I shall never say anything I do not think." We have seen that his students were no longer sure during the last decade of his life, thirty years later, that he had not said things in print that he did not actually believe. And his *opus postumum* lends support to their suspicions. Here we find Kant saying: "God is not a *being outside* me but merely a *thought within me*."[11]

Even if Kant had never deviated from the declaration in his letter, that alone—coupled with his own report of how he outwitted the King of Prussia with a misleading promise—would lead us to expect that Kant sometimes did not mean what he seemed to mean. We should also ask what sort of thing Kant lacked the courage to say—and whether this kind of silence may not poison the whole system.[12]

Kant's admirers, from the biographers of 1804 to Karl Jaspers, have stressed again and again that Kant aimed not so much to teach philosophy as philosophizing or, in the current English idiom, *doing* philosophy. I have tried to show that in this respect Kant was a disaster. One of his contemporaries, on the other hand, really did make an all-out attempt to make his readers think, to the point of frequently not stating his own views, especially in his

[11] Vorländer, II, p. 293.
[12] See Solzhenitsyn, *Cancer Ward*, the chapter "Idols of the Market Place."

abundant theological or antitheological polemics. It was because so many people were unsure about Lessing's beliefs that F. H. Jacobi's aforementioned book on the doctrine of Spinoza (1785) met with so much interest and created such a sensation, as Jacobi reported that Lessing was a Spinozist, which was then widely taken to mean an atheist. But in Lessing's case it was not timidity that kept him from stating his convictions; he clearly felt that stating them would not serve his primary purpose of getting his readers to think seriously and strenuously about important questions. The classical statement he published in 1778 is worth recalling because it furnishes such a contrast to Kant's "critical philosophy":

Not the truth in whose possession some human being is or thinks he is, but the honest trouble he has taken to get behind the truth is what constitutes the worth of a human being. . . .

If God held in his closed right hand all truth and in his left hand only the ever live drive for truth, albeit with the addition that I should always and evermore err, and he said to me: Choose! I should humbly grab his left hand, saying: Father, give! Pure truth is after all for you alone![13]

Lessing cherished development as much as Kant feared change, and he did not assume, like Kant, that the human mind is immutable. He even wrote a short essay on the theme that man's mind might change: "That There Could Be More Than Five Senses for Man." To him, change was exhilarating.

Lessing's untimely death in 1781 was one of the greatest misfortunes ever to befall German literature and thought. If only he had lived a few years longer to publish his reactions to Kant's "critical philosophy"! But at least his legacy was not ignored. Goethe developed it

[13] See sec. 17 above.

not only in *Faust* but also in his polemics against Newtonian science.

Kierkegaard's *Concluding Unscientific Postscript* begins with reflections on something Lessing said, and it would be nice if one could claim that in existentialism Lessing's heritage gained philosophical expression. But Kierkegaard, Jaspers, and Heidegger were never able to emancipate themselves from Kant. They never even recognized that Kant was in important ways the antithesis of Lessing. And gradually it became a cliché that existentialism represented a revolt against Hegel. It is important to see the whole development of philosophy after Kant in a different light, and to that end it was necessary to make a beginning by seeing Kant as he has not been seen before. Actually, there is one short passage in which Kant is seen as here, a few words near the end of Nietzsche's *Twilight of the Idols* (1889). Section 49 is entitled *Goethe:*

> ... He did not retire from life but put himself into the midst of it; he was not fainthearted but took as much as possible upon himself, over himself, into himself. What he wanted was *totality;* he fought the mutual extraneousness of reason, senses, feeling, and will (preached with the most abhorrent scholasticism by *Kant,* the antipode of Goethe); he disciplined himself into wholeness, he *created* himself.
>
> ... Goethe conceived of a human being who would be strong, highly educated, skillful in all bodily matters, self-controlled, reverent toward himself, and who might dare to afford the whole range and wealth of being natural, being strong enough for such freedom. ...

Nietzsche was not the first to see Goethe that way. Schiller's and Hegel's images of him had been similar, and nineteenth-century German philosophy cannot be understood without him, any more than it can be understood without Kant. And Kant was, for all his virtues, in many ways a disaster.

36 ▶▶▶ Looking back upon my account of Kant, I feel like quoting the conclusion of Lessing's *Duplik*, the polemic in which the image of the two hands of God is found:

> I had meant to let the reader gather casually the reasons for this judgment, and yet I have often literally pronounced the judgment myself. What shall I do? Apologize? Ask for forgiveness with the silly mien of an incompetent hypocrite? Promise that next time I'll be more careful?
>
> Can I do that? Promise? Yes, yes, I promise—never even to *resolve* to remain cold and indifferent in certain matters. If a human being is not permitted to generate warmth and take sides when he recognizes clearly that reason and scripture have been abused, when and where is it permitted?

In my juxtaposition of Goethe and Kant I might have taken the time and trouble to conceal my feelings better, but decided against that, not only for the reasons stated by Lessing. It would be perverse to try to discover the minds of several dead writers while taking pains not to discover one's own. By seeing how we react *emotionally* to Goethe and Kant, Hegel and Nietzsche, Heidegger and Buber, Freud and Jung, we can find out a great deal about ourselves. While I see no need to burden my discussion of these men with the discoveries I have made about myself in the course of writing about them, I believe that not hiding my emotions may make it easier for you to discover your feelings and your mind.

Disapproval, of course, can be based on intellectual considerations, but a little observation of ourselves and others shows quickly that the emotion accompanying it is not always proportionate to our reasons. Whenever this is the case, the question arises why we have such strong feelings about some faults and not about others. Usually, though not always, powerful negative feelings are an indication that we sense the same faults in ourselves and have taken some trouble not to give in to them. When this is not the case, we generally associate these faults with someone else or with a group of people whom we dislike intensely, possibly for very good reasons.

I am far from hating Kant and if, contrary to my pronounced opposition to Manichaeism, I were to divide writers into good and evil people, I should certainly include Kant among the good. Why, then, does a certain animus against him come through here and there? And why do I bother to discuss him at such length when I think that in important respects he was a disaster?

I love philosophy and have given much of my life to it, but it seems to me to be in very poor health, and this, as I have tried to show, is due in no small measure to Kant who, with the best intentions, came close to ruining it. To restore its health, we need to understand what has gone wrong.

Actually, I doubt that mainstream philosophy will ever become strong enough to be of much help in the discovery of the mind. Nor do I think, upon reflection, that it was strong enough before Kant came along. In many ways he is an embodiment on a large scale of what is wrong with philosophy, but he also had an enormous influence, and its very enormity makes one wonder what might have happened if he had pushed philosophy in a different direction. Suppose he had not insisted on certainty, necessity, and completeness! This, it seems to me, was his most fateful error, and his obscure style may be considered a mere corollary of that. Suppose he had been more like Lessing! Such questions are obviously unanswerable. If one thing had been different, ever so many others might have been different as well; for example, all the professors of philosophy who took to Kant like fish to water might in that case have found Kant much less attractive. At the very least they might not have followed his example in this respect. One only needs to compare the Nietzsche literature with Nietzsche to appreciate that point, or the Kierkegaard literature with Kierkegaard.

One might well consider reflections of what might have happened if only Kant had done things differently so futile that they are not even worth mentioning if it were not for the fact that reading Hegel makes such questions almost inescapable. For the bizarreness of Hegel's philosophy is due largely to his misguided attempt to reconcile Goethe and Kant, and it is fruitful to separate out these two strains and see what remains when the Kantian elements are eliminated.

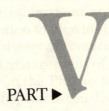

PART ▶ V

Hegel's
Three Conceptions
of Phenomenology ▶▶▶

37 ►►► Schopenhauer, who was probably, next to Hegel, the greatest philosopher of his time, called Hegel "this Caliban of the spirit."[1] He also spoke of "Hegel's philosophy of absolute nonsense (3/4 of it empty and 1/4 in [*sic*] insane notions."[2] *Aberwitzig* (insane) is a word that recurs often in Schopenhauer's remarks about Hegel, along with the assurance that Hegel had no *Geist* at all. Schopenhauer's attacks are very repetitive, and a single long sentence gives a good idea of their tenor:

> *Schelling* was now followed by a philosopher created by the ministry who, with political intent that, moreover, went askew, was certified as a great philosopher from up high—*Hegel*, a flat, witless, disgusting-revolting, ignorant charlatan who, with unexampled impudence, kept scribbling insanity and nonsense that was trumpeted as immortal wisdom by his venal adherents and actually

---

[1] *"Diesen geistigen Kaliban,"* in the Preface to the second ed. of *Die Welt als Wille und Vorstellung.*
[2] In the Introduction to *Über den Willen in der Natur.*

taken for that by dolts, which gave rise to such a complete chorus of admiration as had never been heard before.[3]

Few detractors of Hegel have gone so far, but while it is widely considered bad form to speak irreverently about Kant, disrespect for Hegel is still good form. Many writers and lecturers enjoy making scurrilous remarks about Hegel, while others—and sometimes actually the very same people—make use of his ideas without giving credit to him. Most Hegel scholars, however, ignore these facts and write about the master without as much as allowing for the possibility that he might have made important mistakes. The transitions in his books from one concept or stage to another are presumed to be necessary in some obscure way, and vast amounts of time are spent on discovering what does not meet the eye. As a result of this, much Hegel scholarship seems as mindless as Schopenhauer's total failure to grasp Hegel's genius. It is almost as if we were asked upon entering the world of Hegel scholarship to take leave of our understanding and to walk for once, to borrow one of Hegel's metaphors, on our heads.

Having exerted myself to rehabilitate Hegel and to reawaken interest in his philosophy after World War II, I am not quoting Schopenhauer by way of agreeing with him. But it seems to me that as we approach Hegel we should begin by facing the fact that there is something bizarre and almost incredible about his books. I aim to

[3] This incredible passage is worth quoting in the original, too: "*Auf* Schelling *folgte jetzt schon eine philosophische Ministerkreatur, der, in politischer, obendrein mit einem Fehlgriff bedienter Absicht, von oben herunter zum grossen Philosophen gestempelte* Hegel, *ein platter, geistloser, ekelhaft-widerlicher, unwissender Scharlatan, der, mit beispielloser Frechheit, Aberwitz und Unsinn zusammenschmierte, welche von seinen feilen Anhängern als unsterbliche Weisheit ausposaunt und von Dummköpfen richtig dafür genommen wurde, wodurch ein so vollständiger Chorus der Bewunderung entstand, wie man ihn nie zuvor vernommen hatte.*" *Parerga und Paralpomena* (1851), vol. I, sec. 13, p. 91f.

show that this grotesque quality was due in large measure to his attempt to reconcile Kant and Goethe. Specifically, Hegel's *Phenomenology of the Mind*—or *of the Spirit*—might have become one of the greatest contributions ever made to the discovery of the mind, if it had not been for Kant's disastrous influence. In many ways it is a bold, almost foolhardy book, and the conception underlying it was a work of genius inspired by Goethe. But Hegel was determined to produce a major philosophical treatise and felt that the only way of doing that was to follow in Kant's footsteps.

That the book is deeply at odds with itself and that the author is continually pulled in different directions was noted as long ago as 1857 by Rudolf Haym: "To say everything: the *Phenomenology* is *psychology reduced to confusion and disorder by history, and history deranged by psychology*" (p. 243). I tried to show in 1965 how "instead of mixing only history and psychology, Hegel offers us what Richard Wagner was later to call a *Gesamtkunstwerk,* leaving out little but music" (Section 30). But Haym was right in sensing an underlying dichotomy, though wrong in assuming that the basic duality was that of history and psychology. The fundamental conflict is between Kant and Goethe.

This conflict existed in Hegel's mind, and apart from it we cannot begin to understand his mentality. But the conflict did not exist in an inaccessible realm beyond the phenomenal world, behind Hegel's thought and books. I aim to discover Hegel's mind in his work and hope to show how his books and his thought are misconstrued as long as we fail to understand his mentality. This demonstration will take up the bulk of this chapter, and *Hegel's major contributions to the discovery of the mind will be considered only in the final section.*

The conflict between Kant and Goethe can be traced back to Hegel's earliest philosophical manuscripts, his so-called *Theologische Jugendschriften,* the theological, or rather antitheological pieces he wrote when he was in his twenties, in the 1790s. They were published only in 1907 by one of Wilhelm Dilthey's students, Hermann Nohl, after Dilthey himself had published a major work on this material, "The History of Hegel's Youth," the year before. Since the claim that the *Phenomenology* represents an attempt to reconcile Kant and Goethe might seem farfetched, I shall try first to show very briefly how these two divergent influences operated in the early manuscripts.

Goethe said, as we have seen, "Works of nature and art one does not get to know when they are finished; one must catch them in their genesis in order to comprehend them to some extent"; and in 1899 Otto Pniower inscribed this epigram on the title page of his book on Goethe's *Faust*. Dilthey might just as well have inscribed it on the title page of his *Jugendgeschichte Hegels* seven years later.

On the eve of World War II, in 1938, Theodor Haering published the second and last volume of his history of Hegel's development in which he required 1,300 pages to get to Hegel's first book, the *Phenomenology,* and stopped after devoting a few pages to it. Two years later, Hermann Glockner, the editor of a widely used edition of Hegel's works in twenty volumes, published the second and last volume of his supplementary work on Hegel, in the same binding and designed to go with the set; and it took him 1,000 pages to get as far as the end of the *Phenomenology,* and he devoted only a few pages to Hegel's later writings. Since the war, a veritable industry has developed around Hegel's early writings, not only those of the 1790s but also the abundant manuscripts of the immediately following years. One is sometimes led to wonder if these German scholars are determined to lead Goethe's dictum *ad absurdum*. But they have long departed from its spirit and are for the most part no longer interested in understanding the whole phenomenon of Hegel by way of his development; many of them could say with the scholar whom Nietzsche mocks in Part Four of *Zarathustra* that the motto of their conscientiousness is "Rather know nothing than half-know much!" Zarathustra asks this man whether his aim is to "pursue the leech to its ultimate grounds," and he retorts: "That would be an immensity; how could I presume so much! That of which I am the master and expert is the *brain* of the leech: that is *my* world. And it really is a world, too." Here Nietzsche echoes Goethe's mockery: "That is your world! A world indeed!" (*Faust*, 409).

Goethe's pointer about genesis and development has been taken up with a vengeance; but scholastics are after all scholastics, and from whatever motto they may start they sooner or later become microscopists. Hence it would not be fair to say that no major philosopher has suffered as much from Goethe's suggestion as Hegel. To be sure, Hegel's works have often been forgotten over the studious concern with their genesis and the study of his early manuscripts, but what is at fault is not the concern with development; it is rather the myopia that, not at all in Goethe's spirit, loses sight of the development to get bogged down in relatively trivial details.

Hegel himself saw fit to publish only four works: the *Phenomenology* (1807), the *Science of Logic*, which appeared in three volumes (1812, 1813, and 1816), the *Encyclopedia of the Philosophical Sciences* (1817), and the *Philosophy of Right* (1821). During the last ten years of his life he did not publish another book but thoroughly revised the *Encyclopedia* (second edition, 1827; third, 1830). All four works are of considerable interest, but the first two are unquestionably Hegel's masterpieces, and only the *Phenomenology* needs to be considered at length in connection with the discovery of the mind. The *Encyclopedia*, which contains Hegel's entire system in outline form, covers some of the same ground as the

Phenomenology, but only very briefly, and that part of it needs to be taken into account.

I shall also introduce a few passages from Hegel's introductory lectures on the philosophy of history, but there is no need here to try to deal with the whole system. It seems possible to illuminate both Hegel's role in the discovery of the mind and Hegel's own mentality and thus his philosophy as a whole by concentrating mainly on a single question: What was Hegel's conception of phenomenology?

38 ▶▶▶ Even so, something will be gained by first dealing very briefly with the starting point of Hegel's philosophical reflections, as this was different from what many people still suppose. The point is important but I have dealt with it in detail elsewhere.[4] Here we can concentrate on the most crucial points.

It has been remarked that every philosopher comes to philosophy either from science or from religion, which would seem to be false, as many have come to philosophy from both directions simultaneously, or rather from the conflict of religion and science, like Kant. But Hegel, although the word "science" is found in the titles of all his books,[5] came to philosophy from religion and, all his life long, sought in it a substitute for religion or, as he himself might have put it, that which transcends religion, that which is even higher and comes after it. Many philosophers after World War II are more interested in epistemology or the philosophy of language

[4] Kaufmann (1954); greatly enlarged version in Kaufmann (1959), chap. 8, also reprinted in MacIntyre (1972), chap. 3. See also my *Hegel* (1965) for a full-length portrait.

[5] For the *Phenomenology*, see below. The *Philosophy of Right* had two facing title pages of which the first read: *Naturrecht und Staatswissenschaft im Grundriss.*

and, when they deal with Hegel, are prone to project into him their own concerns. Others do the same with their own interest in politics and social questions. Yet Hegel's writings of the nineties, whether we call them theological or antitheological, leave no doubt whatsoever that his first concern was with religion and morality.

It is a commonplace that Hegel started out from Kant, which is true. But it needs to be added that he did not start from the *Critique of Pure Reason*. His starting point was Kant's *Religion Within the Bounds of Mere Reason Alone* (1793), and next to that his ethics. This was natural enough considering that Hegel was a student at the *Tübinger Stift* at that time, studying theology. Nor is it surprising that the publication of Schiller's reflections on "aesthetic education" in 1795, which dealt with some of Hegel's central problems, left a permanent mark on his thought.[6]

Like Schiller, Hegel had not been satisfied with Kant's book on religion. He was convinced by it that religion must not contain anything that goes against reason, but he wanted something more full-blooded than Kant's purely rational religion. His imagination was nourished on the Greeks, Lessing, Goethe, and Schiller, and he felt that morality was a matter of humanity, of being humane, and could not be divorced from feeling, art, and literature.

His earliest fragments deal with the possibility of a folk religion that would contain nothing offending reason. Under the influence of Goethe's and Schiller's classicism and his own enthusiasm for the Greeks, Hegel looked to ancient Greece for inspiration. His next experiment and first complete essay took the form of a life of Jesus in which everything miraculous and supernatural is stripped away and Jesus preaches Kant's mor-

[6] Kaufmann (1965), sec. 7.

ality. This was a sustained attempt to write a scripture for his folk religion. Two brief quotations suffice to show its tenor. Jesus says, for example:

> What you can will to be a universal law among men, valid also against yourselves, according to that maxim act; this is the basic law of ethics, the content of all legislation and of the sacred books of all peoples.
>   What I teach I do not offer as my ideas or property. I do not demand that anyone should accept it on my authority.... I subject it to the judgment of universal reason.[7]

This is rather grotesque; we should remember that Hegel himself did not publish his early manuscripts; and T. M. Knox omitted "The Life of Jesus" in his English version of Hegel's *Early Theological Writings.* But if a touch of the grotesque adheres to most of Hegel's writings, very much including his *Phenomenology,* we ought to ask whether this was not often due to his ill-advised attempt to follow Kant. To be sure, in the books Hegel published he criticized Kant's doctrines, including his moral philosophy, and Kant's influence is no longer so obvious.

No sooner had Hegel finished this *tour de force* than he wrote "The Positivity of the Christian Religion," also in 1795. This is an essay of considerable originality, a hundred years ahead of its time in its insistence that some of the flaws of Christianity, notably its authoritarianism, go back to Jesus himself. More than any of his other works, excepting only his humorous short article "Who Thinks Abstractly?"[8] the essay on the positivity shows us Hegel's native ability to write vividly, powerfully, and sardonically. Why, then, did he stop writing that way? Obviously, because he became convinced that serious philosophy had to be written in Kant's manner.

[7] Hegel (1907), pp. 87, 89.
[8] Included, complete, in Kaufmann (1965).

The basic philosophical stance in the essay on the positivity is still Kantian, but in his next major effort, which Nohl as editor entitled "The Spirit of Christianity and Its Fate," Hegel turned against Kant, projecting his own dissatisfaction with Kant's rigid moral law into Jesus' alleged dissatisfaction with the rigid Jewish law of his time. Instead of voicing Kant's moral doctrines, Jesus is now identified with Goethe's image of humanity. After picturing the spirit of Judaism in New Testament times in the darkest colors, with a brush steeped in Christian anti-Semitism, Hegel says, in words that come close to Nietzsche's formulations in *Twilight of the Idols:*

> A man who wished to restore the human being again in his totality could not possibly choose such a path [as Kant's] which only adds a rigid conceit to the human being's division against himself. Acting in the spirit of the laws could not mean for him acting from respect for duty and in contradiction to the inclinations; for in that case both parts of the spirit (of this division of the mind against itself one cannot speak in any other way) would no longer act *in* the spirit of the laws but against it . . .

Two pages later (p. 268) Hegel says in his discussion of the Sermon on the Mount: "The agreement of inclination with the law is of such a nature that law and inclination are no longer different; and the expression 'agreement of inclination and law' therefore becomes quite unsuitable."

The turn against Kant is palpable, and so is the desire for harmony and integration. But it might be thought that at this point Hegel discovered true Christianity or the original and undefiled spirit of Christianity. Actually, however, Kant's division of man against himself, like his belief in the "radical evil" of human nature, was derived from the New Testament. It was Paul who had written the Romans (7.15 ff): "I do not do what I want, but I do the thing I hate. . . . I know that nothing good dwells within me, that is, in my flesh. . . . For I do not do the good I want, but the evil I do not want is what I do." And according to the Gospels, Jesus had said: "The spirit is willing, but the flesh is weak."[9] This conception of man divided against himself can be traced back to Plato and beyond him to the Orphics; it is part and parcel of the notion of two worlds, which Kant revived. The world of the flesh and the inclinations is pitted against the realm of the spirit. What is usually called for is a triumph over *this* world and the flesh, or the inclinations.

In Paul there is a notion of harmony attained through faith, but his denigration of *this* world is emphatic and usually explained, no doubt correctly, in terms of his own confidence that this world was about to come to an end, or as the Revised Standard Version puts it, "the form of this world is passing away."[10] In his essay on the spirit of Christianity Hegel speaks of faith, but his conception of it is totally opposed to Paul's, and to the Lutheran and Calvinist traditions as much as to the Roman Catholic. Jesus, according to the young Hegel, "recognized kindred spirits" in those who had faith; for "with such complete trust in another human being, with such devotion to him, with such love which holds back nothing, only a pure or purified soul can throw itself into the arms of one equally pure. . . . Faith is the spirit's recognition of spirit; and only equal spirits can recognize and understand each other."

This is faith without transcendence, faith without another world, faith that precludes any notion that I am impotent filth while God alone is good and omnipotent. What Hegel here calls faith is love and trust between free spirits who are convinced of their essential equality. As I tried to show in 1954, it was Goethe's *Iphigenia* (1787) that inspired Hegel at this point.

[9] Mark 14.38, Matthew 26.41.
[10] I Corinthians 7.31.

In the last part of his essay on the spirit of Christianity Hegel dealt rather opaquely with fate and its reconciliation through love, and these pages, which are strikingly similar to parts of his later *Phenomenology,* read like reflections on the motto that Goethe later gave his play:

> *Every failing that is human*
> *pure humanity atones.*

The central theme of Goethe's play is that Orestes can be reconciled with fate and liberated from the furies without any divine intervention, simply by the humanity of his sister, Iphigenia.

It is a commonplace among Hegel scholars that the highly implausible discussion of brother and sister in Hegel's *Phenomenology* is based on Sophocles' *Antigone,* and the allusions are indeed unmistakable; but most scholars have not been as scandalized as they ought to have been that Hegel should have based such wild generalizations on one play. It hardly lessens this scandal, but it helps to explain Hegel, that he clearly also had in mind Goethe's *Iphigenia* and his own relationship to his sister who never married—and later committed suicide less than three months after Hegel's death. He may also have thought of Goethe's sister, Cornelia, who had married "under pressure, and against her will," and died at twenty-six, while giving birth to her second child; for it was no secret that "Her love of her brother was the only love vouchsafed her."[11]

In 1865 J. H. Stirling published a vast two-volume work under the title *The Secret of Hegel.* It was soon remarked that he had managed to keep the secret. Among scholars, however, it is still a well-kept secret that Hegel drew on his experience of life, on what he saw and what Goethe might have called *Anschauung.* Many scholars still proceed as if Hegel's *Phenomenology*

[11] Friedenthal, p. 27f.

had been developed out of pure concepts, although in the first decade of this century some editors began to point out in footnotes allusions to *texts*, like *Antigone*. But to have called attention to the fact that Hegel himself had a sister would have been considered most indelicate and unphilosophical. Why do Hegel scholars think that it is better to base sweeping generalizations about the relation of brother and sister on one ancient play than it is to base them on at least *two* plays as well as some personal experience?

Two points about the early manuscripts on religion should be kept in mind. First, it has often been remarked that Marxism functions in many ways like a religion. It has not been remarked that Marx unconsciously brought off the feat that Hegel had attempted unsuccessfully. In his earliest manuscripts Hegel sought to develop a folk religion that might supplant Christianity. In his mature work he gave up any hope of reaching ordinary folk but never ceased trying to develop a philosophy that would serve him as a surrogate for religion.

Secondly, Hegel found himself right from the start somewhere between Kant and Goethe. Initially, he put Kant's doctrines into Jesus' mouth and must have noticed how bizarre that was. Then he read Goethe's image of humanity into Christianity, and that did not seem so grotesque. But as he became a professional philosopher like Kant, he turned his back on the vigorous style of his early years and began more and more to emulate not only Kant's impossible style but also Kant's affectation of rigor. For although he agreed with Goethe that the history of science is science itself, he agreed with Kant that philosophy must emulate science and that this precluded formulation of likely hypotheses or bold conjectures and then weighing these against alternatives. Like Kant, he associated science with rigorous deduction, necessity, certainty, and completeness; and the more he claimed to be rigorous the more unreadable he became, as he veiled his overwhelming lack of rigor behind extreme obscurity.

39 ▶▶▶ We are now ready to ask about Hegel's conception of phenomenology. Today the term brings to mind Hegel no less than Edmund Husserl and his followers, and one may well wonder how similar Hegel's conception was to twentieth-century phenomenology. The early Husserl shared the determination of the early Hegel, expressed prominently in Hegel's preface to his *Phenomenology*, to make philosophy a rigorous science. Nevertheless, the similarity almost ends there, and one may hazard the guess that if Hegel's *Phenomenology* had been better known at the time, Husserl would not have used this word to designate his program and his school. For Hegel's *Phenomenology* is anything but scientific and not at all close to what Husserl had in mind.

Actually, the term "phenomenology" had been used before Hegel by J. H. Lambert, Kant, Herder, Fichte, and Novalis; and it was used after him, not in his sense, by Sir William Hamilton, Moritz Lazarus, and Ernst Mach, before Husserl used it.[12] But there is no need here to distinguish all the many meanings that have been associated with it. Hegel was the first to use the term in the title—or rather the subtitle—of a book. The original title page called the work *System der Wissenschaft* (system of science) in large print, followed by the author's name, which in turn was followed by three lines identifying Hegel, and it was only below all this that the words appeared in small print: "First Part: the Phenomenology of the Spirit," or "of the Mind"—*die Phänomenologie*

---

[12] See J. Hoffmeister's introduction to his edition of Hegel's *Phänomenologie* (1952), pp. vii–xxviii; also Hoffmeister (1955), pp. 463–65, R. Eisler (1913), p. 486, and H. Spiegelberg (1971), vol. I, pp. 7–19.

System

der

Wissenschaft

von

Ge. Wilh. Fr. Hegel,

D. u. Professor der Philosophie zu Jena, der Herzogl.
Mineralog. Societät daselbst Assefsor und andrer
gelehrten Gesellschaften Mitglied.

Erster Theil,

die

Phänomenologie des Geistes.

Bamberg und Würzburg,
bey Joseph Anton Goebhardt,
1807.

des Geistes. The book is usually cited as Hegel's *Phenomenology,* and I shall follow that practice.

None of Hegel's predecessors had established a single clear meaning for the term. Hegel, as I hope to show, wavered between at least three different conceptions of phenomenology; moreover, his *Phenomenology* attracted relatively little attention during the nineteenth century, and most of the writers who used the term after him did not associate it with him. Moritz Lazarus' crisp definition shows this at a glance, and Lazarus and H. Steinthal should at least be mentioned in a book on the discovery of the mind as they were cofounders of what they called *Völkerpsychologie,* the psychology of peoples. Lazarus' definition is offered in the second volume of his book *Das Leben der Seele* (1857: The Life of the Soul), p. 219: "Phenomenology is a descriptive portrayal [*eine darstellende Schilderung*], psychology an analytic explanation of the appearances of the life of the soul [or of psychic life: *des Seelenlebens*]." Phenomenology, Lazarus went on to say, "looks for the facts," psychology "for their causes and conditions." Husserl's later usage is much closer to Lazarus than it is to Hegel.

During the century when Hegel's *Phenomenology* was all but forgotten—and he himself was partly to blame for that, as we shall see—Eduard von Hartmann tried to accomplish in his own philosophy a synthesis of Hegel and Schopenhauer and called one of his own books *Phänomenologie des sittlichen Bewusstseins* (1879: Phenomenology of Moral Consciousness). But on the whole those who were interested in Hegel during the nineteenth century paid attention only to the later Hegel, not to his first book.

One might still suppose that the question about Hegel's conception of phenomenology must have arisen as soon as Husserl began to use the term for his new direction in philosophy. But initially Husserl's whole enterprise seemed to be so obviously antithetical to

Hegel's that people were interested in one or the other, if either, but not in both. Husserl had come from mathematics, and his conception of "Philosophy as a Strict Science" (in 1910 he published an important essay with the title, *Philosophie als strenge Wissenschaft*) was opposed as strongly as could be to metaphysics as well as to any attempt to approximate philosophy to psychology or history, religion or literature, or an analysis of culture. Like Kant, and almost totally uninfluenced by Goethe, Husserl craved apodictic certainty. (Initially he had thought of phenomenology as "descriptive psychology," but in 1910 he distinguished phenomenology from psychology, though he still insisted on being purely descriptive; he hoped to describe timeless essences.) If Husserl had been aware of Hegel's *Phenomenology*, he might not have chosen this term for his own philosophy. His discussions of "the transcendental ego" were certainly meant to bring to mind Kant.

Sartre created a new perspective when he entitled a long section of his first major philosophic work in 1943: "Husserl, Hegel, Heidegger." He had been deeply influenced by all three and thus made it necessary for students of the phenomenological movement that had been founded by Husserl to take note of Hegel because the French phenomenologists could not be understood without reference to Hegel.[13] Heidegger's essay on "Hegel's Concept of Experience," which deals with the beginning of Hegel's *Phenomenology*, is of no comparable importance and in any case did not appear until seven years later, in 1950.

Now it might still be assumed that once Hegel was considered in the context of Husserl's school, scholars must surely have dealt with his conception of phenomenology. But although Hegel himself was a

[13] See Spiegelberg.

generalist if there ever was one, generalism has fallen out of favor even among Hegel scholars, and professors who write about Hegel generally prefer questions of detail. They keep arguing about this section or that of the *Phenomenology* and scrutinize some argument or other but rarely ask what the book is all about or what Hegel meant by phenomenology.

To make matters worse, Hegel's own ideas about what he was trying to accomplish in his first book changed while he was writing it; he did not have any clear conception of phenomenology at the time; and the subtitle of the book was an afterthought. The half title on page 1 of the original edition still reads: "First Part. Science of the Experience of Consciousness." The interesting and important Introduction to the book was still tailored to *this* subtitle and did not contain any mention of phenomenology. Nor is that word mentioned or explained anywhere in the book, except for about three references to "the" or "this *Phenomenology of the Spirit*." That phrase puts in a rather belated appearance four pages from the end of the volume (on p. 762 of the original edition), and then also twice (on pages xxxii and xliv) in the ninety-one-page Preface which Hegel wrote in January 1807 after most of the book, which had been finished in October, had already been printed. In the six-page Table of Contents, which was added last of all, the Preface is divided into nineteen unnumbered sections with various headings that do not appear in the text, and here "The *Phenomenology of the Spirit*" appears twice. But this table obviously represents an attempt to impose on the unwieldy text an order that Hegel had not had in mind while writing it.

According to Goethe's dictum, we must consider the genesis of the work in order to comprehend it better (or, as he said, "to some extent"), and the story of the writing of the book is fascinating indeed. But I have recounted it elsewhere, making use of Haering's and Hoffmeister's lengthier treatments.[14] The most important point to note here is that the work was written in very much the same way as was Kant's *Critique of Pure Reason*, "in flight, as it were," without time enough for the author to reread what he was writing.

We may not feel that writing one's first book at thirty-six is rather late in life, but Hegel did. Schelling, his friend, was five years younger but had already published ten books and had won a place in the history of philosophy; Hölderlin, Hegel's closest friend during his early years, had become insane and his life's work was done; while Hegel, full of ideas, had merely published some articles that did not begin to give anyone a notion of what he really had to contribute. In the winter of 1805/06 he signed a contract with a publisher, and it was agreed that the first half of the book was to be printed by Easter 1806.

The similarities to Kant are striking. Again a much shorter book was contemplated at the outset, and the *Phenomenology* actually was meant to be the first half that Hegel committed himself to write in a few weeks. But Easter came around and Hegel still had no manuscript to send to the publisher who, never having been eager to publish the work in the first place, made very clear how he felt about this. Under enormous pressure, Hegel finally mailed him the first half of the *Phenomenology* from Jena on October 8. By that time, Hegel's most loyal friend, F. I. Niethammer—who had been the coeditor of Fichte's journal eight years earlier—had signed a commitment that he would pay for the entire printed edition if Hegel did not furnish the whole manuscript by October 18. Hegel barely managed to get off at least a few hundred pages ten days before the

[14] Kaufmann (1965), sec. 22–23. Further references, also to other authors, are given there.

final deadline and five days before Napoleon entered Jena, having just put an end to the Holy Roman Empire, founded in 800 by Charlemagne. When the eighteenth came around, Hegel wrote Niethammer that he had been advised "that such circumstances set aside all obligations" but that he would send the balance of the manuscript as soon as the mails left again; and he did. The long Preface was added in January. On February 5 a woman whom Hegel did not love in the least gave birth to his illegitimate son, who made Hegel's life even more difficult. In sum, the book was written under an immense strain; Hegel wrote it about as fast as anyone could copy it; and the conception of the book changed utterly while he was writing it.

Obviously, this is relevant to the question about Hegel's conception of phenomenology and also to more detailed problems about Hegel's arguments. Something written carefully and reconsidered again and again needs to be read very differently from something written at breakneck speed without any time out for self-criticism. And it is noteworthy that Kant and Hegel, who claimed to emulate science and promised their readers nothing less than certainty, wrote in the latter fashion.

Philosophers, however, continue on the whole to discount information about how these books were written as merely of biographical interest and obviously not philosophical. And the way in which such information is usually handled tends unfortunately to confirm this harmful and myopic prejudice. Otto Pöggeler, one of the two editors of *Hegel Studien,* published an informative article of more than sixty pages on the composition of the *Phenomenology* that is a case in point.[15] He says:

> It cannot be denied either that, independent of philological research, an immediate understanding [!] of great works takes place, an understanding that is not

[15] Pöggeler (1966), reprinted in Fulda and Henrich (1973), pp. 329–90.

wrong in despising the disintegrating [!] spirit of philology (it is through an understanding of this sort that thinkers like Marx and Heidegger have appropriated [!] the idea of the *Phenomenology* in a creative manner).

Actually, Hegel's *Phenomenology,* like his later works, represents a sustained attempt to show that immediate understanding is an oxymoron, like wooden iron. Hegel insisted that understanding cannot be intuitive but by its nature involves "mediation," study, and concepts. Pöggeler follows up his parenthesis with a cascade of questions—a rhetorical device borrowed from Heidegger—and one of them reads in part: "Couldn't there also be a philology that does not disintegrate"—*die nicht zersetzt,* that is not destructive? (p. 338).

The dichotomy of an immediate understanding and a destructive philology is spurious and at first glance simply does not make sense. One has to recall that this whole Heideggerian hermeneutic is theological in origin—a point that will be taken up in the chapters on Heidegger and Buber—and that both horns of this spurious dilemma are derived from the interpretation of the Bible. In that context it was widely felt that philology was destructive because it destroyed faith and, as practiced by the so-called Higher Critics, dissolved the texts into a mosaic assembled from different sources. Many of the pious therefore condemned any philological approach, as even Kierkegaard did, and claimed to have an immediate understanding of the text, without the benefit of scholarship or of even being able to read the Bible in the original. Martin Buber, of course, translated the Hebrew Bible into German and was a scholar, but his *I and Thou* offers what may well be the most popular and influential celebration of some sort of immediate understanding. It seems reasonable to postpone a detailed discussion of this whole complex of ideas until we get to Buber.

The danger of lengthy inquiries about the composition of Hegel's first book is certainly not that they destroy something. On the contrary, they get bogged down in such a wealth of minute detail that those interested in Hegel's conception of phenomenology are almost bound to dismiss them as irrelevant, the more so because Pöggeler, after another Heideggerian cascade of questions, says very modestly on the last page, in words that sound like an involuntary parody of Heidegger: "Thus we have at most clarified a few preliminary questions that relate to the question about the composition of the *Phenomenology*." Philosophers can hardly be blamed for feeling that while philologists are still arguing about all sorts of small preliminary questions, it is best to ignore them and to seek immediate understanding. But that is a pipe dream. Goethe and Hegel were right that the genesis of a work and its place in the author's development help us to understand it, provided that we do not get mired down in details and miss the connecting principle, the spirit.

It is interesting how little attention most scholars have paid to Hegel's Table of Contents although he is reputed to have been a master builder with considerable architectural skill. The *Phenomenology* is divided into eight parts, each headed by a Roman number and a title, beginning with "I. Sense Certainty; or the This and Opinion," and ending with "VIII. Absolute Knowledge." But the Table of Contents, unlike the text, lumps together I, II, and III under "(A) Consciousness," then inserts "(B) Self-consciousness" before IV, and finally lumps together the last four parts under "(C)" without any title. This last portion without a title comprises pages 162–765! For no good reason, it is subdivided into "(AA) Reason," "(BB) Spirit," "(CC) Religion," and "(DD) Absolute Knowledge," a series of headings that is totally pointless and redundant because they are simply inserted above, respectively, "V. Certainty and Truth of

Reason," "VI. Spirit," "VII. Religion," and "VIII. Absolute Knowledge." Moreover, these four headings are obviously not commensurate either with each other or with the preceding four headings. Art appears only under "(CC) Religion," "VII. Religion," "B: The Art Religion," which refers to the religion of the Greeks, and this is surely an eccentric way of dealing with art—or rather of not dealing with art very much. Nor are we offered any reasons why one of the eight chapters of the *Phenomenology of the Spirit* should be distinguished from the other seven by the heading "Spirit."

The Table of Contents was plainly a product of haste but casts some doubt on the author's claim that he had reached nothing less than absolute knowledge. The internal evidence suggests forcibly that the author finished the book in a state of confusion, that his conception of his own enterprise changed rather drastically in the course of writing, and then again after the whole manuscript, except for the title page, Contents, and Preface had been sent off to the printer. The idea of using the term "phenomenology" was an afterthought that came to Hegel only when the book was almost finished and much of it already in the printer's hands.

To add to the confusion, Hegel used "phenomenology" in an altogether different way when he published his system in outline form in his *Encyclopedia* in 1817, although he never repudiated his first book. In the second and third editions of the *Encyclopedia* "Phenomenology of the Spirit" even appears in the Table of Contents, as it did not in 1817, as one very small subpart of the system. Yet when Hegel died in 1831, he was working on a new edition of his first book and, as far as he got, made no substantial changes whatsoever.[16]

Thus the question about Hegel's conception of

---

[16] The least unimportant changes (all of them are microscopic) are indicated in Kaufmann (1965).

phenomenology turns out to be big and complex enough to be usable as a key to the study of his whole thought and development. But for our purposes it will be quite sufficient to deal briefly with seven questions.

1. What did Hegel say about phenomenology in the Preface of 1807?
2. How does the Introduction to the book illuminate his conception?
3. What did Hegel actually do in his *Phenomenology?*
4. What did Hegel say about phenomenology between 1807 and 1817?
5. What conception of phenomenology do we find in the *Encyclopedia?*
6. How, in view of all this, can we sum up his conception?
7. How did Hegel advance the discovery of the mind?

Some scholars may feel that each of these questions calls for a monograph. Yet such monographs must always stop short of telling us what really was Hegel's conception of phenomenology. It is amazing how remote the Hegel scholastics are from Hegel's spirit, and how little they have learned from him that what is philosophically fruitful is seeing quite a number of problems together.

40 ▶▶▶ What did Hegel say about phenomenology in the Preface of 1807? In the Table of Contents, as remarked earlier, the Preface is divided into nineteen unnumbered sections with subtitles. Each is followed by a page number, but they run on without break. The seventh is called "The Element of Knowledge," the eighth "The Ascent into This Is the Phenomenology of the Spirit," and the eleventh "In What Way the Phenomenology of the Spirit is Negative

or Contains What Is False." In the text, the term is introduced in the first sentence of section 8.[17]

It has often been claimed that Hegel's famous formulation of 1821, "What is rational, is actual; and what is actual is rational,"[18] was designed expressly to please the King of Prussia. Yet this idea is central in the Preface of 1807, long before Hegel took any special interest in Prussia—indeed, a few weeks after he had referred to Napoleon in a letter as "this world soul."[19] In sections 6 and 7 Hegel claims that

> The spiritual alone is the actual. . . . The spirit that, so developed, knows itself as spirit is science. . . . Pure self-recognition in absolute otherness . . . is the ground and basis of science or knowledge in general. The beginning of philosophy presupposes or demands that consciousness dwell in this sphere. But this sphere itself receives its perfection and transparence only through the movement of its becoming.

What Hegel is suggesting is that philosophy really begins only with Part Two, whereas the *Phenomenology of the Spirit* is merely Part One of the *System of Science* and no more than "the movement of its becoming" or, as we might say, the development that leads to it. Yet—and the last quoted sentence is Hegel's way of making much the same point Goethe made in the letter to Zelter—it is only by studying the genesis or development that we can comprehend the result.

Section 8 begins: "This becoming of science in general or of knowledge is what this *Phenomenology of the Spirit* represents as the first part of the same," which obviously refers to the fact that the *Phenomenology* was published as Part One of the *System of Science*. When

[17] The headings are listed in Kaufmann (1965), p. 367, and also inserted in the text at the proper places.
[18] *Philosophy of Right*, Preface.
[19] To Niethammer, Oct. 13, 1806. See Kaufmann (1965), chap. 7.

Hegel prepared the second edition, he deleted "as the first part of the same," clearly because Part Two had never appeared.

On the one hand, Hegel keeps insisting again and again that the beginning of philosophy presupposes the point of view reached only at the end of the *Phenomenology;* on the other, he would have us look at the *Phenomenology* as itself scientific and Part One of the *System of Science,* not merely as an introduction. The conception of the *Phenomenology* as an introduction is stated clearly in an unforgettable image in Section 7: While science (that is, Hegel's philosophy!) "demands of self-consciousness that it should have elevated itself into this ether," meaning "self-recognition in absolute otherness" or, in other words, the recognition that whatever is actual is spirit, "the individual has the right to demand that science should at least furnish him with the ladder to this standpoint." The *Phenomenology* is thus presented as a ladder on which the reader can climb up from the most unsophisticated "sense certainty" to the "ether" of "absolute knowledge." Yet Georg Lasson warned the readers of his excellent edition of the book in 1907, in his splendid hundred-page Introduction, that "it is a complete misunderstanding to see in the *Phenomenology* something like a propaedeutic for philosophy" (p. xcvii).

Obviously, the book fails as an introduction or propaedeutic, as it is one of the most difficult and puzzling works in the whole history of philosophy, and one may be tempted to feel that Hegel began by conceiving of the book as an introduction but then changed his mind as he wrote it and stuffed into it more and more of his philosophy. This is clearly what happened, but in Section 10 Hegel gives a reason for considering the *Phenomenology* itself as part of science and not merely an introduction. This passage is important and represents one of his three conceptions of phenomenology, which I propose to call *the scientific conception:* "The way in which the Concept of knowledge is reached thus also becomes a necessary and complete becoming. Hence this preparation ceases to be a fortuitous bit of philosophizing . . ."[20]

What is supposed to make the *Phenomenology* scientific and the first part of science is the alleged *necessity* of the steps that lead from the first stage to the last, and the account is moreover said to be *complete.* If it were not for these two points, Hegel himself would not consider the *Phenomenology* more than "a fortuitous bit of philosophizing" and an inept propaedeutic. The first section of the Preface bears the title "On Scientific Knowledge," and the second section begins:

> The true form in which truth exists can only be the scientific system of it. To contribute to this end, that philosophy might come closer to the form of science—the goal being that it might be able to relinquish the name of love of knowledge [in fact, "philosophy" means the love of *wisdom*] and be actual knowledge—that is what I have resolved to try.

Alas, Hegel always associated science (*Wissenschaft* in German) with knowledge (*Wissen*), and with certainty and necessity as well as system and completeness. That the Latin *scientia* (science) is also derived from a verb that means "to know" is by no means the most important point to be made on Hegel's side. The Preface is one of the greatest essays in the whole history of philosophy, and I have introduced my own translation of the whole of it, with a commentary on facing pages, with the testimonies of Rudolf Haym, Hermann Glockner, Herbert Marcuse, J. N. Findlay, and G. E. Müller who, for all their differences, seem to agree on that. Among the things that make it so interesting is Hegel's polemic

[20] Kaufmann (1965), p. 410 = (1966), pp. 52–54.

against romantic notions of philosophy as a matter of intuitions, brainstorms, aphorisms, fragments, or in one word as "fortuitous" (*zufällig*). Hegel's polemic is brilliant in places, and his plea for what used to be called holism and what is now called a systems approach is as worthy of consideration as it ever was. It is as opposed to the microscopism of ever so many analytic philosophers as it is to the romantics of Hegel's time, to Kierkegaard, and to many so-called existentialists. Nor is that all there is to Hegel's Preface.

The other main theme in it is the crucial importance of development, which is also voiced at the outset, in the first section: "For the subject matter is not exhausted by any aim, but only by the way in which things are worked out in detail; nor is the result the actual whole, but only the result together with its becoming."

A few sentences earlier, Hegel suggested that the difference between philosophies must be comprehended "in terms of the progressive development of the truth" and, very much in Goethe's spirit, employed a botanical metaphor, or rather example. The bud gives way to the blossom, and the blossom to the fruit, yet the plant is not to be identified with the result; it is "the result together with its becoming" or, in other words, the whole development. As Hegel put it, bud, blossom, and fruit—and different philosophical systems—are "elements of an organic unity in which they not only do not conflict, but in which one is as necessary as the other; and it is only this equal necessity that constitutes the life of the whole."

The point is very close to Goethe's dictum, published three years later in 1810, that "the history of science is science itself." We cannot here resolve the question of influence, but it should be kept in mind that Goethe often did not publish things until years after he had written them, that he was very free with his ideas in conversation, and that I have always tried to quote the best formulations without regard for their dates. Moreover, his memorable formulations are often ways of summing up in an epigram what he had previously demonstrated at length not only in his writings but also in his life.

It was from Goethe that his contemporaries, including Hegel, learned that Storm and Stress, classicism, and romanticism were not simply alternative styles but rather, like bud, blossom, and fruit, stages in a development, and that if you wanted to know Goethe it would never do to read only one of his masterpieces as that would only show you the poet at one stage in his development; to know Goethe, one had to study the whole development.

What is derived from Kant rather than Goethe is Hegel's insistence on necessity and certainty ("absolute knowledge," no less!); and in explaining why the *Phenomenology* was itself scientific he included for good measure the claim of completeness, suggesting that he covered *all* of the stages in the development and demonstrated their necessary sequence, instead of merely dealing "fortuitously" with stages of special interest to him. These are the claims that define the scientific conception of phenomenology; if they are untenable, then the scientific conception is untenable; and they are, and it is.

That Hegel could have made those three claims about necessity, absolute certainty, and completeness, in the Preface to the *Phenomenology*, instead of pleading extenuating circumstances for this book and explaining how it had actually come to be, remains astonishing even if we take into account mitigating circumstances that were still prevailing when he wrote this Preface. Hegel put up a brave front or, to use one of Nietzsche's favorite metaphors, donned a mask; and it remains amazing that many of his readers and nonreaders to this day still take the mask for his real face and think that the author slowly and painstakingly excogitated one after another necessary transition from stage to stage. In defense of Hegel one can only say that in the Preface he spoke more about what in his view needed to be done than about what he had in fact accomplished.

This interpretation makes his claims a little less grotesque, but it leaves them still untenable. A complete account of Goethe's development may be possible, but if the biographer limits himself to a single volume of the length of Hegel's *Phenomenology* he has to be selective and omit a great deal. Indeed, all comprehension depends on selectivity and discrimination. In Goethe's case, one could hardly omit the *Urfaust, Faust: A Fragment, Faust: The First Part of the Tragedy,* and finally Part Two; nor *Götz* and *Werther, Iphigenia* and *Tasso,* and the other major works mentioned above. But even in a volume of 800 pages one would have to leave out most of the material in the 143-volume edition of his writings; and one would *construct* a series of stages that, if one shared Hegel's bias, would give an impression of a single development that in retrospect seems purposive. But when the subject is no longer Goethe but *Geist* and one tries to write the *Bildungsroman* of the human spirit, the notion of completeness is grotesque.

It is understandable that in Hegel's time an educated person in the West should still have thought of human history as a single story leading, more or less, from the beginnings of humanity in the Near East (Egypt, Mesopotamia, and the Old Testament) to the Greeks, the Romans, and the Holy Roman Empire of the German Nation, which Napoleon vanquished the day Hegel finished his book. Again we can plead extenuating circumstances for a man of that time, though it stands to reason that any attempt to reduce that story to an account of something like 800 pages must involve relentless selectivity and a bold construction that makes nonsense of the claim of completeness. And today the very notion of reducing human history to some such single story no longer makes sense. A construction of that sort might still be fruitful in a certain context, but nobody in his right mind would think of offering it with the claim of completeness. What, for example, of Asia, Africa, and pre-Columbian America?

The same considerations apply to necessity and certainty. To begin with the latter, a construction of this sort cannot hope to be certain; at best it will be fruitful, suggestive, and illuminating. It may lead to new insights, new lines of research, and interesting comparisons. But it cannot claim to be certainly true. Here Hegel followed Kant (and, of course, Spinoza and Descartes, Aristotle and Plato).

It was also Kant who, probably more than anyone else, impressed on him the notion that what is scientific must be necessary, and that the business of philosophy is with the necessary. Again one can plead extenuating circumstances. Hegel was by no means the only writer after Kant to use "necessary" loosely as an inclusive antonym of "capricious," or "fortuitous," or "arbitrary." This bad habit is deeply ingrained among Germans. That makes it no less important to realize that Hegel systematically ignored the difference between demonstrating that an event was necessary and merely giving a reason for it that suggests that it was not completely fortuitous.[21]

Hegel's explicit and exoteric conception of phenomenology was what I have called the scientific conception of it, and this is untenable. It obstructed Hegel's discovery of the mind by keeping him from contributing as much as he might have done. Had it not been for Kant, Hegel might have emancipated himself from an unfortunate philosophical tradition. He might have revolutionized philosophy even more than he did. He might have regenerated it by taking his cue from

[21] See Kaufmann (1960), p. 158f., and (1965), sec. 17 and p. 371.

Lessing and Goethe while bringing to their legacy his solid training in philosophy. Of course, every such "might" invites ridicule: if the moon were made of blue cheese, everything might be different. But it is illuminating to see how in Hegel's writings two traditions are at war with each other and how he keeps trying to reconcile the irreconcilable—specifically, Kant and Goethe. Hegel had many brilliant ideas, to be considered in due course, but it was only long after Freud had published his *Interpretation of Dreams* that Hegel's *Phenomenology* began to attract much attention, and by then Hegel had missed the boat. People had ignored the book partly because it was so manifestly bizarre, and it is odd that most of its admirers today simply fail to see this grotesque aspect of the work. When I first studied it in 1942, perforce by myself, there was said to be only one professor in the United States who was interested in it (J. Loewenberg). Now that it has become fashionable, it is highly unfashionable to face up to this side of the *Phenomenology* though it really meets the eye.

The reasons for this are obvious. Those who find a major philosopher very implausible rarely bother to study him in depth, and those who specialize in his work almost invariably deny that he is really implausible in important ways. They are protecting their investment of time, energy, and effort.

41 ▶▶▶ How does the Introduction to the *Phenomenology* illuminate Hegel's conception? Here the word "phenomenology" is not mentioned because Hegel had not yet thought of this label when he wrote the Introduction. But he did say a few things that help us to understand why he liked the subtitle of the book when it did occur to him.

In a rather poetic passage he called "the path of the natural consciousness to true knowledge . . . the way of the soul that migrates through the series of its forms as so many stages prescribed to it by its nature so that it may purify itself and become spirit by attaining through its complete experience of itself the knowledge of what it is in itself."[22]

This is one of the loveliest images in the book; the metaphor of the transmigration of the soul is wonderfully apt; and the suggestion of a gradual refinement and growth of self-knowledge seems plausible. The idea that the soul becomes spirit is partially explained by the gloss that it gains "knowledge of what it is *in itself*," which means knowledge of what it is implicitly but, to begin with, not yet *for itself* or for its own consciousness. It is only at the end of the development that the soul comprehends what it was all along.

Hegel continues:

> The natural consciousness will show itself as merely the Concept of knowledge or not real knowledge. But insofar as it immediately takes itself for real knowledge, this path has a negative significance for it, and it takes for a loss of itself what is [in fact] the realization of the Concept [or a step forward toward eventual knowledge]; for on this path it loses its own truth [or finds that what it took for real knowledge was not real knowledge]. This path may therefore be viewed as the way of doubt [*Zweifel*] or really as the way of despair [*Verzweiflung*].

What happens at the first stage, to which Hegel alludes in this passage, happens again and again, or rather would happen at every stage if Hegel always succeeded in showing how the soul cannot gain the satisfaction it expected because in one way or another it deceived itself and is hence propelled onward to the next stage. The play on words which defies translation suggests that the recurring disappointment is not purely theoretical (doubt) but involves the whole human being (despair). A

[22] (1807), p. 9, end of 5th para.

few lines later Hegel adds: "The series of its forms [*Gestaltungen*] that consciousness passes through on this way is nothing less than the detailed history of the education [*Bildung*] of consciousness itself for science." What he proposed to write really was the *Bildungsroman* of the human spirit—a grandiose poetic conception that invites comparison with Goethe's *Faust*. This comparison would be worth spelling out at length here if I had not included a whole section on it in my *Hegel*.[23] Suffice it to say that we here confront *Hegel's second conception of the phenomenology of the spirit*, which I shall call the *poetic* one. As the scientific conception is derived from Kant, the poetic one was inspired by Goethe.

Near the end of the Introduction, Hegel says once more: "By virtue of this necessity this path to science is itself already science [a point we have discussed at length], and regarding its contents it is the science of the experience of consciousness." We recall that this was what Hegel was then still planning to call this part of his work, and that the half title that immediately precedes the Introduction in the original edition reads: "Science of the Experience of Consciousness."

Now this title and "The Phenomenology of the Spirit" are not synonymous. The former suggests a study of the contents of consciousness at each stage, while the latter suggests a study of the manifestations of the spirit. From the point of view reached in the end both labels are appropriate, but the justification of "The Phenomenology of the Spirit" becomes apparent only in the end when consciousness comes to realize that whatever is actual is spirit. Why did Hegel change the title, or rather the subtitle, at the last moment? Since he changed it only when he came to the end of the book, we must now turn to our third question.

[23] (1965), sec. 28.

42 ▶▶▶ What did Hegel actually do in his *Phenomenology?* In the original edition, Chapter I comprises about fifteen pages, Chapter II, twenty, and Chapter III, forty. In this part of the book, which the Table of Contents subsumes under the heading of "Consciousness," Hegel's approach is reminiscent of traditional theory of knowledge and constantly harks back to Plato and Aristotle.[24] Chapter IV, which the Contents subsumes under "Self-Consciousness," comprises sixty pages and is altogether different. In the first part we encounter Hegel's famous and influential reflections on master and slave, while the second part (B) deals in turn with stoicism, skepticism, and what Hegel calls the unhappy consciousness. None of this is very close to previous books of philosophy. The sketch of master and slave is very dense and compact, but as Hegel's illustrations gain a life of their own, like the characters of a novelist or dramatist, the presentation becomes more and more prolix, and soon Hegel becomes so absorbed in his constant allusions to the allegedly unhappy spirituality of medieval Christianity that one is led to wonder whether he has lost the thread.

It will have been noted that every chapter is longer than the preceding chapter (fifteen, twenty, forty, sixty pages). If the chapters had averaged about twenty pages each, then the whole first part of the system, even if it had comprised eight chapters, as the *Phenomenology* finally did, could easily have been printed in the same volume with the second part, as had been Hegel's plan when he started writing the book. But in Chapter V he got carried away entirely and dealt with "Certainty and truth of reason" in more than 210 pages, including, for example, twenty-eight pages on phrenology. Hegel's claims of scientific rigor and necessity become more and

[24] W. Purpus (1908) has dealt at length with Hegel's debts here to Plato and Aristotle.

more astounding as one reads on. One might compliment the author for being so full of surprises, so utterly unpredictable, so richly imaginative and irrepressibly *geistreich*, or ingenious, but hardly for the qualities on which, according to the Preface, everything depends.

Some scholars find the break between Chapters V and VI even greater than that between IV and V. Chapter VI, "Spirit," runs on for about 250 pages and deals at length with Greek ethical notions, largely in terms of rather fanciful allusions to *Antigone* but without attempting any analysis of that play or of Plato's or Aristotle's ethics. It deals at greater length with the alienation involved in modern life, with the Enlightenment, and with "the absolute freedom and the terror" of the French Revolution, before finally proceeding to a critique of modern *Moralität* and specifically of Kant's ethic.

When Hegel had reached this point (p. 624), any notion that all this might merely be the first half of a one-volume system in which Hegel's Logic would follow upon his Science of the Experience of Consciousness had become absurd. Indeed, the remaining two chapters simply could not become as long as V and VI, or any thought of publishing at least Part One, without the Logic, in a single volume had to be abandoned. One can imagine Hegel's own terror when he thought of his publisher's reactions. He managed to keep Chapter VII down to 115 pages, and the last chapter, "Absolute Knowledge," comprises just under twenty-five pages, if only because time ran out. But the book ends with a bang and not a whimper.

"The goal, absolute knowledge, or spirit that knows itself as spirit, is reached by way of the memory of the spirits as they are in themselves . . ." Hegel then contrasts history, whose domain includes the accidental, with his own "science" and concludes: "Both together, history comprehended, form the memory and the Golgotha [*Schädelstätte*] of the absolute spirit, the actuality, truth, and certainty of his throne, without which he [the absolute spirit] would be something lifeless and lonesome; only

> from the goblet of this realm of spirits
> his infinity foams up for him."

Looking back, all the forms of the spirit that have suffered shipwreck are suddenly seen as so many dead spirits whose skulls form the throne of the absolute spirit. But then this theistic image is turned around; the absolute spirit has no independent existence and would be lifeless without these spirits; their life is all the life he has, and it is only in the realm of so-called finite spirits that the absolute spirit possesses its own infinity. One could say very safely that the book ends with a poetic vision, even if the last two lines were not an adaptation of the last two lines of Schiller's early poem "Friendship" (*Die Freundschaft*).

Actually, Schiller had not included this poem in his own selection of his poems in two volumes (1800–03), but his brief introduction to the second volume shows how much the whole conception of the *Phenomenology* owed to him and Goethe and their whole way of thinking. Thus Schiller said,

> Even what is faulty signifies at least a stage in the education of the spirit [*eine Stufe in der Geistesbildung*] of the poet. The author of these poems has formed himself before the eyes of the nation and together with the nation, like all his fellow artists, nor does he know of anyone who ever was perfect when he entered. Thus he has no qualms about presenting himself to the public *all at once* in the form in which he has already *bit by bit* appeared before it.

The poem, too, is full of images and phrases that show how wrong it is to trace Hegel's ancestry only to other philosophers. But the powerful "only" that Hegel placed before his quotation was Hegel's own and not simply part of the quotation. The last stanza of Schiller's celebration of friendship says, if one may strip it of its rhymes (a,a,b,c,c,b) and meter:

> *Friendless was the great master of worlds,*
> *Felt a lack—and therefore created spirits,*
> *Blessed mirrors of his bliss!*
> *Though the supreme being found no equal,*
> *From the goblet of the whole realm of souls*
> *infinity foams for him.*

That the absolute spirit has its life *only* in the realm of spirits is a point introduced by Hegel. While Schiller spoke here of a realm of *souls,* he did have "spirits" in the second line, and "realm of spirits" in the first stanza. Indeed, spirits are mentioned repeatedly in this poem, and *Geist* and *Geister* were words constantly used by Goethe, Schiller, and Hölderlin. Goethe, of course, was the oldest and came first.

Since the term "phenomenology" occurs in Hegel's book only as part of the phrase "phenomenology of the spirit," and this was introduced only three pages before this finale, we need not hesitate to say that the change of the title from "Science of the Experience of Consciousness" to "Phenomenology of the Spirit" meant a move from Kant to Goethe and Schiller. "Science," "experience," and "consciousness" are terms that bring to mind Kant, while *Geist* is a poetic word with religious overtones that do not commit one to any religion, and "phenomenology" has a saving vagueness, particularly if one is as careful as Hegel was not to define it.

It would fit my theme in this book better if I spoke of "the phenomenology of *mind,*" and since this is also the title of the English translation by J. B. Baillie I could easily get away with that. But ever since my first article on Hegel in 1951—indeed, since my book on Nietzsche the year before—I have insisted that the best rendering is "spirit" because the religious and poetic overtones are so strong in Hegel, and in ever so many passages even Baillie has to have recourse to "spirit." "Phenomenology of the spirit" is the study of the appearances or manifestations of the spirit—and is thus closer to Goethe's *Faust* than to Kant's *Critique of Pure Reason*.

43 ▶▶▶ What did Hegel say about phenomenology between 1807 and 1817? Before anyone claims to understand Hegel better than he understood himself, he should consider how Hegel himself viewed his first book once he had finished it and saw it in print.

Reading the proofs, he wrote Niethammer on January 16, 1807: "I often wished, of course, that I might be able to clear the ship here and there of ballast to make it fleeter.—In the second edition, which is to follow soon—*si diis placet?!*—everything shall become better; this comfort I shall commend to myself and others." But it did not please the gods, and when Hegel finally began to prepare a second edition shortly before his death, two dozen years later, the revisions he made were, without exception, microscopic and in many instances anything but improvements.

A week later, Hegel wrote a former student, C. G. Zellmann:

> ... Science alone is theodicy: it keeps one both from looking at events with animal amazement or ascribing them more cleverly to accidents of the moment or of the talents of one individual—as if the destinies of empires depended on an occupied or not occupied hill—and from lamenting the triumph of injustice and the defeat of right.

Hegel's insistence on demonstrating some *necessity* in his work was not inspired solely by a dubious conception of rigor; it was also born of deep suffering.[25]

[25] See Kaufmann (1965), secs. 12 and 60–62.

When he spoke of elevating philosophy to the status of a science what he had in mind was by no means least of all a surrogate religion or, as he put it in this letter, a theodicy. Literally, it was not a question of justifying God, at least not a transcendent deity that dwells above the world; but what Hegel sought in philosophy, and in his *Phenomenology*, was a view, a demonstration that would reconcile him to the misery of humanity by showing that all the suffering had not been pointless. As he put it later in his introductory lectures on the philosophy of history:

> But even as we contemplate history as this slaughter bench on which the happiness of peoples, the wisdom of states, and the virtue of individuals have been sacrificed, our thoughts cannot avoid the question *for whom, for what final aim* these monstrous sacrifices have been made.[26]

A manuscript written half a dozen years before the *Phenomenology* is also relevant. In 1800 Hegel had attempted to rewrite his essay on the positivity of the Christian religion but had not got beyond drafting a new preface. Here he condemned such demonstrations as his own in his earlier draft, which had traced positive or authoritarian doctrines and commandments in Christianity, as "horrible blabbering" that has become "boring and has altogether lost interest—so much so that it would rather be a need of our time to hear a proof of the opposite. . . . Of course, the proof of the opposite must not be conducted with the principles and methods" of what Hegel called

> the old dogmatics. Rather, one would have to deduce this now repudiated dogmatics out of what we now consider the needs of human nature and thus show its naturalness and its necessity [even then Hegel operated with the spurious dichotomy of the totally fortuitous and the nec-

[26] Hoffmeister's ed. (1955), p. 79f.; Kaufmann (1965), p. 256.

essary!]. Such an attempt would presuppose the faith that the convictions of many centuries—that which the millions, who during these centuries lived by them and died for them, considered their duty and holy truth—were not bare nonsense or immorality.[27]

Hegel was never very clear about what precisely he meant by dialectic. He did not use that term nearly as often as most people suppose, and he did not claim to have a dialectical method.[28] When he used the adjective "dialectical" it was usually followed by the word "movement." Roughly, a dialectical movement leads from one extreme to another or, as the matter is usually put, from one thing to its opposite. (Hegel never once construed what he did in terms of thesis, antithesis, and synthesis, but he did sometimes speak of "the opposite.") Here we have a crucial instance in his own development where he moved from one position to its opposite, and it is palpable that the movement involved a spurious dichotomy. Obviously, something can be neither "bare nonsense or immorality" nor necessary.

What I am trying to show is that Hegel's views are not bare nonsense, that an effort at sympathetic understanding can succeed, that one can discover what he was driving at and what influences were at work in his mind; but it does not follow that I have any wish to prove the "naturalness and necessity" of his views. Nobody could do that! Of course, one could try to show that it "was only natural" or that "it figures" that a man influenced by Kant and Goethe should come up with what we find in Hegel, or that a man who has written a long manuscript criticizing Christianity should get bored with that and feel that what was really needed now was just the opposite, a reinterpretation of Christianity. In Berlin *is' ja logisch*, "it's logical," is an idiom like "it figures." But in

[27] Nohl's ed. p. 143; Kaufmann (1960), p. 158.
[28] Kaufmann (1965), sec. 37.

a philosophical analysis one ought to keep in mind that this is an exaggeration. There is no necessity. Hegel's confusion about necessity is rooted in a psychological confusion, in a troubled and confused state of mind, in his need for what in his letter to his former student he calls a theodicy.

One other psychological factor is at work here that helps to account for the wide appeal of Hegel's confused use of "necessity." Why, we must ask, does this simple error cast such a powerful spell? Why are most Hegel scholars so reluctant to face up to Hegel's error and be done with it? And why has it captivated millions by way of Karl Marx? Elsewhere (1973) I have given a detailed analysis of men's dread of fateful decisions, which I call *decidophobia*, and have distinguished ten typical strategies, including moral rationalism and the faith that one is riding the wave of the future. Hegel furnishes a typical example of a man filled with anxiety by the notion of the fortuitous and accidental. In his more rational moments he realized that all he could hope to show was that various developments were not totally capricious, that there were some reasons for them, and that one could *construe* them as organic. But his central stance called for much more. "Science alone is theodicy"! Nothing less than necessity would do. Ultimately, Hegel's insistence on a rigor that he himself failed utterly to exemplify and his affectation of deductions that he obviously came nowhere near accomplishing were rooted in decidophobia. Like Kant, Hegel was afraid of uncertainty and insecurity (*Unsicherheit*).

Any study of the *Phenomenology* ought to begin with the admission that the book is grotesque and that the author, who could write a life of Jesus in which Jesus spouts Kant's formulas, had a flair for the grotesque but lacked the courage to develop his natural talents and tried to force himself into a mold that did not fit. One only needs to read his essay on positivity and "Who

Thinks Abstractly?" to realize that the style he affected in his philosophical works was neither natural nor necessary for him—except as a defense mechanism, a mask, a device born of fear of himself.

A mask? Does that mean that the style is a cloak that could be removed, as if content and form were entirely separate? No, the masks men use are not altogether inorganic and cannot be exchanged easily for other masks. The concept of the mask is so important for the discovery of the mind that it will have to be considered at length in connection with the writer who first gave it a central place in his philosophy—Nietzsche. Here it must suffice to note that Hegel with another mask would not have been the Hegel we know. This does not involve any retraction on my part: Hegel liberated from his fear of himself would not have been the Hegel we know. He would not only have written better, he would also have thought differently!

To Hegel scholars this may sound like sacrilege, and other philosophers are apt to be apprehensive about such an approach, too. Where would it leave them? But one of Hegel's and Hölderlin's friends, Isaak von Sinclair (whose last name Hermann Hesse used as a pseudonym when he first published *Demian* in 1919), wrote Hegel frankly that, trying to read the *Phenomenology*, he had got lost in Chapter IV. "You seemed to me to be diverted into a point of view that is too historical and even, if I may express myself this way, too pathological, where you were guided more by your gift of combination than by the calm observation that prevailed in the beginning."[29] That is surely a very tactful and kind way of putting it. When Hegel wrote Schelling about the book, May 1, 1807, he was full of apologies and spoke of the "unfortunate confusion . . . that has affected the whole process of publishing and printing, and in part even the

[29] Pöggeler (1966), p. 336f.

composition itself. . . . Getting into the details has damaged, as I feel, the synopsis of the whole," and more in the same vein.

On October 28, 1807, Hegel's advertisement for himself appeared in the Jena cultural supplement. Such *Selbstanzeigen* usually appeared before the book, but Hegel's one-page description of the *Phenomenology* was delayed.

> . . . The Phenomenology of the Spirit is to replace psychological explanations [Hegel was to change his mind about this] as well as the more abstract discussions of the foundation of knowledge [presumably meaning Kant and Fichte]. It considers the *preparation* for science from a point of view which makes it a new, an interesting, and the first science of philosophy. It includes the various *forms of the spirit* as stations on the way on which it becomes pure knowledge or absolute spirit. . . . The wealth of the appearances of the spirit, which at first glance seems chaotic, is brought into a scientific order which presents them according to their necessity. . . . A *second volume* will contain the system of *Logic* as speculative philosophy, and of the other two parts of philosophy, the *sciences* of *nature* and the *spirit*.[30]

Every advanced student of Hegel knows that the second volume never appeared and that the *Science of Logic* alone took up three volumes when it finally appeared in 1812, 1813, and 1816. Yet it is noteworthy how the *Encyclopedia*, published in 1817, fits the description of Volume 2 and how easily it could have been presented that way. The fact that Hegel chose not to do this suggests that he no longer felt comfortable with the *Phenomenology*, and he actually called one small part of the *Encyclopedia* "phenomenology" and placed it below, not above, psychology, which it was obviously no longer intended to "replace."

[30] Complete translation in Kaufmann (1965), p. 366.

Encyklopädie

der

philosophischen Wissenschaften

im Grundrisse.

Zum Gebrauch seiner Vorlesungen

von

D. Georg Wilhelm Friedrich Hegel,

Professor der Philosophie an der Universität
zu Heidelberg.

Heidelberg,
in August Oswald's Universitätsbuchhandlung.
1817.

Encyclopädie

der

philosophischen

Wissenschaften

im Grundrisse.

Zum Gebrauch seiner Vorlesungen

von

Dr. Georg Wilhelm-Friedrich Hegel,

ordentl. Professor der Philosophie an der Universität
zu Berlin.

Zweite Ausgabe.

HEIDELBERG.
Druk und Verlag von August Oßwald.

1827.

Hegel's frequent changes in sequences that are supposed to be "necessary" make a mockery of the way he has all too often been read. Comparisons of the *Phenomenology* with the *Philosophy of Right* or of the *Science of Logic* with the corresponding portion of the *Encyclopedia* or even of the second edition of Volume I of the *Science of Logic* with the first or, finally, of the three editions of the *Encyclopedia* show how Hegel kept changing his sequences. Of course, there is not the slightest objection to that. On the contrary, it does him credit that he kept thinking about his ideas after he had published them and that he was never satisfied with his work. But every sequence was presented by him as if it were necessary, and he did *not* consider it necessary to explain why he had changed the sequence. Obviously, all the talk about necessity cannot be taken seriously, and all Hegel really tried to offer each time was an especially plausible *construction*. Certainty and necessity were out of the picture, nor was what he offered very rigorous. It was more like a series of thought experiments, but unfortunately conjectures and constructions, hypotheses and experiments, had no place in his conception of science.

It was actually a very peculiar experiment that led Hegel to revise his conception of phenomenology between 1807 and 1817. In 1808 he had moved to Nuremberg to become the headmaster of a boys' secondary school (*Gymnasium*), and he decided to teach the boys some philosophy. During his first year there "he wanted to teach pneumatology or doctrine of the spirit together with logic as a kind of introduction to philosophy; he divided this pneumatology into . . . phenomenology and psychology. A surviving disposition shows that initially he meant to present his whole *Phenomenology*, but he subsequently broke off at some point in the chapter on Reason—evidently because [surprise!] the students were not able to follow him. During the following years he limited Phenomenology to" the first five[31] of the eight chapters, finishing with Reason and omitting Spirit as well as Religion and Absolute Knowledge.

Obviously, the unsuitability of the *Phenomenology* for teenage students need not have changed Hegel's mind about the book. But in fact it did prove to be a turning point, and it helped to precipitate the birth of the third conception of phenomenology, which we encounter in the *Encyclopedia* in 1817.

44 ▶▶▶ What conception of phenomenology do we find in the *Encyclopedia?* The *Encyclopedia*, though published by Hegel himself, is not a full-fledged book in the same sense as the *Phenomenology* and *Science of Logic*. It is, like *The Philosophy of Right*, essentially an elaborate syllabus that was intended to meet the requirement of the ministry of education that every course must be based on a textbook. Naturally, Hegel did not want to use a text written by someone else. When he finally obtained a professorship at Heidelberg, he therefore quickly wrote the *Encyclopedia* as a text that could be used in any course he would give. It contained his whole system in outline form, arranged in 477 consecutively numbered sections on 288 uncrowded pages. Many sections begin with a brief statement that is then elaborated in an indented paragraph that far exceeds the opening statement in length. The whole was designed, as is stated clearly but not very elegantly on the title page—also of the second and third editions—"For the Use of His Lectures" (*Zum Gebrauch seiner Vorlesungen*). *The Philosophy of Right* has a similar notation on the title page. The point was that his students could in this way gain a general idea of

---

[31] Pöggeler (1966), p. 330f. slips in speaking of "the first three chapters," so strong is the hold of triads on the minds of Hegel's interpreters!

what Hegel was up to, an overview that would keep at least some of them from getting lost in details, while Hegel himself could use the book by asking his students to turn to such and such a section and then discuss it at length.

Hegel used the *Encyclopedia* in this way for ten years, then issued a radically revised edition, comprising 574 sections on 534 pages, in 1827, and a third edition, again radically revised, in 1830, a year before he died. It is to Hegel's credit that he kept revising his system and made as many changes as he did. It is also understandable that, having once published his system in outline form, he did feel some commitment to it and hence did not make more changes, nor called attention to the changes by producing arguments to back them up. Hegel scholars have for the most part ignored what his son said when he edited the second posthumous edition of his father's lectures on the philosophy of history. Rebuking "those who identify the rigor of thought with a formal schematism," Karl Hegel pointed out "that *Hegel clung so little to the subdivisions he had once made that he changed them every time he gave a course.*"[32] Of course, that does leave the question where the vaunted rigor is to be found and what precisely is supposed to be necessary when the transitions from one subdivision to the next obviously are not.

The reasons for the new place of phenomenology in Hegel's system were plainly pragmatic. The *Phenomenology* had been intended as an introduction to the system and a ladder on which one could climb up to the point of view from which the Logic was to be studied, but when teaching teenage boys Hegel discovered that it did not work very well as an introduction. Of course, it might still have been a good introduction for more advanced students, but Hegel evidently no longer

[32] Kaufmann (1965), sec. 53. For the quotation see p. 234. Italics added.

felt that it was. If he had called the *Encyclopedia* Part Two, he would have implied that one could not very well tackle it until one had read the *Phenomenology* first. On the other hand, Hegel had found it worthwhile to teach parts of the first chapters of the *Phenomenology* and hence wished to include these in outline form in his syllabus and hence had to find a place for them. But the best place, not to say the most logical place, was not at the beginning, before the brief outline of the Logic, nor obviously in the Philosophy of Nature that followed; it had to be somewhere in the last part, the Philosophy of Spirit.

Omitting a few subheads, this is the way Hegel subdivided his Philosophy of Spirit in the edition of 1817:

First Part. *Subjective* spirit
   A. *Soul*
   B. *Consciousness*
      a. Consciousness as such
      b. Self-consciousness
      c. Reason
   C. *Spirit*
      a. *Theoretical* spirit
      b. *Practical* spirit
Second Part. *Objective* spirit
   A. *Right* [or Law: *Das Recht*]
   B. *Morality* [à la Kant: *Die Moralität*]
   C. *Ethics* [à la Goethe and Schiller: *Die Sittlichkeit*]
Third Part. *Absolute spirit*
      a. Religion of art [Greek religion; art was still omitted!]
      b. Revealed religion
      c. Philosophy

Such little incongruities as using small *a*, *b*, and *c* in the final part, where symmetry would call for capitals, are not only found in the original Table of Contents as well as the text but were never caught by Hegel even in the third edition. But as of the second edition the title and

contents of *a* was changed to Art, and that part of Hegel's system, particularly in the form of his lectures on aesthetics, is still widely regarded as one of its strongest points. The subdivisions of *Sittlichkeit*, which should be preceded by *a*, *b*, and *c*, are actually preceded in the last edition by *AA*, *BB*, and *CC*, suggesting that Hegel kept trying out different arrangements without a perfectly clear view of the whole.

The *Phenomenology* of 1807, of course, had represented an attempt to cover the whole Philosophy of Spirit. In the system of 1817, however, the opening paragraph of "*Subjective* spirit," which precedes "A. *Soul*," suggests how phenomenology can be fitted into the system:

> Subjective spirit is a) the immediate spirit or *spirit of nature*—the subject of what is usually called *athropology* [*sic*] or the *soul;* b) spirit as identical reflection into itself and into what is other, *relation* or specification; *consciousness*, the subject of the *phenomenology* of the spirit; c) *the spirit that is for itself* or spirit as *subject;* the subject of what is usually called *psychology*.

It is easy to imagine Hegel lecturing on this section (307), trying to explain it to his students; but it remains a dreadful muddle for all that. We are asked to believe that the study of the soul is usually called anthropology, while the study of the spirit as subject is usually called psychology, and the phenomenology of the spirit is said to deal with consciousness. Since he had written a whole book on the phenomenology of the spirit, one might have expected Hegel to explain at least briefly why he had changed his mind about it and now meant something altogether different when he used this term. But while Hegel remained open-minded enough to keep changing his mind, he wore the mask of absolute knowledge and refused to mention that he had changed his mind, let alone explain why. And his students obviously did not dare to point out to him even the most trivial slips, not to speak of what looked like major contradictions.

Down through the reflection on master and slave, the highly condensed paragraphs on Consciousness in the *Encyclopedia* of 1817 bear some relation to the *Phenomenology* of 1807; but stoicism, skepticism, and the unhappy consciousness are no longer mentioned and Reason, to which Hegel had devoted almost 250 pages in 1807—almost twice as much space as he had allotted to the preceding four chapters taken together—is now covered in half a page. Reason, moreover, is thus taken up before, and in some sense below, psychology!

Another ten years later, in the second edition of 1827, a great deal is changed in the *Encyclopedia*. But in the outline given above, Hegel made only two changes. He substituted Art for the Religion of Art, and the three divisions of Subjective Spirit are now A. Anthropology, B. Phenomenology, and C. Psychology. In the third edition, in 1830, he made one further change. Psychology, which in the second edition still had only two subdivisions, is finally promoted to equality with all the other subheads of the Philosophy of Spirit by the addition of c. The free spirit after theoretical and practical spirit.

Thus Hegel's final conception of phenomenology needs to be distinguished from both the scientific and the poetic conception. One might call this one *the restricted or the* Encyclopedia *conception,* but it represents a terrible anticlimax and can safely be ignored, as indeed it has been. My reason for calling attention to it at some length is that while it contributes nothing to the discovery of the mind, this episode helps greatly to illuminate Hegel's mind, and one of the central themes of this study is the attempt to discover the minds of the major figures we consider here. Hegel's mind was clearly very different from what has been generally assumed.

Dritter Theil.

Die Philosophie des Geistes
§. 377 — §. 577.

45 ▶▶▶ How, in view of all this, can we sum up his conception? If Hegel had really been the systematic philosopher he is widely supposed to have been, the way in which he worked phenomenology into his system should obviously take precedence over the book of 1807. Yet scarcely anybody today would consider that a reasonable suggestion. For phenomenology, about which he had thought so long, was obviously incorporated into his system in an ill-considered and arbitrary fashion that requires explanation in pragmatic terms and cannot be justified in terms of any conceptual necessity.

In sum, not only the scientific conception of phenomenology maintained *by* Hegel in his first book but also the scientific conception *of* Hegel that is still popular is utterly untenable. In 1951 I published an article, "The Hegel Myth and Its Method," attacking Hegel's detractors in general and Karl Popper's caricature of Hegel in particular. That attack met with rare success and, along with my subsequent work on Hegel, helped to bring about what is now sometimes called the American Hegel renaissance. J. N. Findlay's *Hegel*, published in England in 1958, played an important role in this development, too. But what proved most important was the explosion of interest in Marx and the paucity of philosophical material in Marx, which forced those with philosophical interests to concentrate on Marx's early manuscripts, which were written when he was still very much preoccupied with Hegel and which were not rich enough philosophically for philosophers to stay with them. Now the renewed interest in Hegel is an international phenomenon and keeps being fed by interest in Marx.

Here I am in effect attacking another Hegel myth, the notion that he was a rigorous or scientific philosopher. The present chapter is of a piece with my book on Hegel, but that was not designed to prove or disprove some one thesis. It was an attempt at a full-length study. Now I am trying to drive home some striking conclusions.

The first of these concerns much Hegel scholarship. After Hegel's death his students interlarded selections from their lecture notes into the third edition of the *Encyclopedia* and thus transformed it into a three-volume work that few people could ever be expected to read through. More recently a very erudite English translator has taken the second and shortest of the three major parts of the *Encyclopedia*, the Philosophy of Nature—less than eighty pages in the original edition and 160 in the third edition—and by adding notes and commentaries has made of that alone three volumes. It is easy to appreciate so much devotion as well as the additions to our knowledge; but it has become more and more difficult and hence unusual for anyone to recall the fluidity of Hegel's thought and to experience his ideas as he experienced them.

The trouble with much recent scholarly and editorial work is not that such work is destructive and dissolves what was whole, as Pöggeler has suggested, but rather that it freezes what was fluid. Fleeting thoughts and doubtful notions that pass through a great mind and are put on paper to be reexamined in the light of day (Nietzsche's case), or words once spoken in a lecture and perhaps not even recalled by the speaker afterwards, or even phrases that were heard wrong find their way into volumes in which they do not look any different from ideas that were carefully considered (Hegel's case).

This process began with Hegel himself. He wrote his *Phenomenology*, and later also his *Encyclopedia*, under circumstances and pressures that did not allow for much weighing of words or reexamining whole passages and indeed the overall arrangement, and especially in his first book he came to write at such a pace that he put fleeting thoughts and doubtful notions down on paper and then had to send them to the printer without any opportunity to rethink what he had written.

This makes a mockery of the scientific conception of phenomenology. It may be objected that although Hegel's book falls far short of that, the conception remains noble and superior to the book he actually wrote. But any such claim depends on one's ability to show that *any* single series of stages leading from sense certainty to absolute knowledge *could* be shown to be complete and necessary. I have tried to show why no such series could possibly be necessary and complete.

That leaves us with the poetic conception. Opponents of this conception may plead that it is not "philosophical" and rigorous enough.[33] Before I offer my own reply to that, it may be of some interest to note that Friedrich Engels offered some brilliant formulations that go very well with my view. I am under no illusions that his agreement could prove me right, but he put the matter so well that it would be a shame to ignore his formulations.

First having read that William Thomson had called a book by a French mathematician a mathematical poem, Engels jotted down, in English: "Hegel a dialectical poem."[34] "Science," in other words, can be poetic (shades of Goethe)—and on the facing page Engels vilified Newton. Three of Engels' letters to Conrad Schmidt are also pertinent. Speaking of one of Hegel's critics, he writes:

> To suppose that he is criticizing Hegel when he tracks down one of the false leaps that H, like any other systematic thinker, has to use to construe his system! The colossal discovery that H sometimes confounds contrary and

[33] See, *e.g.*, Klaus Hartmann (1972), p. 399.
[34] *Werke*, vol. 20, p. 477 (*Dialektik der Natur: Notizen und Fragmente*).

contradictory opposition! I could show him far worse tricks if that were worth the trouble! He is, as we say in the Rhineland, a raisin-shitter; he transforms everything into minutiae; and as long as he does not get over this habit he will, to speak with Hegel, "come from nothing through nothing to nothing."[35]

The second letter, dated November 1, 1891, is similar:

Under no circumstances should you read Hegel the way Herr Barth has read him, namely in order to discover the paralogisms and rotten tricks that serve him as levers of construction. That is work for schoolboys. What is much more important is to discover under the incorrect form and in the artificial context what is correct and bears the marks of genius. Thus the transitions from one category or one opposite to the next are almost always arbitrary— and often accomplished by means of a joke, as when positive and negative in section 120 *zugrunde gehn* [perish] to enable Hegel to reach the category of the *Grund* [ground]. To subtilize about that is a waste of time.

The third letter, February 4, 1892, makes much the same point and concludes: "In every language one would have to do this differently. Just try to translate the sequence in the Doctrine of Essence into another language, and most of the transitions become impossible."

All this is indeed a scandal, but one cannot diminish it by claiming that Hegel really was rigorous after all. At first glance, of course, the poetic conception seems soft compared to the tougher scientific conception. It is widely felt nowadays that a philosopher should be satisfied with nothing less than solid arguments. But anyone who knows what a rigorous argument about *Antigone* or

---

[35] July 1, 1891, *Werke,* vol. 38, p. 129. The Rhenish word is *Korinthenscheisser.*

Sittlichkeit would look like must retort that no "scientific" interpretation of the *Phenomenology* could possibly be tough or rigorous. On the contrary, any such reading must depend on an extremely feeble conception of "science," rigor, and argument. One simply has to put on blinders and immerse oneself in carefully selected details to avoid the discovery that the book is utterly unscientific and lacking in rigor.

It does not follow that the book is therefore not philosophical. I have a tough conception of rigor and solid arguments but not of philosophy. A great deal of philosophy has been utterly lacking in rigor, and what troubles me is not that but the widespread failure of philosophers, including Kant as well as Hegel, to realize this and their affectation of a rigor that is not there.

Consider three memoirs, inspired by great love and admiration for two very remarkable recent philosophers who might almost be called patron saints of analytical philosophy. George Pitcher observes in his memoir of J. L. Austin, to whom he had dedicated his first book, which was on Wittgenstein:

> I was ready to follow him to the moon. There were others, too, just as willing. Ideally, perhaps, this effect should have been brought about by means of overwhelming philosophical arguments, but in fact it was not, for Austin produced none. Indeed, I cannot recall anything I ever heard, or read, of Austin's that contained a straightforward, old-fashioned philosophical *argument*. . . . It is certain that we would not have reacted . . . as we did but for the quite extraordinary . . . authority that seemed uncannily to still all critical doubts while he spoke . . .[36]

Wittgenstein's *Tractatus* is a stunning example of an affectation of rigor. The wealth of symbols and the way

[36] *Essays on J. L. Austin* by Sir Isaiah Berlin *et. al.* (Oxford, 1973), p. 20f.

the propositions are numbered to indicate their precise weight gives the unwary reader the impression that everything is proved beyond a doubt, although in fact we are offered an often capricious sequence of aphorisms. Despite Wittgenstein's towering reputation for integrity, it is hard to escape the conclusion that he and Austin used the immense authority of their personalities and their very superior intellects to "still all critical doubts." One did not dare; one was intimidated. Austin's manner was different from Wittgenstein's, and both men were very different from various German professorial types, but what they had in common with many German professors was that certain questions—including many of the most important critical questions—simply could not be asked.

Norman Malcolm, who knew the later Wittgenstein, says in his beautiful memoir: "one had to attend [his lectures] for quite a long time (at least three terms, I should say) before one could begin to get *any* grasp of what he was doing."[37] Surely that is a way of saying that Wittgenstein did not offer rigorous arguments in which conclusions were derived from stated premises. And in the "Biographical Sketch" that appears in the same volume, Georg Henrick von Wright, one of Wittgenstein's literary executors, says of him: "He once said that he felt as though he were writing for people who would think in a quite different way, breathe a different air of life, from that of present-day men."[38]

Hegel did not think along those lines. He operated with a Kantian conception of philosophy and felt that he ought to be rigorous in a way in which he obviously did not manage to be rigorous. But for all that he *was* developing a new way of thinking that owed a great deal to Goethe. He did not do this very well by any standards,

[37] (1958), p. 28.
[38] *Ibid.*, p. 2.

certainly not by his own; but that may be generally true of philosophers who try as much.

46 ▶▶▶ How did Hegel advance the discovery of the mind? By accepting all of the four points discussed in connection with Goethe (they will be recapitulated in a moment) and developing them in a most fruitful way. This was a stupendous achievement, and Hegel would confront us as an even far greater man than he was if he had not also accepted three of the five points discussed in connection with Kant. Although Hegel rejected Kant's model of the mind and his grotesque notion of autonomy, he was corrupted by Kant's impossible style, his misguided method, and his insistence on certainty, completeness, and necessity. We have seen the disastrous results.

It is only fair to add that Kant was not Hegel's only model, that he helped H. E. G. Paulus prepare a scholarly edition of Spinoza before he wrote the *Phenomenology,* and that he was steeped in Plato, including such late dialogues as the *Parmenides* and *Sophist,* and above all in Aristotle. But it was Kant who had begun the attempt to create a special brand of German for serious philosophy. Hegel wrote J. H. Voss, the great translator, in May 1805, shortly before he wrote the *Phenomenology:*

> Luther has made the Bible speak German; you, Homer—the greatest present that can be given to a people—I should like to say of my aspirations that I shall try to teach philosophy to speak German. Once that is accomplished, it will be infinitely more difficult to give shallowness the appearance of profound speech.

Hegel worked hard on this letter. Three drafts have survived although the letter itself is lost, and this quotation comes from the final draft. But the last sentence is certainly a howler. Hegel's misguided accomplishment certainly made it *easier* for shallow people to affect profundity, and Heidegger's similar attempt has had still worse results. In details, Hegel, like Heidegger after him, was often translating from the Greek, with Aristotle as the great source; but the notion that philosophy requires a special brand of German came from Kant.

Yet Hegel also accepted Goethe's model of autonomy; his idea that man is his deeds and that a history of the deeds gives us the essence; the all-important point that the mind can be understood only in terms of development; the opposition to Newtonian science and the bold notion that "the history of science is science itself"; and finally also the disparagement of mathematical certainty, which turns up in the Preface to the *Phenomenology*. In some cases the Goethean formulations I have cited were published after 1807, but I assume, knowing something of both men and taking into account the fact that Goethe became world famous when Hegel was four years old, that Goethe did not take these ideas from Hegel. If he had, I do not doubt that Hegel would have called attention to it, with great pride, as he did when he said in his lectures on the philosophy of history: "For a valet there are no heroes, says a familiar proverb. I have added [in the *Phenomenology*][39]—and Goethe repeated this two years later [in Ottilie's diary in *Elective Affinities*]—not because there are no heroes but because he is a valet."[40]

Although I believe that Goethe's influence on Hegel was overwhelming, it would not matter greatly if at one point it would be more appropriate to speak of an elective affinity rather than influence. What we are dealing with is after all not four independent points but an

[39] About five pages before the end of chap. VI: Spirit.
[40] Hoffmeister's edition, p. 102f.

organic syndrome, and what is remarkable is how these ideas function together in Hegel.

Again I shall concentrate on five points, but they can all be stated summarily, and in view of what has already been shown they require no lengthy elaboration at all. After the charges preferred against Hegel, it may be felt that his contribution would have to be immense to justify our prolonged discussion of him, and the time has come to show briefly that it was.

First, although Hegel's systems approach has come in for a good deal of ridicule, beginning with Kierkegaard, it was a stroke of genius. Hegel maintained that views and positions have to be seen as a whole, that the theoretical and moral belong together as aspects of a single standpoint, and that, in effect, atomism and microscopism miss the spirit that holds everything together.

Contemporary philosophers could still learn a great deal from Hegel in this respect. Too often, the history of philosophy that is taught in our colleges and universities is merely the history of epistemology; and ethics, political philosophy, aesthetics, and philosophy of religion are left out, to be taken up, if at all, in various systematic courses. It is not at all unusual for courses on Kant to get approximately halfway through the *Critique of Pure Reason* and stop short of the refutation of the traditional proofs of God's existence, not to speak of Kant's other works. What is stressed is more often than not the discussion of single arguments that do not seem to be tenable as they stand but that can be reconstructed in a number of ways. At that point *philosophy becomes similar to chess:* if we made this move, then, ten moves later, we would get into trouble in this way or that; hence we must try to find a better move; and when that also does not work, we make yet another attempt. According to ever so many contemporary philosophers, that, written out with so many numbers and letters (such as F and a and y) that the text becomes unreadable and has to be puzzled out, is the way to "do philosophy." As Mephistopheles said to the newly arrived student, it "lacks nothing except the spirit's connections" (see section 10 above). Hegel was supremely interested in "the spirit's connections" or, as *we* might say, in the way Kant's theory of knowledge, his ethics, his aesthetics, and his philosophy of religion hang together and are products of the same mind.

Obviously, Hegel himself did not explore these connections or Kant's mind in anything like the way attempted in the present book. But in principle he was, I think, on the right track and we can still learn from him.

Secondly, Hegel tried to show in his *Phenomenology* how each view must be seen in relation to the person holding it. What he had in mind was, of course, not a reductionist psychology; it was more nearly a way of transcending the split between subject and object. Instead of concentrating exclusively either on views and positions, as most philosophers still do, or on the human being who holds these views, Hegel, at least in principle, tried to see at every stage a whole that included subject and object, thinker and thought.

Here Hegel was hampered not only by his lack of psychological sophistication but also by his failure to reach any clarity about the place of psychology in his system. As we have seen, he said in his own advertisement for the *Phenomenology* that it was intended to "replace psychological explanations," but then placed psychology above phenomenology in his *Encyclopedia.* His brilliant idea that each view or position must be seen together with the person holding it remains at the level of a fascinating suggestion or program but is never worked out well in detail.

Third, Hegel suggested that every position should be seen as a stage in a development—the development of mind or spirit. That should mean first of all the development of the mind of the individual who maintained this position, and here once again Hegel was not at his best. But it also means the development of the human spirit or mind through history. Each position has to be seen not only as a whole but also as a part of a still larger whole—in relation to what came before it and after it. Short of that, we do not fully understand its meaning and are still blinded by myopia. A position derives its meaning in part from its developmental context.

Hegel did succeed quite remarkably in impressing this lesson on those who followed after him, and in the course of the nineteenth century this idea gradually came to dominate the study of philosophy and religion, literature and art—to such an extent that the so-called "new criticism" and "analytical philosophy" may be seen as protests, if not revolts, against the excesses committed by scholars who drowned works or ideas in their developmental context. While this suggestion concedes that these revolts were justified in some measure, it is nevertheless essentially Hegelian: the "new criticism" and "analytical philosophy" have to be understood as stages in a development.

Fourth, a position needs to be seen in relation to opposing views that help us to see not only its motivation but also the partiality and inadequacy of both sides. While a little of this insight has rubbed off on later proponents of "dialectic," most members of philosophical schools have never absorbed the whole lesson. School philosophers, whether they are Thomists or Marxists, phenomenologists or analytical philosophers, usually match their wits against other members of their own school, relying on an unquestioned consensus and concentrating on relatively minute differences.

Hegel's philosophy spawned its share of scholastics, in keeping with Schiller's distich on "Kant and His Interpreters":

> *One who is opulent offers*
> *legions of famishing beggars*

food. When the kings construct,
teamsters find plenty of work.

Yet Hegel himself was really a quintessential anti-scholastic. He recognized clearly that what is most important is not the minutiae on which people who belong to the same school happen to disagree but rather the relation of fundamentally different positions to each other. Perhaps Hegel still has as much to contribute to the discovery of the mind as he has contributed already.

Fifth and last, he himself applied these insights not only in his *Phenomenology* but also in his vastly influential lectures on the philosophy of history, aesthetics, religion, and the history of philosophy. These lectures were published posthumously by his students on the basis of students' lecture notes, and one can raise no end of objections to the ways in which they were edited; yet Hegel revolutionized the study of all of these fields. His most important contribution was the same in all of these areas. He taught people to see history and art history as well as the history of religion and of philosophy as disciplines through which we can try to discover the human mind or spirit or, in one word, man.

Here Hegel left his mark on the whole nineteenth century, by no means only on *German* scholarship or on *scholars* only but also on the way educated people generally came to think. In fact, he left a permanent mark on all of these disciplines down to our own time. There has been no dearth of anti-Hegelians, and it is fruitful to see much intellectual history since Hegel as a series of revolts against him, from Kierkegaard and Marx to the new criticism and analytical philosophy, which G. E. Moore, who spearheaded analytical philosophy, saw as a revolt against Hegelianism. Many of Hegel's critics absorbed easily as much of Hegel as they disowned, and the continual resurgence of revolts bears testimony to the vitality of his influence.

Of course, what his critics as well as his admirers took from him was by no means always what was best in him. What happens to all great spirits is that their worst qualities are easiest to imitate and hence aped most frequently. All kinds of mannerisms are copied and in Hegel's case also his extraordinarily obscure style and his spurious deductions, but many followers are quite blind to the major contributions of their master, and few, if any, approximate his originality or have any deep insights of their own.

In sum, Hegel was far more successful in advancing the discovery of the human mind through historical studies than he was in advancing the discovery of the individual human mind. He did not manage to apply his stupendous insights to the individual, as he might have done in the *Phenomenology,* because he was held back at every turn by his Kantian heritage. He thought he knew how a major philosophical work must be written, and he felt that he had to be scientific in a way that was really absurd, aspiring to certainty, necessity, and completeness. At every transition from one stage to another he tried to approximate a deduction, but his deductions were not logically compelling. His admirers have often called them "dialectical." Hegel himself was never clear about *what* they were nor did he ever give a clear account of "dialectic," a failing shared by almost all who have used that term since. It is still, or once again, a fashionable word and used by all kinds of people who do not feel called upon to specify their meaning. In Hegel's defense it must be said that he himself did not often speak of dialectic. In most of the relatively few passages in which this concept appears, Hegel used the adjective "dialectical" and did not speak of arguments but rather spoke of a "dialectical movement." Yet he, too, did not consider it necessary to state precisely what he meant by that.

In the present context, however, it is much more

important to recall that it is widely agreed that Hegel's lectures on the philosophy of history, which are probably his most popular and perhaps also his most influential book, and his lectures on aesthetics, the philosophy of religion, and the history of philosophy are much easier to read than the books he himself published. Moreover, some of the best of Hegel is found in these lectures and in the "additions" to the paragraphs of his *Encyclopedia* and *Philosophy of Right* that his students compiled from his lectures and inserted in the posthumous editions of these books. Why should this be so? Nothing like this is true of Kant or Schopenhauer, Nietzsche or any of the major French or British philosophers. Has anyone even asked this question before? Once we do pose it, the answer seems clear enough.

When he wrote his books, Hegel was hampered by Kant's legacy, wrote as Kant had written, and aspired to certainty, completeness, and necessity. He affected a rigor that was spurious. But when he lectured he managed to get away from this heritage and frequently developed his insights in ways that were really much more congenial to him.

He still provides plenty of work for teamsters, and since the 1960s more scholars than ever before are turning out articles and books on him. But Hegel also had insights that are still waiting to be developed and applied. A quotation from his lectures on the philosophy of history is downright Freudian. For once I shall translate *Geist* as mind: "The stages that the mind seems to have left behind it also possesses in its present depth. As it has run through its stages in history, it has to run through them in the present . . ."[41]

A scholastic might read his own discoveries or those of later thinkers into Hegel and appear not to go beyond him even when he did. But it seems far better to ac-

[41] Hoffmeister's ed., p. 183.

knowledge that Nietzsche and Freud went far beyond Hegel and made contributions to the discovery of the mind that he had not dreamed of. Nietzsche will be considered, along with Heidegger and Buber, in the second volume of this trilogy; Freud, along with Adler and Jung, in the last.

Goethe and Hegel advanced the discovery of the mind immensely, and yet one feels that when they died in 1831 and 1832 psychology had not yet been born. Hegel was held back by his Kantian heritage, and his *Phenomenology* is often as grotesque as the early essay in which he placed his paraphrases of Kant's ethics in the mouth of Jesus. What was needed was a thinker who would develop Goethe's legacy without trying to reconcile it with Kant's. This is what Nietzsche did and, after him, Freud.

It may seem that, if this is so, one might just as well begin *Discovering the Mind* with Nietzsche and skip Goethe, Kant, and Hegel. But if Goethe and Hegel were right when they insisted that what is of the mind must be caught in its genesis to be comprehended, then it makes sense to go back to the beginnings. And if Hegel was right, that a position needs to be seen in relation to opposing views, then our juxtaposition of Goethe and Kant makes sense, the more so because the faults I have found in Kant are encountered again and again in contemporary reflections on the mind.

Finally, we may have advanced the understanding of the minds of three very remarkable individuals. Kant and Hegel did more than anyone else to create the image and model of the modern philosopher, who is a professor and takes pride in being academic and writing for his professional colleagues rather than popularly. Yet we have seen how their works are the creations of very human writers and reflect their character no less than their genius. Far from standing above their fellow men and seeing the human mind from the vantage point of gods, they were resolving their own personal problems in their books. And we can still learn from Goethe's insistence on the crucial importance of development and from his conception of science. Being a poet as well as a scientist, he knew that poetry and science are not totally different but creations of the same mind. Those who would discover the mind cannot afford to ignore poetry and art.

Bibliography ▶▶▶

Bibliographies for Goethe, Kant, and Hegel could easily fill one volume each. The first item in the Bibliography shows how large the secondary literature on Kant was even in the nineteenth century. A two-volume *Goethe-Bibliographie* is listed under Goethe. My own *Hegel* contains an eighteen-page Hegel bibliography, divided into Hegel bibliographies, Hegel's writings (including English translations), and writings about Hegel; but since this book appeared in 1965 there has been a veritable explosion of interest in Hegel, and well over a thousand books and articles on Hegel were published in 1970–75. *Hegel-Studien*, listed below, tries to keep its readers informed about this flood.

The following bibliography is confined almost entirely to a few representative editions of the collected works of the major authors discussed in this volume and to articles and books that are cited in the text.

Adickes, Erich. "Bibliography of Writings by and on Kant which have appeared in Germany up to the End of 1887," in

The *Philosophical Review*, II (1893), 257–92, 426–49, 557–83, 670–709; III (1894), 31–55, 176–92, 305–36, 434–58, 583–600, 689–716. The last part appeared in *Supplement to the Philosophical Review*, n.d., 253–380.

———. *Kant und das Ding an sich.* Berlin: Pan Verlag Rolf Heise, 1924.

———. *Kant und die Als-Ob Philosophie.* Stuttgart: Fr. Frommans Verlag, 1927.

Amelung, Heinz, ed. *Goethe als Persönlichkeit: Berichte und Briefe von Zeitgenossen.* Vol. 1: *1749–1797.* Munich: Georg Müller, 1914. Vol. II: *1797–1823.* Berlin: Propyläen-Verlag, 1923. Vol. III: *1823–1832.* Berlin: Propyläen Verlag, 1925.

Arnoldt, Emil. *"Die äussere Entstehung und die Abfassungszeit der Kritik der reinen Vernunft,"* in *Kritische Excurse im Gebiete der Kant-Forschung.* Königsberg: Ferd. Beyer's Buchhandlung, 1894, pp. 99–652.

Bartley, William W. III. *Wittgenstein.* Philadelphia: J. B. Lippincott Company, 1973.

Beck, Lewis White. *A Commentary on Kant's Critique of Practical Reason.* Chicago: University of Chicago Press, 1960.

———. *Early German Philosophy.* Cambridge, Mass.: Harvard University Press, 1969.

———. *Essays on Kant and Hume.* New Haven: Yale University Press, 1978.

———, ed. *Kant Studies Today.* LaSalle, Ill.: Open Court, 1969.

———, ed. *Kant's Theory of Knowledge:* Selected papers from 3rd International Kant Congress, Dordrecht. Boston: D. Reidel, 1974.

———. *Studies in the Philosophy of Kant.* Indianapolis: Bobbs-Merrill, 1965.

———, trans. and ed. *Kant's Critique of Practical Reason and Other Writings in Moral Philosophy.* Chicago: University of Chicago Press, 1949.

———, trans. *Critique of Practical Reason* by Immanuel Kant. New York: Liberal Arts Press, 1956.

———, trans. *Foundations of the Metaphysics of Morals* by Immanuel Kant. Indianapolis: Bobbs-Merrill, 1959.

————, ed. and trans. with others. *On History* by Immanuel Kant. Indianapolis: Bobbs-Merrill, 1957.

Bergmann, F. *On Being Free.* Notre Dame, Ind.: University of Notre Dame Press, 1977.

Berlin, Sir Isaiah et. al. *Essays on J. L. Austin.* Oxford: Oxford University Press, 1973.

————. "Herder and the Enlightenment," in *Vico and Herder.* New York: The Viking Press, 1976.

Blankenburg, Captain von. Report on Lessing's *Faust* in *Litteratur und Völkerkunde*, Vol. 5. Dessau and Leipzig: 1784, pp. 82–84.

Borowski, Ludwig Ernst. *Darstellung des Lebens und Charakters Immanuel Kants. Von Kant selbst genau revidirt und berichtigt.* Königsberg: Friedrich Nicolovius, 1804. Reprinted in Gross.

Bradley, F. H. *Appearance and Reality.* 1893. Oxford: Oxford University Press, 1930.

Brittan, Gordon G., Jr. *Kant's Theory of Science.* Princeton: Princeton University Press, 1978.

Buber, Martin. *Ich und Du*, Leipzig: Insel-Verlag, 1923.

————. *I and Thou*, trans. Walter Kaufmann. New York: Charles Scribner's Sons, 1970.

Byron, Lord. *Sardanapalus.* London: J. Murray, 1821.

Cassirer, Ernst. *Goethe und die geschichtliche Welt.* Berlin: Bruno Cassirer, 1932.

————. *Kants Leben und Lehre.* Berlin: Bruno Cassirer, 1918.

————. *Rousseau Kant Goethe.* Princeton: Princeton University Press, 1945.

Cohen, Hermann. *Kommentar zu Immanuel Kant's Kritik der reinen Vernunft.* Leipzig: Felix Meiner, 1907.

Deussen, Paul. *Die Geheimlehre des Veda.* Leipzig: F. A. Brockhaus, 1907.

————. *Der Kategorische Imperativ.* Kiel: Universitätsbuchhandlung, 1891.

————. *Das System des Vedânta.* Leipzig: F. A. Brockhaus, 1906.

Dewey, John. *Theory of Valuation.* Chicago: University of Chicago Press, 1939.

Dilthey, Wilhelm. *Judendgeschichte Hegels.* Berlin, 1906. Leipzig: B. G. Teubner, 1921.

Eckermann, Johann Peter. *Gespräche mit Goethe in den letzten Jahren seines Lebens*. 2 vols. Leipzig: Brockhaus, 1836. 3rd vol., Magdeburg, Heinrichschofen'sche Buchhandlung, 1848. Often reprinted in one volume.

Eisler, Rudolf. *Handwörterbuch der Philosophie*. Berlin: Ernst Siegfried Mittler und Sohn, 1913.

———. *Kant-Lexikon*. Berlin, 1930. Hildesheim: Georg Olms, 1961.

Elias, Julius. Article on Schiller in *The Encyclopedia of Philosophy*, ed. Paul Edwards. 8 vols. New York: Macmillan, 1967.

Engelmann, Paul. *Letters from Ludwig Wittgenstein with a Memoir*, 1967. New York: Horizon Press, 1968.

Engels, Friedrich, and Karl Marx. *Werke*. Berlin: Dietz, 1957ff.

Feuerbach, Ludwig. *Das Wesen des Christentums*. Leipzig: Otto Wigand, 1841.

———. *The Essence of Christianity*, trans. George Eliot, 1854. Reprinted New York: Harper & Brothers, 1957.

Fichte, Johann Gottlieb. *Sämtliche Werke*. 8 vols. Berlin: Veit und Comp. 1845–46.

———. *Leben und literarischer Briefwechsel*, ed. Immanuel Hermann Fichte. Zweite sehr vermehrte und verbesserte Auflage (2nd ed., revised and expanded), 2 vols. Leipzig: Brockhaus, 1862.

———, ed. *Philosophisches Journal einer Gesellschaft Teutscher Gelehrter*. Jena and Leipzig: Christian Ernst Gabler, 1798.1.

Findlay, J. N. *Hegel: A Re-examination*. London: George Allen & Unwin, 1958.

Freud, Sigmund. *Gesammelte Werke*. 18 vols. London: Imago, 1941–68.

Friedenthal, Richard. *Goethe: His Life and Times*. Cleveland and New York: World Publishing, 1965.

Fulda, Hans Friedrich and Dieter Henrich. *Materialien zu Hegels "Phänomenologie des Geistes."* Frankfurt am Main: Suhrkamp Verlag, 1973.

Goethe, J. W. *Werke: Vollständige Ausgabe letzter Hand*. Stuttgart and Tübingen: Cotta, 40 vols., ed. under Goethe's supervision, 1827–31, plus 15 vols. of *Nachgelassene Werke*,

1833–34, and 5 more vols. 1842. Index vol. for vols. 1–55, ed. C. T. Musculus, 1835.

————. *Sämtliche Werke. Propyläen-Ausgabe.* 45 vols, plus 4 supplementary volumes (see Amelung). Munich, Georg Müller, and later Berlin, Propyläen-Verlag, no dates. Arranged chronologically, this edition also includes large numbers of letters.

————. *Werke: herausgegeben im Auftrage der Grossherzogin Sophie von Sachsen.* 143 vols. Weimar: Böhlau, 1887–1919. Includes diaries, 15 vols., and letters, 50 vols.

————. *Gedenkausgabe der Werke, Briefe und Gespräche,* ed. Ernst Beutler. 24 vols. Zurich: Artemis, 1949.

————. *Gespräche,* ed. Woldemar Freiherr von Biedermann. 10 vols. in 5, F. W. von Biedermann, Leipzig, 1889–91. Rev. ed., 5 vols., ed. Flodoard Freiherr von Biedermann *et al.,* *ibid,* 1909–11.

————. *Briefwechsel zwischen Goethe und Zelter.* 6 vols., Berlin, Duncker & Humblot, 1833–34. Often reprinted.

————. *Briefwechsel zwischen Schiller und Goethe.* 6 vols. Stuttgart and Tübingen: Cotta, 1828–29. Often reprinted.

————. *Goethes Faust in ursprünglicher Gestalt nach der Göchhausenschen Abschrift herausgegeben* von Erich Schmidt. Weimar: Hermann Böhlau, 1887. The so-called *Urfaust,* often reprinted.

————. *Faust: A Drama, by Goethe and Schiller's Song of the Bell,* trans. Lord Francis Leveson Gower. London: John Murray, 1823. See also Kaufmann.

————. *Faustus from the German of Goethe.* London: Boosey and Sons and Rodwell & Martin, 1821. Translator anonymous.

————. *Radirte Blätter nach Handzeichnungen von Goethe,* ed. C. A. Schwerdgeburth. Weimar, Magdeburg: Caesar Mazzucchi, 1821.

————. *Reise–Zerstreuungs–und Trost-Büchlein vom September 1806 bis dahin 1807 ihro der Prinzess Caroline von Weimar durchl. unterthänigst gewidmet von Goethe.* Facsimile, limited ed. Leipzig: Insel-Verlag, n.d.

Goethe-Bibliographie. Begründet von (Begun by) Hans Pyritz ... Fortgeführt von (Continued by) H. Nicolai & G. Burkhardt ... 2 vols. Heidelberg: Carl Winter, 1965–68.

Goethe und die Naturwissenschaften: Eine Bibliographie von Günther Schmidt. Halle, 1940. 4,554 publications relating to Goethe and the natural sciences are listed.

Goethe-Jahrbuch, vols. I–XXXIV, ed. Ludwig Geiger. Frankfurt: Rütten & Loening, 1880–1913. *Jahrbuch der Goethe-Gesellschaft,* vol. I, ed. H. G. Gräf. Leipzig: Insel-Verlag, 1914; vol. XXI, ed. M. Hecker, Weimar, 1935. *Goethe: Vierteljahresschrift der Goethe-Gesellschaft: Neue Folge des Goethe-Jahrbuchs,* vol. I, Weimar, 1936. And eventually: *Goethe Jahrbuch,* ed. Karl-Heinz Hahn, Weimar, 1976, vol. 93 of the *Gesamtfolge.*

Gram, Moltke S., ed. *Kant: Disputed Questions.* Chicago: Quadrangle, 1967. See Vaihinger and Paton.

Gross, Felix, ed. *Immanuel Kant: Sein Leben in Darstellungen von Zeitgenossen: Die Biographien von L. E. Borowski, R. B. Jachmann und A. Ch. Wasianski.* Berlin: Deutsche Bibliothek, 1912.

Hartmann, Eduard von. *Phänomenologie des sittlichen Bewusstseins: Prolegomena zu jeder künftigen Ethik.* Berlin: Carl Duncker, 1879.

Hartmann, Klaus. *Hegel-Studien,* 7 (1972), book review p. 399.

Haym, Rudolf. *Hegel und seine Zeit.* Berlin, 1857. Hildesheim: Georg Olms Verlagsbuchhandlung, 1962.

———. *Herder nach seinem Leben und seinen Werken dargestellt.* 2 vols. Berlin: Gaertner, 1877–85.

Hegel, G. W. F. *Gesammelte Werke.* Critical edition. Hamburg: Meiner, 1968 ff.

———. *Sämtliche Werke: Jubiläumsausgabe in 20 Bänden,* ed. Hermann Glockner. Stuttgart: Frommann, 1927–30.

———. *Sämtliche Werke: Kritische Ausgabe,* ed. Lasson, Hoffmeister, *et. al.* 18 vols. Hamburg: Felix Meiner, 1917–1944.

———. *Werke: Vollständige Ausgabe durch einen Verein von Freunden des Verewigten.* 18 vols. Berlin: Duncker and Humblot, 1832–45. 2nd ed., partly revised, 1840–47.

———. *Briefe von und an Hegel,* ed. Johannes Hoffmeister. Vols I–III, 1952–54; vol. IV, ed. Rolf Flechsig, 1960. Hamburg, Felix Meiner.

———. *Phänomenologie des Geistes,* ed. Johannes Hoffmeister. Hamburg: Felix Meiner, 1952.

————. *The Phenomenology of Mind*, trans. J. B. Baillie. 2nd ed., revised, London: Allen & Unwin; New York: Macmillan, 1931.

————. *Phenomenology of Spirit*, trans. A. V. Miller, with Analysis of the Text and Foreword by J. N. Findlay. Oxford: Clarendon Press, 1977.

————. *Theologische Jugendschriften*, ed. Hermann Nohl. Tübingen: Mohr (Paul Siebeck), 1907.

————. *Die Vernunft in der Geschichte*, ed. Johannes Hoffmeister. Hamburg: Felix Mainer, 1955.

Hegel-Jahrbuch, ed. W. R. Beyer. Meisenheim am Glan: Anton Hain, 1972ff.

Hegel-Studien, ed. F. Nicolin and O. Pöggeler. Bonn: Bouvier, 1961ff. There are also many *Beihefte*: #15 appeared in 1976.

Heidegger, Martin. *"Hegels Begriff der Erfahrung"* in *Holzwege*. Frankfurt: Klostermann, 1950.

————. *Kant und das Problem der Metaphysik*. Bonn: Cohen, 1929. 3rd. ed., Frankfurt: Klostermann, 1965.

Heisenberg, Werner. *Das Naturbild Goethes*. Bad Godesberg: Alexander von Humboldt-Stiftung, 1967.

Herder, Johann Gottfried von. *Sämtliche Werke*, ed. Bernhard Suphan. 33 vols. in 30. Berlin: Weidmann, 1877–1913.

Hoffer, Eric. *The True Believer*. New York: Harper & Brothers, 1951.

Hoffmeister, Johannes, ed. *Wörterbuch der philosophischen Begriffe*. 2nd ed. Hamburg: Felix Meiner, 1955.

Husserl, Edmund. *"Philosophie als strenge Wissenschaft"* in *Logos*, I (1910), 289–314.

Ibsen, Henrik. *En Folkefiende*, Copenhagen: Gyldendal, 1882.

————. *An Enemy of the People*, trans. Michael Mayer. London: Eyre Methuen, 1974.

Jachmann, Reinhold Bernhard. *Immanuel Kant geschildert in Briefen an einen Freund*. Königsberg: Friedrich Nicolovius, 1804. Reprinted in Gross.

Jacobi, F. H. *Ueber die Lehre des Spinoza in Briefen an den Herrn Moses Mendelssohn*. Anonymous. 1st ed., Breslau, Gottl. Löwe, 1785. 2nd ed., Breslau, Gottl. Löwe, 1789.

Jacoby, Günther. *Herder als Faust*. Leipzig: Meiner, 1911.

James, William. "Does Consciousness Exist?" in *Essays in*

Radical Empiricism, 1912. New York: Longmans, Green, 1943.

Kant, Immanuel. *Gesammelte Schriften,* herausgegeben von der Königlich Preussischen Akademie der Wissenschaften: *Werke* vols. I-IX; *Briefwechsel,* vols. X-XIII; *Handschriftlicher Nachlass* vols. XIV-XXIII; *Vorlesungen,* vols. XXIV-XXVIII; plus index vols. in progress. Berlin: Georg Reimer, 1902 ff. (now Walter de Gruyther). Now sponsored by the Deutsche Akademie der Wissenschaften zu Berlin. This edition is cited as "Akademie."

———. *Critique of Practical Reason,* etc. See Beck.

———. *Critique of Pure Reason,* trans. Max Müller. London: Macmillan, 1881; trans. Norman Kemp Smith, London: Macmillan, 1929. The best two translations. Have often been reprinted.

———. *Philosophical Correspondence, 1759–99,* ed. and trans. Arnulf Zweig. Chicago: University of Chicago Press, 1967.

Kantstudien. Vol. 1, ed. Hans Vaihinger, 1897. Vol. 68, ed. Gerhard Funke and Joachim Kopper, Berlin and New York: Walter de Gruyter, 1977. Supplementary issues (*Ergänzungshefte*) have appeared frequently: # 100, Bonn: Bouvier, 1970.

Kantzenbach, F. W. *Herder.* Hamburg: Rowohlt Taschenbuch Verlag, 1970.

Kaufmann, Walter. "Coming to Terms with Hegel" (review article prompted by Charles Taylor's *Hegel*), in *The Times Literary Supplement,* London, January 2, 1976.

———. *Critique of Religion and Philosophy.* New York: Harper, 1958. Later editions, most recently Princeton: Princeton University Press, 1978, have the same section numbers.

———. *Existentialism, Religion and Death.* New York: New American Library, 1976.

———. *The Faith of a Heretic.* Garden City, N.Y.: Doubleday, 1961; New York: New American Library, 1978. Section numbers are the same in all editions.

———. *From Shakespeare to Existentialism.* Boston: Beacon Press, 1959; rev. ed., Garden City, N.Y.,: Doubleday, 1960;

Princeton: Princeton University Press, 1980. Includes 4 chapters on Goethe and 3 on Hegel.

————. *The Future of the Humanities.* New York: Reader's Digest Press, 1977. Distributed by McGraw-Hill.

————. *Goethe's Faust: The Original German and a New Translation and Introduction.* Part One and Sections from Part Two. Garden City, N.Y.: Doubleday, 1961.

————. *Hegel: Reinterpretation, Texts and Commentary.* Garden City, N.Y.: Doubleday, 1965; Anchor Books ed., 1966. 2 vols., Notre Dame, Ind., University of Notre Dame Press, 1977–78: *Hegel: A Reinterpretation* and *Hegel: Texts and Commentary. Hegel's Preface to His System in a New Translation with Commentary on Facing Pages, and "Who Thinks Abstractly?"*

————. "Hegel's Early Antitheological Phase" in *The Philosophical Review*, LXIII.1 (Jan. 1954). Expanded version in *From Shakespeare to Existentialism* and in *Hegel: A Collection of Critical Essays*, ed. Alasdair MacIntyre. Garden City, N.Y.: Doubleday, 1972.

————. "The Hegel Myth and Its Method" in *The Philosophical Review*, LX.4 (Oct. 1951). Rev. version reprinted in same 2 books as last entry.

————. *Man's Lot: A Trilogy. Photographs and Text.* New York: Reader's Digest Press, 1978. Distributed by McGraw-Hill. Includes *Life at the Limits, Time Is an Artist,* and *What Is Man?* also issued simultaneously in 3 softcover volumes.

————. *Nietzsche.* Princeton: Princeton University Press, 1950. 4th ed., rev. and expanded, Princeton: Princeton University Press, 1974.

————. *Twenty-Five German Poets.* New York, W. W. Norton, 1975.

————. *Without Guilt and Justice.* New York: Peter Wyden, 1973. New York: Dell, 1975, with same section numbers.

————, ed. *Existentialism from Dostoevsky to Sartre.* New York: Meridian Books, 1956. Rev. and expanded, New York: New American Library, 1975.

————, ed. *Hegel's Political Philosophy.* New York: Atherton Press, 1970.

Kierkegaard, Søren. *Concluding Unscientific Postscript,* trans. David F. Swenson and Walter Lowrie. Princeton: Princeton University Press, 1944.

————. "That Individual" in *The Point of View, etc.,* trans. Walter Lowrie, London: Oxford University Press, 1939.

Klopstock, Friedrich Gottlieb. *Der Messias.* First 3 cantos, 1748; 4 vols., 1751–73. Often reprinted.

Kuhn, Thomas. *The Structure of Scientific Revolutions.* Chicago: University of Chicago Press, 1962.

Kulenkampff, Jens. *Materialien zu Kants "Kritik der Urteilskraft."* Frankfurt am Main: Suhrkamp, 1974.

Lasson, Georg. *"Einleitung"* in *Phänomenologie des Geistes* by G. W. F. Hegel, ed. Georg Lasson. Leipzig: Dürr'sche Buchhandlung, 1907, pp. XVII–CXVI.

Lazarus, Moritz. *Das Leben der Seele.* 3 vols. Berlin: Heinrich Schindler, 1856ff.

Lessing, G. E. *Gesammelte Werke,* ed. Lachmann and Muncker. 23 vols. Stuttgart: Göschen, 1886–1924.

————. *Werke,* ed. George Witkowski. 7 vols. Leipzig: Bibliographisches Institut, 1934.

Lewes, George Henry. *Life and Works of Goethe.* London: D. Nutt, 1855.

Liebmann, Otto. *Kant und die Epigonen.* Stuttgart: Schober, 1865.

Luther, Martin. *Sämtliche Schriften,* ed. J. G. Walch. 24 vols. Halle, 1740–53. Pagination of this ed. indicated in St. Louis reprint, 1881–1910.

————. *Sämmtliche Werke,* ed. Johann Konrad Irmischer, vols. 57-62: *Tischreden.* Frankfurt and Erlangen: Heyder & Zimmer, 1854.

Malcolm, Norman. *Ludwig Wittgenstein.* London: Oxford University Press, 1958.

Marius, Richard. *Luther.* Philadelphia: J. B. Lippincott, 1974.

Mendelssohn, Moses. *Jerusalem.* Berlin: Friedrich Maurer, 1783.

Müller, Max, ed. *The Sacred Books of the East.* 50 vols. Oxford: Clarendon Press, 1879–1910.

Niebuhr, Reinhold. *An Interpretation of Christian Ethics,* 1935. New York: Meridian Books, 1956.

Nietzsche, Friedrich. *Gesammelte Werke, Musarionausgabe,* 23 vols. Munich: Musarion Verlag, 1920–29.

———. *The Birth of Tragedy, Beyond Good and Evil, On the Genealogy of Morals, The Case of Wagner,* and *Ecce Homo,* plus selections, in *Basic Writings of Nietzsche,* trans. and ed. Walter Kaufmann. New York: Random House, 1968. Also in 3 softcover vols.

———. *Thus Spoke Zarathustra, The Antichrist, Twilight of the Idols, Nietzsche Contra Wagner,* plus selections, in *The Portable Nietzsche,* trans. and ed. Walter Kaufmann. New York: Viking Press, 1954; Penguin Books, 1976.

———. *The Gay Science,* trans. and ed. Walter Kaufmann. New York: Random House, 1974.

———. Letter to Heinrich Köselitz, Dec. 8, 1888. Quoted and discussed in Kaufmann, *Nietzsche,* 4th ed., p. 435.

Orwell, George. *Nineteen Eighty-Four.* New York: Harcourt, 1949.

Paton, H. J. *The Categorical Imperative: A Study in Kant's Moral Philosophy.* London: Hutchinson, 1947.

———. *Kant's Metaphysics of Experience.* 2 vols. London: Allen & Unwin, 1936.

———, trans. *The Moral Law: Kant's Groundwork of the Metaphysic of Morals.* New York: Barnes & Noble, 1963.

———. "Is the Transcendental Deduction a Patchwork?" in *Proceedings of the Aristotelian Society,* XXX (1930). Reprinted in Gram.

Plato. *The Collected Dialogues of Plato including the Letters,* ed. Edith Hamilton and Huntington Cairus. Bollingen Series LXXI, 1961, now Princeton University Press. Most convenient ed. of the works in English.

Pniower, Otto. *Goethe's Faust: Zeugnisse und Excurse zu seiner Entstehungsgeschichte.* Berlin: Weidmannsche Buchhandlung, 1899.

Pöggeler, Otto. *"Die Komposition der Phänomenologie des Geistes,"* in *Hegel-Studien,* 3 (1966). Reprinted in Fulda & Henrich.

Purpus, Wilhelm. *Zur Dialektik des Bewusstseins nach Hegel.* Berlin: Trowitzsch & Sohn, 1908.

Rousseau, Jean Jacques. *Du contrat social.* Amsterdam: M. M. Rey, 1762.

————. *Social Contract,* trans. H. J. Tozer. 3rd ed. London: Allen & Unwin, 1920.

Ryle, Gilbert. *The Concept of Mind.* London: Hutchinson's University Library, 1949.

Sartre, J.-P. *Critique de la raison dialectique.* Paris: Librarie Gallimard, 1960. *Critique of Dialectical Reason,* trans. Alan Sheridan-Smith, ed. Jonathan Rée. London: NLB, 1976.

————. *La Diable et le Bon Dieu.* Paris: Librarie Gallimard, 1951. Trans. by Kitty Black in *The Devil and the Good Lord and Two Other Plays,* New York: Alfred Knopf, 1960.

————. *L'Être et le Néant.* Paris: Librarie Gallimard, 1943. *Being and Nothingness,* trans. Hazel E. Barnes. New York: Philosophical Library, 1956.

————. *L'Existentialisme est un humanisme.* Paris: Les Editions Nagel, 1946. Trans. Philip Mairet in Kaufmann, ed., *Existentialism from Dostoevsky to Sartre.*

————. "Portrait of the Anti-Semite," in *Existentialism from Dostoevsky to Sartre,* ed. Walter Kaufmann. Trans. and adapted by Mary Guggenheim from *Réflexions sur la Question Juive.* Paris: Paul Morihien, 1946.

————. "Sartre at Seventy: An Interview [with Michel Contat]" in *The New York Review,* Aug. 7, 1975. Reprinted with minor stylistic differences in *Life/Situations: Essays Written and Spoken.* Trans. Paul Anster & Lydia Davis. New York, Pantheon, 1977.

Schiller, Friedrich. *Sämtliche Werke: Säkular-Ausgabe,* ed. Eduard von der Hellen. 17 vols. Stuttgart, 1904–05.

————. *On the Aesthetic Education of Man in a Series of Letters.* Ed. and trans. Elizabeth M. Wilkinson and L. A. Willoughby, Oxford: Clarendon Press, 1967.

Schlick, Moritz. "*Erleben, Erkennen, Metaphysik,*" in *Kant-Studien,* 31, Berlin, 1930. Reprinted in *Gesammelte Aufsätze 1926–1936.* Vienna: Gerold & Co., 1938.

Schopenhauer, Arthur. *Sämtliche Werke.* Leipzig: Grossherzog Wilhelm Ernst Ausgabe. 5 vols. Leipzig: Insel Verlag, n.d.

Schultz, Uwe. *Kant.* Reinbek bei Hamburg: Rowohlt Taschenbuch Verlag, 1965.

Shelley, P. B. "Scenes from the *Faust* of Goethe." The Walpurgis Night first published in *The Liberal,* No. 1, 1822; both scenes (the other one being The Prologue in Heaven) in *Posthumous Poems*, 1824. Included, e.g., in *The Complete Poetical Works*, ed. Thomas Hutchinson. London: Oxford University Press, 1921, pp. 740–53.

Simmel, Georg. *Goethe*. Leipzig: Klinkhardt & Bermann, 1913.

———. *Kant*. Leipzig: Duncker & Humblot, 1904.

———. *Kant und Goethe*. Berlin: Bard, Marquardt, 1906.

Smith, Adam. *Inquiry into the Nature and Causes of the Wealth of Nations*. London: W. Strahan, 1776. Chicago: University of Chicago Press, 1976.

Smith, Norman Kemp. *A Commentary to Kant's "Critique of Pure Reason,"* 1918. 2nd rev. ed., 1923. Atlantic Highlands, N.J.: Humanities Press, 1962.

Smith, Vincent A. *A History of Fine Art in India and Ceylon from the Earliest Times to the Present Day*. Oxford: Clarendon Press, 1911.

Solzhenitsyn, A. *Cancer Ward*, trans. Rebecca Frank. New York: Dial Press, 1968.

Spiegelberg, H. *The Phenomenological Movement*. 2nd ed. 2 vols. The Hague: Martinus Nijhoff, 1971.

Spinoza, B. *Ethica* in *Opera Posthuma*, 1677. Often reprinted.

———. *Opera quae supersunt omnia . . .*, ed. H. E. G. Paulus (with Hegel's assistance). Jena, 1802–03.

Stirling, J. H. *The Secret of Hegel*. Edinburgh: Oliver & Boyd, 1898.

Strauss, David Friedrich. *Das Leben Jesu*. Tübingen: Osiander, 1835. Often reprinted. *Life of Jesus Critically Examined*, trans. from 4th German ed. by George Eliot. London: Chapman, 1846.

Strawson, P. F. *The Bounds of Sense: An Essay on Kant's Critique of Pure Reason*. London: Methuen & Co., 1966.

Taylor, Charles. *Hegel*. Cambridge: Cambridge University Press, 1975.

Tetens, J. N. *Über die allgemeine speculativische Philosophie: Philosophische Versuche über die menschliche Natur und ihre Entwickelung*. 1775–77. Berlin: Reuther & Reichard, 1913.

Vaihinger, Hans. *Goethe als Ideal universeller Bildung*. Stuttgart: Meyer, 1875.

———. *Die Philosophie des Als Ob . . . Mit einem Anhang über Kant und Nietzsche.* Leipzig: Felix Meiner, 1911. Often reprinted.

———. *Die Transcendentale Deduktion der Kategorien.* Halle: Niemeyer, 1902. Expounds his "patchwork theory." Trans. in Gram.

Vorländer, Karl. *Die ältesten Kant-biographien: Eine kritische Studie.* Berlin: Reuther & Reichard, 1918.

———. "Goethes Verhältnis zu Kant in seiner historischen Entwicklung," I and II, in *Kantstudien,* 1879, pp. 60–99 and 325–51.

———, ed. *Grundlegung zur Metaphysik der Sitten* by Immanuel Kant. Leipzig: Felix Meiner, 1906.

———. *Immanuel Kant: Der Mann und das Werk.* 2 vols. Leipzig: Felix Meiner, 1924.

———. *Immanuel Kant's Leben.* Leipzig: Felix Meiner, 1911.

———. *Kant, Schiller, Goethe.* 2nd ed., rev. and enlarged. Leipzig: Felix Meiner, 1923.

———. *Die Philosophie unserer Klassiker: Lessing, Herder, Schiller, Goethe.* Berlin: T. H. W. Diek, 1923.

Voss, Johann Heinrich. *Homers Odyssee übersetzt.* Hamburg: auf Kosten des Verfassers, 1781. Often reprinted.

Ward, Keith. *The Development of Kant's View of Ethics.* Oxford: Basil Blackwell, 1972.

Warda, Arthur. *Die Druckschriften Immanuel Kants (bis zum Jahre 1838).* Wiesbaden: Heinrich Staadt, 1919.

Wasianski, E. A. Ch. *Immanuel Kant in seinen letzten Lebensjahren.* Königsberg: Friedrich Nicolovius, 1804. Reprinted in Gross.

Wilcox, John T. *Truth and Value in Nietzsche.* Ann Arbor: University of Michigan Press, 1974.

Wilkinson, Elizabeth M. and L. A. Willoughby. *Goethe, Poet & Thinker.* London: Edward Arnold, 1962.

Wittgenstein, Ludwig. *Tractatus Logico-Philosophicus.* London: Routledge & Kegan Paul, 1922; New York: The Humanities Press, 1951.

Wolff, Robert Paul. *The Autonomy of Reason: A Commentary*

on *Kant's Groundwork of the Metaphysic of Morals*. New York: Harper & Row, 1973.

———. *Kant's Theory of Mental Activity*. Cambridge, Mass.: Harvard University Press, 1963.

Wood, Allen W. *Kant's Moral Religion*. Ithaca, N.Y.: Cornell University Press, 1970.

Acknowledgments ▸▸▸

Some of these ideas were worked out and presented at the Research School of Social Sciences, Australian National University, in the fall of 1974. I am grateful to Eugene Kamenka, who invited me there, and to those who attended my seminars and participated in the discussion. A brief preliminary version of the Hegel chapter appeared in *Phenomenology and Philosophical Understanding*, edited by Edo Pivčević (Cambridge University Press, 1975). A first draft of the entire trilogy was completed in 1976 but laid aside to permit me to complete *Man's Lot*. When I returned to the task of revising this draft for publication, which involved extensive changes, I was helped by the detailed comments of several friends. Jill Anderson commented on the Goethe chapter, Moshe Barasch and Lewis Beck on Kant, Raymond Geuss on Goethe and Kant, David Hoy on Hegel, Jo Kaufmann on the Prologue and the Goethe chapter, and Alexandros Nehemas on the whole manuscript. Professor Nehemas' comments were especially extensive, and our long discussions were an utter delight.

Lewis Beck's reaction to my treatment of Kant calls for a special word of thanks. When I mailed my manuscript to him, I asked myself how I would feel if somebody sent me an essay of such length in which he tried to show how Nietzsche had been "a disaster." When one has given much of one's life to translating a man's work and writing studies and commentaries, one can hardly be expected to be very sympathetic to such an effort. But it is one of the beauties of the academic scene, which is bleak in many ways, that it favors the growth of affectionate criticism of the work of others, and when such criticism is truly friendly it constitutes one of the most delightful forms of human intercourse. This applies to all of those to whom I have just stated my indebtedness, but in Lewis Beck's case it went far beyond anything I could have expected. In fact, his very kind comments helped to restore my faith in a book in which, after such a long interruption, I had begun to lose interest. Nobody could have hoped for such encouragement from the leading American Kant scholar.

Once again, it is a pleasure to express my gratitude to Princeton University for granting me leaves and working conditions that have allowed me to proceed with my research and writing.

✳   ✳   ✳

This posthumous edition would not have been possible without the help of Prof. Saul Goldwasser and Prof. Irving Louis Horowitz.